Getting Your Way Every Day

Getting Your Way Every Day

Mastering the Lost Art of
Pure Persuasion

Alan Axelrod

AMACOM

American Management Association

New York • Atlanta • Brussels • Chicago • Mexico City • San Francisco
Shanghai • Tokyo • Toronto • Washington, D.C.

Special discounts on bulk quantities of AMACOM books are available to corporations, professional associations, and other organizations. For details, contact Special Sales Department, AMACOM, a division of American Management Association, 1601 Broadway, New York, NY 10019.
Tel: 212-903-8316. Fax: 212-903-8083.
E-mail: specialsls@amanet.org
Website: www.amacombooks.org/go/specialsales
To view all AMACOM titles go to: www.amacombooks.org

This publication is designed to provide accurate and authoritative information in regard to the subject matter covered. It is sold with the understanding that the publisher is not engaged in rendering legal, accounting, or other professional service. If legal advice or other expert assistance is required, the services of a competent professional person should be sought.

Various names used by companies to distinguish their software and other products can be claimed as trademarks. AMACOM uses such names throughout this book for editorial purposes only, with no intention of trademark violation. All such software or product names are in initial capital letters or ALL CAPITAL letters. Individual companies should be contacted for complete information regarding trademarks and registration.

Library of Congress Cataloging-in-Publication Data

Axelrod, Alan, 1952–
       Getting your way every day : mastering the lost art of pure persuasion / Alan Axelrod.
          p.   cm.
     Includes index.
     ISBN-10: 0-8144-7335-0 (pbk.)
     ISBN-13: 978-0-8144-7335-1 (pbk.)
      1. Persuasion (Psychology)   2. Rhetoric.   3. Influence (Psychology)
     4. Business communication   I. Title.

     BF637.P4A94   2007
     153.8'52—dc22

                                                        2006018487

Printing number

   10   9   8   7   6   5   4   3   2   1

For Anita,
who almost always gets her way every day.

Contents

Getting Your Way
Every Day

To the Reader

The language of business, they say, is money. Everything else is just words.
Or so they say.

But money, of course, is never just money. It is a marker of plans, dreams, hopes, and decisions, and behind those plans, dreams, hopes, and decisions are words. Money is never spent or invested, made or lost, without someone persuading and someone else having been persuaded. Master the strategy, tactics, and tools of persuasion, and you speak the language of business. You speak the language of money.

If there were a dictionary of this language, a manual of persuasion, a rule book of rhetoric, it would fly off bookstore shelves.

In fact, this is the book. Not that its author has a monopoly on the secrets of persuasion. Actually, those secrets have been with us and available for the taking for the past 2,500 years. No one thought harder or as thoroughly and effectively about how to persuade the mind, win the heart, and move the will than the ancient Greeks, beginning some two-and-a-half millennia ago.

What the Greeks invented, the Romans often perfected, and in no instance was this truer than the art and science of rhetoric. The prosecution of one Gaius Verres, the notorious governor of Sicily, is an example.

Born about 115 B.C., Gaius Verres became Rome's poster child for extravagant political corruption and stupefying misgovernment, combined with apparently limitless power. An embezzler, extortionist, and art thief with a nasty penchant for executing anyone who got in his way, he did not so much govern Sicily as suck it dry like ripe fruit, which he clearly meant to fling aside when nothing more was left. Yet his political connections were so powerful and so extensive that no authority could dislodge him. He was destined, it seemed, to rule forever.

In desperation, the people of Sicily sought help from a youthful orator named Cicero. He was, the Sicilians knew, a student of the world's most famous teacher of oratory, Molo of Rhodes, and if anyone could persuade a court of Roman law to oust Verres, it was, they believed, this young man.

The trial took place in 70 B.C. Cicero made a single speech, framing his case in words so compelling that the defendant's lawyer simply refused to reply, and Gaius Verres fled Rome before the verdict was even handed down. Deposed and powerless, he lived in exile until the year 43 B.C., when Mark Antony, with a covetous eye on the old crook's art collection, had him murdered.

The Greeks and the Romans knew very well that the right words, said the right way, could move the world. And, since their time, innumerable masters of verbal

1

persuasion have followed their example. While it is no wonder, then, that for nearly 2,500 years rhetoric was the foundation of all education, it is utterly baffling that this subject has disappeared from the classrooms of today.

Getting Your Way Every Day: Mastering the Lost Art of Pure Persuasion will introduce business people—and everyone else who has an everyday need to speak and write clearly, vividly, and persuasively—to the art and science of rhetoric, the classical secrets of making your case and getting your way. First formulated by the Greek orators including Aristotle, then brought to perfection by Cicero and the rhetoricians of the Middle Ages and Renaissance, this powerful system of persuasion is now very nearly a lost body of knowledge. *Getting Your Way Every Day* will reveal the system to a new generation of business professionals in a form that is streamlined and bottom-lined, customized for the twenty-first century using nonacademic, real-world, case-by-case, and application-by-application examples.

PART I

Get Ready to Win

Profit from Ancient Wisdom

*A practical, compact history of classical rhetoric
and why it's still the most effective way to make
your case and get your way today and every day.*

In most modern dictionaries the definition of *rhetoric* begins nobly enough: "The art or study of using language effectively or persuasively." Nothing wrong with that. Who doesn't want to use language effectively or persuasively? But read on. The third or fourth definition typically runs something like this: "Language that is elaborate, pretentious, insincere, or intellectually vacuous." It is this third- or fourth-string definition, not the primary one, that most people today associate with rhetoric. In fact, most people don't even use the word on its own anymore, but invariably attach qualifiers such as *mere* or *just* to it. "You're not giving us a valid reason. It's *mere rhetoric.*"

RHETORIC IS NOT A FOUR-LETTER WORD

The fault is not really in the interpretation of a word. Suspicions concerning persuasion run deep in our culture. Remember the story of Adam and Eve? The Serpent brings an end to paradise on earth through a persuasive speech he makes to Eve, convincing her to eat the forbidden fruit. We are wary of the salesman with "the gift of gab" or the dictator who happens to be a "silver-tongued orator," capable of making lies seem to be the truth.

Well, here is the truth. Rhetoric—by which I mean nothing more or less than the effective use of speech or writing to inform, persuade, or motivate listeners or readers in order to get your way—is a tool that, like any other tool, can be used constructively or destructively. Give a mechanic a screwdriver and she'll build you something. Give the same tool to a burglar and he'll break into your house to rob you blind. The moral value of the screwdriver is what the user brings to it. The same is true of rhetoric. There is nothing inherently immoral, dishonest, or evil about persuasion. In itself, it is morally neutral. The user applies, for better or worse, his own values and motives when trying to persuade others.

5

CLASSICAL PERSUASION

Based on the written record—which is, of course, all we have to go by—the ancient Greeks were the first to make conscious, deliberate use of rhetoric: the art of persuasion. So much is evident from the epics of Homer, which were probably composed during the eighth or ninth century B.C., or the works of the great Greek dramatists such as Sophocles, or the writings of the earliest historians, Herodotus and Thucydides, all active during the fifth century B.C.

As the Greeks were apparently the first to practice rhetoric, so they were the first to study, formulate, and codify it—to attempt systematic answers to what was, in effect, a question both simple and profound: *How do I get my way?* Historians identify Corax of Syracuse, who lived during the second quarter of the fifth century B.C., as the first formulator of the art of rhetoric. He created an aid to help ordinary citizens effectively plead property claims in court, and his most enduring contribution to the art of rhetoric was his prescription for the proper form of a plea. He wrote that it should include a *proem*, or introduction; a *narration*, which presents the historical facts of the case in question; *arguments*, both confirmation and refutation; and a *peroration*, which, based on everything that has gone before, puts the plea in an "actionable" form.

Corax apparently had students or followers who may have written their own rhetoric handbooks, but none of these survives. The next big name among the ancient Greeks is Gorgias of Leontini, who, as Sicily's ambassador to Athens, dazzled Athenians with his ability to make persuasive speeches and excited an intense and enduring interest in rhetoric throughout this great and influential Greek city-state. The Athenian Isocrates probably studied under Gorgias, as did the seminal philosopher Socrates. Gorgias began his professional career as a *logographos*, a hired writer of courtroom speeches. Around 392 B.C., he opened his own school of oratory and made a fortune from it. He left to posterity twenty-one discourses and nine letters concerning rhetoric and is especially remembered for what he had to say about elegance, eloquence, speech delivery, and the effective use of figures of speech.

Now, by this time, the art of rhetoric was flourishing in Greece, especially in the Athenian cultural center. Orators and rhetoricians were highly esteemed and handsomely paid, and their runaway success aroused a certain degree of suspicion. No less a figure than Plato criticized rhetoricians such as Gorgias for being more interested in opinions and appearances than in philosophical truth. Ironically, Plato made his argument against rhetoricians by means of the masterful practice of rhetoric. Whatever blow Plato might have dealt to the prestige of the art of persuasion in Athens, his low estimate of rhetoric helped incite his most famous student, Aristotle, to write an entire book called *Rhetoric*. This treatise codified the art of persuasion and elevated it to the lofty status it would enjoy for thousands of years, even into the Middle Ages and Renaissance.

In competition with Isocrates, Aristotle operated a school of oratory in Athens and, by 333 B.C., completed his book on the subject. The first two major parts of *Rhetoric* were devoted to what classical rhetoricians call the "discovery" of arguments—that is, the very basis from which a persuasive discourse is composed. Aristotle went on to expound three modes of proof of an argument: the appeal to reason, the appeal to emotion, and the ethical appeal. They form the foundation of virtually all rhetorical theory that followed Aristotle. In *Rhetoric*, Aristotle set out to counter Plato's criticism by showing how rhetoric was, in fact, intimately connected to truth as an indispensable bridge between reality on the one hand and human perception, thought, and action on the other.

After Aristotle, the next giant of classical rhetoric was Roman rather than Greek. Cicero was born in 106 B.C. and wrote seven works on oratory and rhetoric, the most important of which are *De Oratore*, *Brutus*, and *Orator*. He expanded the scope of rhetoric beyond what even Aristotle had suggested, arguing that a competent rhetorician had to have a great breadth of knowledge, so that the study of rhetoric was really the study of what today would be called the liberal arts. Thanks to Cicero, rhetoric found its way to the heart of higher education—at least for the next 1,500 years or so.

With Cicero, another giant of Roman rhetoric was M. Fabius Quintilianus, better known as Quintilian, whose work greatly influenced higher education through the Middle Ages and Renaissance. He covered the preliminary education required for the proper study of rhetoric; the nature, aims, and scope of rhetoric; the art of oratory (including finding and structuring the material of arguments); style; and the role of memory and delivery in effective oration.

WHEN THE *TRIVIUM* WASN'T TRIVIAL

Schoolbook histories too often stereotype the medieval period as the Dark Ages, during which humankind suddenly and deliberately "forgot" all the knowledge gained during the classical era. In fact, medieval scholars revered classical learning and used it to build what was called the *trivium*, the four-year undergraduate course of studies that led to the equivalent of a bachelor of arts degree. The three legs of the trivium were grammar, logic, and rhetoric. (Graduate school, by the way, came after the trivium and consisted of the *quadrivium*: music, arithmetic, geometry, and astronomy.)

During most of the Middle Ages, rhetoric formed the basis of effective letter writing and sermon composition and delivery. These were very important skills for educated men (and, during the Middle Ages, all college graduates were men) who needed to communicate effectively (letters were the chief form of serious communication). For the most part, the history of rhetoric during this long period consisted of transmitting the body of rhetorical thought originally created by Aristotle and Quintilian.

RENAISSANCE PEOPLE

The most notable rhetorician of the Renaissance was the single greatest scholar of the era, Desiderius Erasmus, who put emphasis on variety and style of expression

rather than on strict rules of argument, and perhaps his soundest and most enduring advice for novice writers was to "write, write, and again write."

Other rhetoricians also wrote influential handbooks during the Renaissance,
including the Spaniard Juan Luis Vives (1492–1540) and Philippus Melanchthon
(1497–1560) of Germany, who was a scholar closely associated with Martin Luther
and, not surprisingly, greatly interested in the mechanics of eloquence.

In the later Renaissance, a host of English scholars, including Roger Ascham,
Sir John Cheke, and Sir Thomas Elyot (a distant relative of the great twentieth-
century Anglo-American poet T. S. Eliot), returned directly to Aristotelian rhetoric
and popularized it in the education of young British gentlemen. Other English
scholars focused more on the Romans, Cicero and Quintilian. By the sixteenth
century, English students were being taught by adherents of one of three schools
of rhetoric. The Traditionalists imparted the full course of classical rhetoric, emphasizing both logic and style. The Ramists, followers of the celebrated French
rhetorician Pierre Ramé—who lived from 1515 to 1572 and whose Latinized name
was Ramus—opposed the Aristotelians by dividing rhetoric from logic, which they
considered a separate subject to be taught by others. The Ramists devoted themselves to style and, in oral speech, to delivery. Finally, another group of rhetoricians, the Figurists, taught the whole range of metaphors, similes, and figures of
speech.

One man during the late Renaissance made a bold departure from the three
schools of English rhetoric. This was the scientist and philosopher Francis Bacon
(1561–1626), who was the first student of rhetoric since the Greeks to view rhetoric as a genuine instrument for manipulating thought and transforming it into action. He reduced the "duty and office of Rhetoric" to what he called the application
of "Reason to Imagination for the better moving of the Will." According to Bacon,
imagination and reason were two distinct faculties of mind, and he defined the
function of rhetoric as a kind of bridge between the two, a means of applying the
imagination to reason in order to produce a desired action. Put another way, rhetoric could be used to enliven logic with language sufficiently appealing to the imagination to move the will to action. Thus, rhetoric was an indispensable catalyst in
the art of persuasion.

THE DIVORCE OF ELOQUENCE FROM LOGIC

Whereas scholars and writers of the late Renaissance and early Enlightenment were
highly interested in rhetoric at the highest levels of education and expression, those
of the eighteenth century, especially in England and France, were more concerned
with it as an aspect of elementary education. At the same time, they were less
enamored of the relationship between rhetoric and logic than between rhetoric and
what they generally called eloquence. Rhetoric was regarded less as a verbal system
for rigorous or persuasive discourse than as a means of demonstrating aesthetic
taste and creating "beauty" of language.

In the course of the eighteenth century, ideas on literature and verbal expression underwent a profound transformation as the Romantic era came into being. This literary and artistic period elevated feeling, emotion, sentiment, and the imagination above logic and logical expression. Moreover, writers as well as teachers and theoreticians during this period tended to divorce eloquence from logic. They even suggested that truly meaningful expression, which they defined as language capable of inspiring feelings and the imagination, was incompatible with merely logical expression, or language that appealed to rationality. By the beginning of the nineteenth century, this division between emotion and logic—and between writing suited to the emotions and that suited to logic—became a yawning gulf that has never really been bridged. Even today, most of us hold the prejudice developed during the late eighteenth and early nineteenth centuries, which is that there is emotionally eloquent language on the one hand and coolly rational language on the other, and never the twain shall meet.

THE SECRET REDISCOVERED

The great value of rhetoric today is that it can reintroduce into your writing and speech what the classical Greeks first formulated so long ago: a convenient bridge between emotion and logic and logic and emotion. Despite what many writers of the eighteenth and nineteenth centuries have led us to believe, these two realms are neither naturally separate nor mutually exclusive. Rhetoric electrifies logic. It makes argument compelling.

A PLAN FOR WINNING OTHERS OVER

The purpose of this book is not to revive classical rhetoric for its own sake, interesting though that might be. It is, rather, to offer to modern people, whose lives and livelihoods depend to a high degree on their ability to move, motivate, and persuade others, the benefit of a set of tools that have been never quite been lost but that have certainly been misplaced for a long time. Now you can sort through these same tools, dust them off, and at long last, put them back to work to bring logical clarity to expression, add passion to logical expression, give logical expression to persuasion, and ultimately, persuade others to act so that you can get your way every day.

CHAPTER 2

Look for an Argument

The powerful art of cutting to the chase: deciding
what you want to say and saying it clearly, vividly,
precisely, economically, and convincingly.

My mother used to say that nothing was more pointless than an argument. This was a wise opinion, at least based on her understanding of the word *argument*, which, as she saw it, meant nothing more than trading prejudices with another person at maximum volume. For her, an argument was a verbal way station between harmonious agreement on the one hand and a fistfight on the other. Words were substitutes for bare knuckles.

Words can be nothing more than harsh sounds, like the barking of dogs. As such, they can be pretty unpleasant and quite powerful; some people are intimidated by loud noises. Holler loudly enough and you may, in fact, get your way—unless, of course, your opponent has a bigger chest and a more formidable set of pipes.

A JOURNEY THROUGH THE FOG OF WORDS

For most people most of the time, arguments consist of a barrage of words that raise a smoky fog of emotion. Words should define and clarify, crystallizing action. They should not obscure the relevant issues and reduce the possibility of action to nothing more than blind flailing. Let's begin by cutting through the fog of words.

. . . AND THE GREATEST OF THESE IS CLARITY

The first word to clarify is *argument* itself. Begin by ridding the definition of its negative connotations. *Argument* should not be used as a synonym for *fight*. It is not impolite or unpleasant, something to be avoided; rather, it is an essential tool by which the world does most of its meaningful work. The better you use the tool, the more you can achieve. An argument is a set of reasons or a body of evidence offered in support of a point of view, a proposal, or a conclusion.

You can use three things to try to get your way with others: faith, hope, or clarity. With apologies to the apostle Paul, the greatest of these is clarity.

You may be able to move some people by asking them simply to have faith in you and what you say. Others may be willing to hope that you and your opinions are right and good. But if you can create an argument that supports your views with compelling reasons, you can be certain that you are making the most persuasive appeal of all, the appeal of clarity. Enable others to *clearly see* your point and you give them a reason to make up their minds for themselves, but in the direction you point them.

THE THESIS, OR HOW TO PIN YOUR POINT

We've encountered fresh definitions of two familiar words: *argument* and *conclusion*. An argument is not a verbal fight, but a set of reasons or evidence in support of a conclusion. Now, we usually think of a conclusion as the end of something, but an argument actually begins with the conclusion. So here's another new definition: In an argument, a conclusion is a thesis, a proposition that must be supported by the argument. In constructing an argument, the terms *thesis* and *conclusion* can be used interchangeably. The reason to use one word instead of the other is to avoid confusion between beginnings and endings. When you *begin* an argument with your *conclusion*, it is more convenient to call the statement of that conclusion your *thesis*.

Clearly formulating a thesis is the first step in making a convincing argument, just as laying a solid foundation is the first step in building a sound structure, no matter how elaborate it may finally be. The beauty of the most beautiful tower will not save it from collapse if the lowly foundation is faulty.

Begin by distinguishing a conclusion—or thesis—from mere facts. Not everything needs to be argued. In any situation, there are certain givens on which everyone can agree. If your company has 100 employees, you do not need to construct an argument to support the thesis that your company has 100 employees. It is a given, a fact. However, if you have reached the conclusion that your company desperately requires an additional ten employees, you need to fashion as precise a thesis statement as possible—*Our company needs an additional ten employees to process orders for the new line*—and build an argument to support it. The need for ten new employees is not a fact. It is your conclusion and therefore must be expressed as the thesis of an argument intended to persuade others of the validity of your conclusion and motivate them to take the necessary action to hire ten more people. Once the ten have joined the company, there will be no need to argue that the company has 110 employees. It will have become a fact, a given.

As a prerequisite for building a sound, persuasive argument, you must distinguish between conclusion and fact. It is also necessary to distinguish between premises and conclusions. This is not an academic exercise. It is the answer to a straightforward, although not always simple, question: *What are you trying to prove? What is your conclusion?* Or, put another way, *What is your thesis?*

The thesis (or conclusion) is the statement for which your argument will provide supporting reasons. The statements that actually give these reasons are called *premises.* "Always tell your wife (or husband) the truth. She (or he) will find out anyway." In this statement, the first sentence is the thesis, the second is the premise—the reason in support of the first sentence.

AT ISSUE AND AT STAKE

In the course of this book, we will have a lot more to say about formulating a thesis, but first you must ensure that you have one and that it is clearly stated.

In most real-world situations—especially in business—a reliable way of ensuring that you have found a compelling or worthwhile thesis is to examine it and make sure that it clearly states what is at issue and what is at stake. "Our company needs an additional ten employees" is a reasonable thesis, but not a compelling one. "Our company needs ten additional employees to process orders for the new line" is a better thesis because it clearly indicates what is at issue: the processing of orders for the new product or service line. "Our company needs an additional ten employees to process orders for the new line so that we do not suffer a cash-flow crunch because of a lag between orders, delivery, and payment" is the best thesis statement of the three. It not only makes clear the issue, but also what is at stake—namely, cash flow, something on which the financial health of the company depends.

The stronger you build your foundation, the stronger the finished building will be. The more accustomed you become to thinking in terms of theses, the more persuasive you will be at making arguments. With that as your objective:

* Think in terms of having a thesis, which is a statement that can (and must) be supported by arguments.
* Link your thesis to a clear issue.
* Link the issue to a benefit or consequence: something that is at stake.

The classical Roman rhetoricians provided a helpful guide to moving through these three steps to constructing a compelling or worthwhile thesis. They required a writer or speaker to ask three questions about a thesis. (*Warning: They spoke Latin.*)

1. *An sit?* Is it? This is a question of fact.
2. *Quid sit?* What is it? This is a question of definition.
3. *Quale sit?* What kind is it? This is a question of quality.

If the basic thesis is that "our company needs an additional ten employees," you could use these questions to develop a more compelling statement:

1. Does our company really need ten more employees? Why? (Question of fact)
2. If it is agreed that our company really needs ten more employees, what will each of these employees do? What will their roles be? (Question of definition)
3. Assuming these ten new employees adequately perform their roles, how will they improve our company? Will there be a genuine benefit, and will the added benefit outweigh the added cost? (Question of quality)

Effective, persuasive arguments begin with a dialogue—between you and yourself. Ask yourself the questions necessary to transform a thesis into a compelling thesis, one worth supporting with an argument.

FIX PROBLEMS, NOT PEOPLE

Every enterprise has problems. Every enterprise consists of people. Problems are much easier to fix than people. Effective arguments focus on problems, not people.

Joe just failed to close a sale. You could present the following thesis to him: "Joe, you are a lousy salesman." Will this lead to an argument that will change Joe by transforming him into a great salesman? Almost certainly not.

Alternatively, you could try saying something like this: "Joe, it would be more effective to focus your presentation on value rather than cost." Upon this thesis you could build an argument about effective salesmanship rather than an argument about Joe. The fact is that you really don't want to change Joe. (Joe is Joe.) What you want is to help him to become a more effective salesman. And that's a good thing, because it is much easier to learn a repertoire of sales techniques than it is to transform your personality.

Chapter 6 will explore the common fallacies that typically torpedo arguments. Among the most common is the "ad hominem fallacy," the mistake of basing an argument on some attribute of personality rather than on the issues and stakes involved in the matter at hand. "Joe is a bad salesman because he's a doofus" is an ad hominem thesis. The Latin phrase *ad hominem* means "to the man," and by turning our attention to the person we are addressing, we are distracted from the real issues. Ad hominem arguments are almost never valid and are rarely persuasive. Persuading others means changing how they look at something or how they respond to something or how they do something. It does not mean changing who they are or criticizing them for failing to be someone else.

OPEN YOUR MENU, PLEASE

In Chapter 3, you will learn that anyone who needs to persuade anyone else of anything will have to make use of one or more of three basic modes of appeal: an appeal to reason, to ethics, or to emotion. Beginning with that chapter, we'll get into what each of these modes of appeal involves and requires. But before you can decide what mode or combination of modes of appeal to use, you need to either *have* something to argue about or *find* something to argue about.

Now, someone writing a book on *how* to argue might be justified in telling readers that *what* they argue about is strictly their business and none of his. Yet the classical rhetoricians, especially the Romans Cicero and Quintilian, made it *their* business. They came up with what they called "The Topics," and it is very much worth passing on as a highly effective way to organize your thoughts and discover just what you have to say. Your arguments may use one or more of the "topics" from the menu that follows to open up, explore, and present your persuasive discourse.

Topic 1: Definition

Many arguments use or even begin with definitions. Some arguments consist entirely of definition. Definition can serve as a way of sorting out the salient elements of a complex or confusing issue. Many arguments degenerate into fruitless verbal fistfights because the opponents, having failed to define the basic issues, talk at cross-purposes. John and Mary think they are arguing about fruit, but John understands this word in this case to mean apples while Mary assumes it means oranges. The argument has failed to define the issue.

At the very least, then, persuasive discourse should begin by making sure everyone is on the same page with regard to the definition of the basic issues. However, it is also possible to use definition as the topic of the entire argument. In this case, definition is subdivided into one of two types.

Definition by *genus* is a thesis on which an argument can be based. "Driving while drunk is a crime against society." This statement defines drunk driving as a member of the genus of crimes against society. We employ the genus subtopic of the definition topic frequently and casually. For example: "Sushi is overpriced food," "Men are from Mars," "Women are from Venus," "All power corrupts," "Policemen are lovers of the doughnut." Used thoughtfully, the genus subtopic can be a most effective and compelling means of finding the thesis of your argument.

The second subtopic of the definition is *division*. Return for a moment to Paul the apostle, who, in the First Epistle to the Corinthians, offers this thesis about the three qualities that should abide in the mature soul: "And now abideth faith, hope, charity, these three; but the greatest of these is charity." Maturity, Paul has concluded, is defined by three things: faith, hope, and charity. That in itself is a definition by division—X is divided into A, B, and C—and it is also a thesis, something that can be supported by means of an argument. The apostle adds an additional thesis to this definition by division, concluding that the greatest quality of the three is charity.

As with the subtopic of genus, we often use the subtopic of division in the everyday speech of business and pleasure. Sometimes this subtopic is merely necessary groundwork for an argument. You may begin an argument in support of a thesis about what makes a great martini by saying, "A martini consists of gin, dry vermouth, and an olive or lemon twist." However, in and of itself, this statement is not a thesis, but a definition necessary to establish a fact, a given. (Please discount for the moment that some would argue that a drink substituting vodka for gin is still a martini.) To transform this definition by division into a genuine thesis, we would have to say something like, "A great martini consists of five parts gin to one part dry vermouth and a twist of lemon rather than an olive." This could be the entire basis of an argument and is therefore worthy of being called a thesis.

Topic 2: Comparison

Few intellectual activities are more common than comparison. The Roman rhetoricians recognized three subtopics within this topic.

Similarity is the detection of the likeness of two or more things. It is the basis of two general types of argument: induction and analogy.

Induction takes note of a similarity among a number of things and uses this similarity to make an inference about some unobserved thing:

> I touched a hot pan and burned my finger. I touched a hot pot and burned my finger. I touched a hot plate and burned my finger. If I touch a hot kettle, I will burn my finger.

Analogy argues that if two things are alike in one or more ways, they are probably alike in other ways as well. Whereas induction argues from similarities among similar things, analogy argues from similarities among dissimilar things. The hot pan, pot, and plate warrant an inductive conclusion about a fourth similar object at a similar temperature, the kettle. The experience of getting physically burned is also analogous to the superficially quite dissimilar experience of being jilted by a lover, as the old saying "Once burned, twice shy" attests. This expression is a thesis that is based on analogy, which is a subtopic of comparison.

Induction and analogy are important methods by which we make arguments concerning the nature of reality and the benefits and risks of proposed actions. Here is a thesis supported by induction:

> We should hire ten new employees now. The last two times we hired new employees, the added productivity not only paid for the additional salaries, it increased profits by 4 percent.

Here is a thesis based on analogy:

> Hiring new employees is a habit, like eating popcorn.

Later in this book, we will have more to say about induction and analogy. For the present, note that they are very common, very useful, often quite persuasive, and subject to all manner of abuse and error. They must be used with care.

Difference is another subtopic of the comparison topic. Difference identifies the contrasts between two or more things or situations and allows you to formulate or support a thesis based on those contrasts. For example:

> "While it is true that in 1998 and 2001, adding employees to the payroll resulted in a profitable increase in productivity, the nature of the widget market back then was different from what it is today. Between 1996 and 1998, the market grew by 10 percent. Between 1999 and 2001, it grew by 7 percent. Since 2002, the market has actually contracted by 2 percent. Therefore, hiring ten new employees now will not produce the same profits we enjoyed as a result of the hiring in 1998 and 2001."

Degree is the third and final subtopic of the topic of comparison. At issue in many arguments is the effect of having, buying, allowing, or creating more or less of something. "More employees will create more productivity" and "More employees will create more cost" are both theses concerning degree.

While the subtopic of degree is common and basic to many arguments, it presents many difficulties, since questions of degree can be hard to settle satisfactorily. Consider these two statements:

> The martini: the more vermouth the better.
>
> The martini: the less vermouth the better.

Which argument is valid or more valid? Judgments involving degree are often subjective or involve a number of complex variables.

Topic 3: Relationship

The classical rhetoricians divided this topic into four subtopics:

1. Cause and effect
2. Antecedent and consequence
3. Contraries
4. Contradictions

Cause and effect is basic to many arguments because it seeks to answer one of the most essential of all human questions: "Why?"

Because "why?" is so basic a question, arguments that offer answers are automatically compelling—but not necessarily persuasive. After all, it is not always easy to answer the "why?" question and answer it convincingly. Whenever you base an argument on a cause-and-effect thesis, you must consider it in the light of five principles:

1. *A given effect may be produced by a number of causes.* Are you certain that you have determined the correct cause?

2. *The cause you propose in your thesis must be adequate to produce the effect.* You simultaneously discover your mantel clock smashed to bits on the floor in front of the fireplace *and* a beetle scurrying across the mantel. Knowing that the beetle is insufficiently powerful, you do not conclude that it knocked over the clock, but you don't rule out the possibility that your twenty-pound tomcat, attracted to the beetle, jumped up on the mantel, knocked the clock off, then fled the scene.

3. *Having identified a cause that is both probable and adequate, you must not fail to consider other equally probable and adequate causes.* A huge truck rumbled by on the street a few minutes ago, rattling everything in the house. Perhaps the vibration could have sent the mantel clock to its destruction.

4. *Consider whether the circumstances were such that the proposed cause could actually produce the effect.* Wait a minute, could Tom have been outside hunting for birds?

5. *Consider whether the proposed cause always produces the same effect, or is at least likely to do so.* When a twenty-pound cat rubs into a clock on a ten-inch-wide mantel, the clock is almost certain to fall.

As mentioned, Chapter 6 covers the fallacies that sometimes bedevil arguments. Among the most common relating to cause and effect is the one known by the Latin name *post hoc ergo propter hoc,* which means "after this, therefore because of this."

> Breaking a mirror means seven years of bad luck. John broke a mirror and spent the next seven years plagued by bad luck.

There is no compelling evidence that John's problems were caused by the mishap with the mirror. The post hoc fallacy is the greatest danger in cause-and-effect arguments.

Antecedent and consequence is a less rigorous relationship than cause and effect.

> "We should double our regular order of romance novels," the bookstore assistant manager says to the manager, "because the height of beachgoing season is coming, and a lot of people love to read romance novels when they sunbathe."

The assistant manager is not arguing that sunbathing causes people to read romance novels, but that beach season is conducive to—an antecedent of—romance novel reading.

Contraries are opposites. The most obvious example is *yes and no,* and a great many arguments center on advocating one or the other of this pair. For better or worse, political arguments are often built on a thesis that poses contraries:

> "The choice is simple. Vote for me and enjoy liberty. Vote for my opponent and be condemned to slavery."

Powerful arguments can be built on contraries, but this subtopic may also lead to oversimplification and exaggeration, a tendency to render gray areas in unwarranted terms of black and white.

Contradictions negate one another, but they are not contraries. For example:

"Abortion is a woman's right" is the *contrary* of "Abortion is murder" (because no one has the right to commit murder), but "Abortion is a woman's right" *contradicts* "Abortion is not a woman's right."

It is important to recognize the difference between contraries and contradictions. Contraries require making two positive assertions or theses: "The soup is hot" versus "The soup is cold." Contradictions merely require negation: "The soup is hot" versus "The soup is not hot," which leaves open the possibility that it might be lukewarm.

It is almost always more compelling to make two positive statements than it is to make a positive statement and its negation. We are more eager to decide which of these two positions is correct—"Hiring ten more employees *will increase profits*" versus "Hiring ten more employees *will erode profits*"—than which of these two is correct: "Hiring ten more employees *will increase profits*" versus "Hiring ten more employees *will not increase profits.*"

However, it is not always possible to argue validly a thesis built on contraries.

"The Constitution guarantees the right to privacy" can be reasonably argued, as can its contradiction, "The Constitution does not guarantee the right to privacy," whereas one cannot reasonably argue the contrary: "The Constitution denies the right to privacy." That statement is factually untrue. There is nothing in the Constitution that forbids this right.

Topic 4: The Possible, the Impossible

Sometimes the first step in persuading someone to do something is successfully arguing that the proposed action is possible. Sometimes the first step in persuading someone to refrain from doing something is successfully arguing that the proposed action is impossible.

The circumstances of possibility and impossibility can make for a compelling thesis.

You are selling a diet program. Your thesis is that by spending $100 on your program, weight loss of twenty-five pounds is possible in three months. Persuade your potential customer of this possibility and you may well have a sale.

Here's another example:

Your boss wants to save money by eliminating three subordinate positions from your department. You argue that it is impossible to maintain the present level of productivity and, therefore, revenue without the contribution of the employees in those three positions.

Arguing on the basis of possibility has another distinct advantage. In many circumstances, it is possible to argue deductively, rather than inductively, about issues of possibility. By removing the element of subjectivity, logic can put to rest some areas of potential dispute. According to Aristotle, there are six major deductive truths concerning possibility:

1. *If one pair of contraries is possible, the other is also possible.* If you can make money, you can also lose money. If you can lose money, you can also make money.

2. *If one of a pair of similar things is possible, the other thing is also possible.* If you can play tennis, you can play badminton.

3. *If the harder of two things is possible, the easier is also possible.* If you can play one of Chopin's *Ballades*, you can play "Chopsticks."

4. *If a thing can have a beginning, it can have an end; if it has an end, it can have a beginning.* This principle has gotten many a parent through many a PTA meeting.

5. *If the parts of something are possible, the whole is possible; if the whole is possible, the parts are possible.* "I can build a motor, a steering system, a transmission, and a set of brakes; therefore, I can build a car, and if I can build a car, I certainly can put together a transmission for you."

6. *If something can be created without skill, art, or preparation, it can be created with the aid of skill, art, and preparation.* This is similar to proposition number three.

Topic 5: Past Fact, Future Fact

This topic is used to construct arguments about whether something has happened or will happen. Police officers, lawyers, and judges use it in their everyday work, and since so many arguments have as their object persuading others of the probability of something having occurred or occurring in the future, the topic is very often useful outside of the courtroom. In many cases, there is no doubt about something having occurred and very little doubt about something occurring in the future. When such events are facts, there is no need to construct arguments to support them. The "past fact, future fact" topic is useful when you are arguing the *probability* (not the factual existence) of an event.

This topic is governed by the following assumptions, all of which were first stated by the classical rhetoricians:

• *If the less probable of two events has occurred, the more probable event is also likely to have occurred.* Rhetoricians and logicians call this an argument *a fortiori,* using a Latin phrase meaning "from the stronger." We use *a fortiori* reasoning all the time. "If I can manage the budget of a Fortune 500 company, certainly I can manage the budget of this household!"

• *If an event that naturally follows another event has occurred, then that other event has also occurred. Conversely, if the antecedent event occurred, then its natural consequence also occurred.* The old saying "Where's there's smoke, there's fire" is an example of a thesis based on this assumption. Smoke is the natural consequence of fire; therefore, the sight of smoke implies the existence of fire, even if the fire is unseen. If you come across the burned-out remains of a building, you can make two reasonable arguments concerning the antecedents of this fact: 1) There was a fire and 2) there was also smoke.

• *If a person possesses the power, desire, and opportunity to do a thing, the person has done it.* This is the basis of the cop's golden rule for identifying suspects. The most likely suspect in a crime is the person who had the means (power), the motive (desire), and the opportunity. Note, however, that these three factors do not prove guilt. All they do is form the basis of suspicion. Always remember that the past fact, future fact topic is all about probability, not fact.

• *If the capability and the desire to do a thing are present, that thing will be done.* This assumption is more of a stretch than the first three and represents certain assumptions concerning human nature. "I applied for a credit card, but I promise I will never use it." (*Right . . .*)

• *If the antecedents of an event are present, then the event will occur.* This is not an absolute statement of inevitability, but it is a strong thesis concerning probability. "With all those oily rags you've been throwing into the garage, we're going to have a fire sooner or later."

• *Given the means, the end will be accomplished.* We act in accordance with this thesis on a daily basis. You climb into your car in the morning assuming that it will get you to work. You have good reason to believe that your car is an adequate means to that end. Of course, you cannot be entirely certain. You may have an accident. The bridge may be out. But it is reasonable to assume that you'll make it.

Topic 6: Testimony, Authority, Statistics, Law, Proverbs, and Precedent

Testimony is another powerful topic on which to base an argument. We rely on it frequently. The most important forms of testimony—the four leading subtopics— are authority, statistics, law, and precedent.

Authority relies on testimony from a specially qualified source to persuade others of the validity of your thesis.

> Ms. Johnson is a distinguished tax attorney, and she is confident that the tax shelter I propose we invest in is perfectly legal.

This subtopic threatens to break down when conflicting authorities dispute one another.

The defense attorney brings in a psychiatrist who claims that his client is not guilty by reason of insanity. The prosecutor brings in another psychiatrist who delivers his opinion that the accused is perfectly sane.

In choosing an authority to back up your argument (or when you are evaluating the use of authority in someone else's argument), ask the following questions:

- Is the authority's opinion internally consistent, or is it self-contradictory or illogical?
- Is the authority clearly unbiased? (Consumer organizations have criticized drug testimonials from physicians who are paid consultants for drug companies.)
- Is the authority's opinion based on the most up-to-date data?
- Is the authority's opinion generally accepted by other authorities in the field, especially by the most eminent authorities in the field?
- Is there anything obviously wrong with the basic assumptions behind the authority's opinion? (The so-called authority states that "based on tests, I am convinced that Medicine X is highly effective." However, the tests involved only a dozen patients.)

There is another question to ask: *Is the authority really an authority?* While you might listen to a basketball player giving advice about what sneakers to buy, why would he know any more than you do about soft drinks? And then there is the drug advertiser that provides a testimonial spoken by a man in a white lab coat who begins, "I'm not a doctor, but I play one on TV . . . ." So what?

Statistics can be extremely persuasive in any argument, because, like numbers, they seem manifestly objective and therefore wholly reliable. When you have good statistics, use them. Just be certain they are good and valid, and genuinely support your argument.

Before you use statistics in an argument, be aware of their cardinal limitation. Provided that statistical information has been carefully and legitimately compiled, the resulting numbers do confirm certain facts; however, they do not necessarily support inferences made on the basis of those facts.

"Sixty percent of the electorate voted for Smith" may be a factually accurate statistic, from which it is reasonable to argue that candidate Smith appealed to more voters than candidate Jones. It is not reasonable, however, to conclude—on the basis of this statistic alone—that Smith will make a better president than Jones.

Other questions to ask about statistics include:

- What is the source of the data? Is it competent? Qualified? Unbiased?
- What was the process by which the statistics were compiled?
- What is the size of the statistical sample? Where and when were the statistics compiled?

- Who was interviewed? Is the sample truly representative?
- Are the statistics up-to-date?

Law settles many arguments. "Let's just not pay the taxes on it" is easily defeated by a counterargument based on law: "The law says we have to."

Of course, applying laws to specific cases is not always obvious, easy, or cut-and-dried—and so we have lawyers. This subtopic also encompasses such controlling principles as contracts, records, deeds, and a variety of other legal documents.

Proverbs and maxims are often used in arguments as if they bear the force of law. Insofar as proverbial wisdom reflects an accumulation of human experience, it can be a persuasive and useful basis for a thesis or a bolster to an argument:

> "I understand that you expect sales of the new widgets to replenish our cash reserves. But we should delay the expenditure until those widgets actually sell through. After all, never count your chickens before they're hatched."

The problem with proverbs and maxims is that for any given saying, it is almost always possible to find another that contradicts it:

> "Yes, but nothing ventured, nothing gained."

It is also possible for just about anyone to coin a slogan that sounds very much like a proverb:

> "You can never be too rich or too thin." (This may be a very unhealthy thesis.)

And while most proverbs are anonymous, and therefore enjoy the status of expressions of collective wisdom, some can be traced to highly dubious sources.

> "Strength lies not in defense but in attack" is a most persuasive maxim. Too bad it comes from Adolf Hitler in *Mein Kampf.*

Precedent is so persuasive a subtopic on which to build a thesis that it is the basis of American jurisprudence. In this country, most legal decisions (in other words, the resolution of most legal arguments) are based on case law and precedent, referring to judicial decisions that were made in the past. In a broader context, people base all sorts of decisions on precedent, a word that means "what went before." Indeed, we value "experience" (that is, a knowledge of precedent) above almost everything else when we seek advice from a doctor, a lawyer, or an auto mechanic.

Consider, however, this maxim from Ralph Waldo Emerson: "A foolish consistency is the hobgoblin of little minds." Precedent for the mere sake of precedent makes for a weak—that is, unpersuasive—argument. You must show that the precedent is valuable.

"The last time we confronted this problem, we did X, Y, and Z, which averted a crisis and even created a spike in revenue. I propose the same solution now."

Arguing on the basis of precedent does not necessarily require finding a precedent that exactly duplicates present circumstances. Past circumstances, events, or actions can often be used as examples or models for present circumstances and events and for proposed actions.

"When America faced crisis and panic during the Great Depression, Franklin D. Roosevelt spoke frankly and reassuringly over the radio in his famous Fireside Chats. These talks worked wonders to hold the country together. Ms. Jones, I suggest that you, as CEO, follow this example and conduct a frank and reassuring videoconference with all of our employees. We need to avert panic and pull everyone together to get through this crisis."

MOTHERS OF INVENTION

In classical rhetoric, the first step in composing a persuasive discourse—an argument—was *inventio*, a Latin term meaning "invention" or "discovery." The topics we have just discussed are aids to inventing or discovering arguments. The Greek rhetoricians would call them the "artistic means" of persuasion (*entechnoi pisteis*) because they specifically constitute the *art* of rhetoric. As the methods and principles of rhetoric, they are encompassed within rhetoric. But invention also relies on "nonartistic means" of persuasion (what the Greeks termed *atechnoi pisteis*): resources that are outside of the art of rhetoric and that are available to anyone, whether skilled in the processes and procedures of argumentation or not.

External aids to invention include encyclopedias, dictionaries, handbooks, professional journals, bibliographies, newspapers, magazines, statistical sources (such as government records), and Internet sources. Constructing persuasive arguments often requires research in appropriate subject areas.

GET SMART

Prepare to be persuasive by learning about the field in which you are making your argument. What follows are some starting-point suggestions for finding external sources and aids to invention. Step one: Get a library card.

Trade and Professional Sources

Know your field. Talk to people you work with. Join a professional group or organization in your field. If necessary, go to the public library and consult *National Trade and Professional Associations of the United States* (Washington, D.C.:

Columbia Books), which lists associations that are likely relevant to your industry, profession, business, or enterprise, as well as any publications these associations may issue. Consult those publications.

While you are at the library, you might also check out the *Readers' Guide to Periodical Literature* (New York: H. W. Wilson Company), which is available in almost all reference departments. This invaluable resource allows you to look up individual articles relevant to your field or even your individual company or institution.

Your public library (or even the reception area of your place of business) may well have copies of relevant trade and professional journals. You should also consider personally subscribing to the most important journals.

Lives Lived

Biographies are an important source of information for building many arguments. When you need biographical information, start with the two standard directories, both available in public library reference departments: *Dictionary of National Biography* is a compendium of noteworthy Britons (Oxford, England: Oxford University Press) and *Dictionary of American Biography* (New York: Scribner), which covers important Americans. One qualification for inclusion in either of these massive, multivolume works is death. Living persons do not make their way into these dictionaries. For biographical information on living persons, see the annual editions of *Who's Who* (London and New York: A&C Black Publishers) for Britons and *Who's Who in America* (New Providence, N.J.: Marquis). Biographies of figures of world renown are published in the *International Who's Who* (London: Routledge) and *Current Biography* (published in New York by H. W. Wilson as a monthly magazine and also in annual yearbook volumes). The *Biography Index* (New York: H. W. Wilson) is found in library reference departments and is a very helpful guide to biographical material, including books and periodicals, in English. Living authors are covered in *Contemporary Authors* (Detroit: Thomson Gale).

Reference Tools

The public library reference department offers a wealth of important indexes that will lead you to key sources that are helpful in building arguments. The *Readers' Guide to Periodical Literature*, already mentioned, is a comprehensive annual guide, by subject and author, to articles published in leading periodicals. More specialized guides concentrating on academic areas are the annual editions of the *Humanities Index* and the *Social Sciences Index* (both New York: H. W. Wilson).

Important indexes to specialized literature (all issued annually by H. W. Wilson) include the *Biological and Agricultural Index*; the *Art Index*; the *Education Index*; the *Applied Science and Technology Index*; the *Business Periodicals Index*; and the *Essay and General Literature Index*.

Many major newspapers publish indexes that are often available online as well as in printed form in library reference departments.

Standard bibliographies include *A World Bibliography of Bibliographies* (Switzerland: Lausanne, Societas Bibliographica) and *Bibliographic Index: A Cumulative Bibliography of Bibliographies* (New York: H. W. Wilson). *Books in Print* (New Providence, N.J.: R. R. Bowker) is available in book form and online.

All these major indexes and bibliographies are costly, multivolume works that you probably won't want to purchase for your collection at home or even in the office. The following general reference books and handbooks should, however, find a place in any writer's or speaker's personal library:

> *The World Almanac and Book of Facts* (New York: World Almanac Books, published annually)

> *Information Please Almanac* (Boston: Pearson Education, published annually)

In addition, you should own a good dictionary—any of the standard available dictionaries are authoritative—and a good encyclopedia. *Encyclopaedia Britannica* and *World Book Encyclopedia* are available in fairly expensive traditional multivolume-book form or, quite inexpensively, on CD-ROM or DVD-ROM for use with personal computers.

Bartlett's and Others

Quotations are useful to illustrate, elaborate on, or even substantiate some aspect of an argument. *Bartlett's Familiar Quotations* (Boston: Little, Brown and Company, 1992) is an indispensable resource. Also highly useful is *Quotationary*, edited by Leonard Roy Frank (New York: Random House, 1999).

Dictionaries of quotations are enormous time-savers for researchers, as are concordances to the Bible. Various concordances are now available, free of charge, online. The best-known printed concordance is James Strong's *Exhaustive Concordance of the Bible* (Nashville, Tenn.: Thomas Nelson Publishers). This work was first published in 1894 and has been frequently reprinted since.

Surfing Cyberspace

For at least the past decade, no single research tool has been more powerful than the Internet and World Wide Web. Like most powerful tools, the Internet has its dangers. The first is, quite simply, information overload. So many resources and sources are available that sometimes one hardly knows where to begin. The second danger is actually the flip side of one of the great strengths of the Internet: Just as anybody can access the Web to find information, virtually anyone can contribute information to the Web. In traditional book publishing, publishers by and large take pains to purchase and publish the works of recognized authorities on various subjects. Certainly, this is no guarantee that everything in print is reliable, accurate, and truthful, but there is some assurance that the authors whose works are published have verifiable credentials and can lay reasonable claim to authority. Online, there are no such controls. You must be very vigilant in considering, judging, weighing, and filtering the information you find.

A good place for prospective Internet researchers to begin is with a *printed* book, *Find It Online: The Complete Guide to Online Research,* Fourth Edition, by Alan M. Schlein (Tempe, Ariz.: Facts on Demand Press, 2004). Of course, the Internet itself provides the most powerful tools for mining the information you need: search engines. They allow you to search out information on subjects merely by typing a keyword or keywords. The best-known search engines are Google (www.google.com), Yahoo! (www.yahoo.com), and Ask Jeeves (www.askjeeves .com). In addition, you might try AllTheWeb (www.alltheweb.com), AOL Search (search.aol.com), Lycos (www.lycos.com), and MSN Search (search.msn.com).

AUTOBIOGRAPHY AND COMMON SENSE

Encyclopedic, professional, and other research is indispensable to many arguments, and it is a valuable adjunct to many others. Very often, though, your best "external" resources for invention are yourself, your own experience, and your own common sense and judgment.

C H A P T E R   3

Lay It All Out

An explanatory start-up inventory of communication
strategies, tactics, and tools.

Having found your argument—what you want to persuade others of—you need next to decide how you will present the argument. There would seem to be an infinite number of ways to persuade people, but Aristotle recognized only three: the appeal to reason, the ethical appeal, and the appeal to emotion. We will explore these three modes of persuasion in detail in the next two chapters, but for now, let's survey them as the first step in organizing your argument, once you have formulated your thesis.

THE THREE MODES OF PERSUASION

The three modes of persuasion are not mutually exclusive. Depending on the issues and audience involved, an argument may use one, two, or all three modes. When it is possible to combine appeals to reason, ethics, and emotion, the result promises to be a highly persuasive argument. Indeed, it is often impossible to separate the three modes neatly. An argument that appeals to reason may tend to make an ethical and an emotional appeal as well. When people perceive that an argument "makes sense" (that is, seems eminently rational), they may also feel that the speaker is trustworthy (appeals to their sense of ethics) and that the argument is also satisfying (makes people feel good, thus appealing to the emotions).

An Appeal to Reason

Most people, most of the time, regard the appeal to reason as the gold standard of persuasion. We feel best about a decision when we can say, "This makes sense"—in other words, it appeals to our rational self. Of the three modes of appeal, therefore, the appeal to reason is almost always the most powerful and persuasive.

Arguments that appeal to reason employ one or more of the topics (and subtopics) discussed in Chapter 2: definition; comparison; relationship; the possible and the impossible; past fact and future fact; and testimony (including authority, statistics, law, proverbs, and precedent). Ideally, an appeal to reason is based on the sound use of deductive and inductive logic, as explained in Chapter 4, although it is not always possible (or necessary or even desirable) to haul out the full range of formal logical proof. Logical shortcuts are not only permissible, they often contribute to a more readable or readily comprehensible argument and, therefore, a more persuasive argument. In fact, whereas formal logicians employ the syllogism that states formal premises and derives formal conclusions (typically taking some variation of the form, "If A is true and B is true, then C must be true"), rhetoricians commonly construct verbal arguments using a less formal, abbreviated version of the syllogism called the *enthymeme*, in which there is a conclusion and one premise—the other premise, which would be explicitly stated in a syllogism, being understood or implied. For example, "John must be a Republican because he favors a lowered rate on corporate income taxes" is an enthymeme, which includes a conclusion (John must be a Republican) and a premise (because he favors a lowered rate on corporate income taxes) but leaves unstated the implicit premise: "All Republicans favor lowered rates on corporate income taxes."

The usefulness of the enthymeme is readily apparent; it saves words, time, and awkward statements of the obvious. But it should also be obvious that there are dangers in the enthymeme and, indeed, in all appeals to reason. It is quite possible that broad generalizations and unwarranted assumptions lurk behind an argument that has a perfectly logical form, making it therefore wrong, even as it exercises its apparently rational appeal. Do all Republicans favor lowered rates on corporate income taxes? Do at least some Democrats favor them as well? Chapter 6 discusses the pitfalls, or fallacies, that beset all three modes of appeal but are special hazards of the appeal to reason.

An Appeal to Ethics

Anyone who has spent much time in sales has heard a definition that goes something like this: A *good* salesman sells the merchandise. A *great* salesman sells himself. This formula defines great salespeople as experts in the ethical appeal. They possess the ability to persuade others—strangers—that they are trustworthy and of good character and will not knowingly present a false argument.

The ethical appeal creates an ethical image of the speaker or writer. It must present this person as a trustworthy source of information, opinion, and judgment. Ultimately, the persuasiveness of the ethical appeal can be summed up in a single plea: "Take my word for it." It is up to the speaker or writer to provide reasons for receiving that plea affirmatively. As we will see in Chapter 5, these reasons are conveyed exclusively through words in written discourse, but also through nonverbal cues in speech. Indeed, in a famous 1971 study by psychologist Albert Mehrabian, people who listened to a live speech were asked to rate the factors that made the speaker persuasive. On average, the audience attributed 55 percent of the persuasiveness to the speaker's appearance and gestures (body language), 38 percent to the speaker's tone of voice, and only 7 percent of the persuasiveness to the words actually spoken.

If the appeal to ethics seems flimsy, superficial, and subject to all manner of abuse, it is. Yet this mode of appeal is important, especially in presenting arguments dealing with matters that offer no certainty and on which opinions are divided.

An Appeal to Emotion

Most of us are embarrassed to admit that our opinions can be strongly affected by an appeal to our emotions. We tend to take pride in our rationality and feel a bit ashamed of our emotions, as if rationality were more likely to be right and the emotions commensurately apt to be wrong. Where rationality is concerned, we feel in control; where emotions dominate, we feel out of control, as if our emotions have a life of their own and are even somewhat alien to us. This is a cultural prejudice. Our emotions, no less than our faculty of reason, are part of us, and there is nothing abnormal or regrettable, let alone shameful, about being moved by emotion. In fact, very few of the major decisions we make are based purely on reason or purely on emotion. Even the most rational of decisions typically have an important emotional component, and many emotionally motivated decisions are quite reasonable.

More than either of the other two modes of appeal, successfully making the emotional appeal requires sensitive and skillful writing, whether the appeal is made on the page or in person. Through mere words, we must earn not just intellectual agreement or assent, but the emotional sympathy of our audience. This is the province of the great poet and the successful novelist as well as the accomplished speechwriter. Naked expressions of pity or outrage rarely succeed in making this appeal; the writer or speaker must instead paint with words a picture that evokes the desired emotions, which, in turn, move the audience to act as the speaker or writer wants it to.

THE FIVE PARTS OF ORGANIZATION

Having formulated your thesis and decided on a mode or modes of appeal, the task that remains is presenting your argument in a comprehensible and persuasive form. Arguments in the most commonly understood sense of the word—that is, arguments as verbal fistfights—rarely have any recognizable or, at least, useful structure, except that they tend to get louder and less coherent the longer they continue. In contrast, arguments in the sense intended by rhetoricians are always characterized by clear and effective organization.

Building on Aristotle, the Roman rhetoricians generally divided persuasive discourse into five parts: *exordium, narratio, confirmatio* (sometimes called *probatio*), *refutatio,* and *peroratio.*

Take a Bow

The Latin word *exordium,* which is the classical label for the first part of a persuasive discourse, is worth examining. It means "beginning a web." In this context "web" refers to the first step in weaving a cloth, which is either to mount the woof or lay the warp. No matter how complex a pattern you intend to weave, the cloth must begin with the foundation of a good woof and warp. Similarly, a persuasive discourse must lead the audience into its subject without unsettling, confusing, or disorienting readers or listeners. Expressed in more positive terms, the audience must feel that it is in capable hands and that it is about to invest its time and attention in something of value. At minimum, the exordium or introduction should tell the audience the purpose or objective of the discourse and, simultaneously, should render the audience receptive to what is about to be presented. We will go into more detail concerning the introduction in a moment, but first, let's continue with an overview of the other four parts of the classical persuasive discourse.

Give 'Em the Facts

What the classical rhetoricians called the *narratio,* the second part of a persuasive discourse, is most accurately described as a statement of fact or facts. In this section, the writer or speaker provides the readers or listeners with a summary narrative of the circumstances that they need to know about the subject at hand. This requires sensitivity to the identity and needs of the reader or the audience. One of the first pieces of advice expert writers give to novices is to *know who your reader is* and to write specifically *for* that reader. The author of an elementary math textbook knows that he is writing for a different reader than the author of an advanced calculus text. Similarly, if you are presenting an argument concerning material you know to be largely unfamiliar to your audience, you will need to devote adequate time and space to the statement of facts. On the other hand, if you are making an argument about an issue in a field that is very familiar to your audience, you will want to devote significantly less time and space to this section, and you may even want to eliminate it entirely. An argument intended to persuade a patient to undergo a new kind of treatment for bunions will include a far more extensive statement of fact than an argument intended to promote the new procedure to a group of podiatrists.

Confirm This

The third section of the classical persuasive discourse is the *confirmatio* or *probatio.* Both Latin terms may be translated in this context to mean the English word *proof.* This section is the make-or-break part of the argument, in which you must marshal your reasons and support for your thesis. This is really the heart of the discourse, because it tells the readers or listeners why they should agree with you or why they should do what you ask them to do.

Key to success is not only marshaling all of the relevant reasons and supports, but doing so in a persuasive sequence. Generally, it is best to begin with the weakest reason and work your way up, crescendo-like, so that you end with your strongest reason. This builds persuasively in the mind of the audience, whereas beginning with the strongest point and descending through to the weakest tends to tear down or diminish the argument. However, a useful variation on this order may be employed if you have a certain number of strong reasons and a certain number of relatively weaker ones. You may want to begin with a strong reason and then enumerate some of the weaker reasons, only to end with the strongest reason of all. This organizational scheme introduces an element of surprise that can sometimes stir a reader or audience.

In cases where your reasons are of approximately equal strength or force, it is best to begin with the reasons that are the simplest, the most obvious, or the most likely to be familiar to your audience, then progress to the more complex, novel, unexpected, or original reasons.

Refute That

Following the presentation of proofs, you may need to refute arguments that oppose your own. In a live debate, your opposition is present onstage with you, but in a speech or written argument, you have to represent the other side (or sides) and then refute any opposing positions. Some writers and speakers are reluctant to include this part in their presentation because they do not want to air the points of view of opponents, even if it is to refute them. Some may also fear that the refutation will not be sufficiently convincing. These are both legitimate reservations, but the fact is that if significant opposition to your argument exists or is likely to exist, your audience either is already aware of it or will be sooner or later. You need to deal with it.

In classical rhetoric, the *refutatio* always follows the *confirmatio*, the presentation in support of your own position. Sometimes, however, it is desirable to depart from this order. If you are entering disputed territory in which the opposing view is the prevailing one (that is, it's the view generally held by the audience or, at least, much more familiar to them), it is more persuasive to begin by presenting and refuting this position. The refutation complete, you then proceed to present and support your own alternative position or proposal.

Wherever you insert the refutation, there are four ways to go about it.

1. You can refute by an *appeal to reason*, either by demonstrating that the contradictory of the opposing proposition is true or by tearing down the arguments that usually support the opposing position.

2. You can refute by an *emotional appeal*, provided that you can accurately gauge the emotional temper of the audience. "It is true that legalizing marijuana will reduce the burden on law enforcement, but how will you feel when your children have unfettered access to this drug? As loving, responsible parents, how will

you feel?" This approach (in this context) may work well, unless you are speaking to an audience consisting mainly of young, unmarried college students.

3. You can refute by an *ethical appeal*, staking your character and trustworthiness against the opposition. The risk here is twofold. You may fail to sell yourself adequately. Also, this type of argument readily degenerates into an ad hominem attack on the opposition, an assertion that your character is superior to that of your opponent. So-called political debates all too frequently descend into the ad hominem arena, and voters voice their disgust with "political mudslinging."

4. You can sometimes refute the opposition by *wit*, using sarcasm, ridicule, or irony to denigrate, devalue, or otherwise belittle the opposing position. This is obviously a high-risk strategy since some audiences will see sarcasm, ridicule, or irony as a poor substitute for a "legitimate" refutation by appeal to reason. Nevertheless, against some opponents and some positions, wit can be effectively deflating and therefore a powerful means of persuasion.

Wrap It All Up

Peroratio, from which our word *peroration* derives, is the Latin term for the final part of a persuasive discourse. It means literally a "finishing off," and the Roman rhetorician Quintilian specified that this "finishing off" should be accomplished in two parts: An *enumeration* (a summary) should immediately follow the refutation to recapitulate your principal points, and an *affectus* should bring the entire presentation to a close by producing an appropriate emotion ("affect") in your listeners or readers and leaving them with this feeling. In most persuasive discourse, the purpose of the *affectus* is to motivate the audience to whatever action the speaker or writer desires it to take.

INTRODUCTORY MENU

The introduction to an argument always serves to inform your reader or audience. Often, it also serves to ingratiate you, as the advocate of a position, with the audience; that is, the introduction may introduce an element of the ethical appeal into any argument. There are five approaches to an effective introduction. An introduction may use one or more.

The Inquisitive Approach

Begin with a question and you create hunger for an answer. A question naturally engages an audience or readers, commanding their time and attention. The question "Can we increase profits?" is more interesting than the statement "We can increase profits." Beginning with a question makes you and your listeners or readers partners in a quest for the answer, whereas beginning with a declaration tends to divide or at least distinguish you from your audience.

The Paradoxical Approach

Paradoxes, like riddles, create curiosity, titillate the imagination, and just naturally draw interest.

> "Although our sales are up and our manufacturing costs are down, our revenues for this quarter are flat."

Like the introduction that asks a question, the paradoxical approach is dynamic, pushing your listeners or readers to solve the riddle and resolve the paradox. Like a question, a paradox presents a situation that is off-balance, creating a natural and inevitable desire to restore balance. In this way, the paradoxical approach motivates attention and thought.

The Problem-Solving Approach

You may think of the introduction that presents a problem as another variation on the question approach and the paradoxical approach. Like these, a problem is a system that is out of balance. The problem weighs down one end of the seesaw and cries out for a solution to restore equilibrium.

> "Our sales are up and our manufacturing costs are down, but our revenues for this quarter are flat. That, ladies and gentlemen, is our problem."

Opening a persuasive discourse by presenting a problem gives you the opportunity to create common cause with your listeners or readers. For that reason, make it abundantly clear that the problem belongs to you *and* your audience. It is far more persuasive to begin by saying "We have a problem" than "You have a problem" or "I have a problem."

The Preparatory Approach

Sometimes, especially in the case of arguments involving complex subjects, it is desirable to begin by preparing your readers or listeners in order to prevent their jumping to an erroneous conclusion, erecting a defensive prejudice, or raising an objection without hearing you out.

> "My purpose in what I am about to say is not to fix blame on anyone, but to make certain that we all understand the crisis facing us and to propose a course of action that will require all of us to work together."

The preparatory approach can be quite simple, serving as a kind of roadmap for your audience.

> "I have three ideas to share with you about marketing our widgets. The first involves market research, the second design, and the third distribution. Let's begin with market research."

Or Just Tell a Good Story

Beginning with an anecdotal narrative directly relevant to your argument is a time-honored opening strategy. People like to hear or read a good story.

Tom Sanders manages the customer service department of a large corporation. He is addressing the customer service reps in his department. The purpose of his talk is to motivate excellent customer service by persuading his staff that they must make the customer's problem *their* problem and that they own the problem until it is resolved. Tom introduces this argument with a story about one of his staff members:

> "Last week, Jane Hawthorne, whom you all know very well, handled a problem at the ABC Shipping account in a way that I just love to talk about.
>
> "At 3:30 on Wednesday afternoon, someone at ABC called in a total panic because nobody could bypass a software security roadblock. Somehow, someone had improperly set the password coding. They were in a panic because they couldn't execute any transactions for their customers, and expedited shipments were piling up on the dock.
>
> "'Okay,' Jane said. 'I understand. Listen, we will work the problem, and we'll work it together.'
>
> "She stayed with this tough one, and what is really important are some of the things she did and the hard decisions she had to make.
>
> "First, of course, she needed to protect ABC's security as well as our own. As you all know, it's not easy to solve bypass problems on the phone because of the potential for a major security breach. Jane understood the customer's panic, but she refused to get caught up in it. She worked fast, but she successfully took the time that was needed to maintain security protocol, and she did so without increasing the panic at ABC. She went by the book, getting all necessary confirmations from ABC to ensure she was speaking only to authorized people at the company before helping them get through the roadblock.
>
> "Let me share a few details. . . ."

The key to the narrative introduction is to ensure that the story you tell is directly relevant to your argument. Amateur speech makers love to pepper their talks with anecdotes fished out of the newspaper or borrowed from some book, purely for entertainment value. Save these stories for the break room or the cafeteria. If you tell a story, make it work—and work hard—for you.

MATTERS OF FACT

After the introduction comes the statement of fact. As mentioned previously, this section may be quite brief—or even dispensed with altogether—if you know that your reader or audience is fully acquainted with the facts relevant to your argument. If you are arguing the merits of a new software program for your accounting department, you do not need to present a brief course in accounting or the role of the computer in accounting. However, if you are promoting accounting software for use by nonaccountants (say, small-business owners), this section of your argument could be used to outline the basic issues and features of accounting with the aid of a personal computer.

Expose

The power and relevance of your argument may depend on exposing facts—data, conditions, problems, opportunities, and so on—of which your audience is unaware. This puts you in the powerful position of being the bearer of news. Present the news without bias, but do make clear the importance—to your audience—of the facts you reveal.

> "I've just finished reading a new study you may not be aware of. It details how our sales tax dollars—yours and mine—are being spent. Let me go over with you three important figures. This is information we all need to have and need to keep in mind as the election approaches."

Inform

In many arguments, your task in stating facts is simply to inform your readers or listeners, bringing them, as it were, up to speed so that they are in a position to understand, appreciate, and evaluate your argument. If your purpose is to persuade your technophobic boss to invest $1,000 per unit for twenty personal computers instead of $500, you'd better present the information clearly, completely, and in a manner that demonstrates, in nontechnical terms, just what benefits the additional $500 per unit will buy. Your job here is to provide your boss with the same information (albeit adapted to someone who may have a lower level of technical savvy) that persuaded you to recommend spending twice as much on new computers than is apparently necessary.

Be Lucid, Brief, and Plausible

The Roman rhetorician Quintilian advised constructing the statement of fact so that it was lucid, brief, and plausible.

Lucidity requires providing enough information to make your argument comprehensible to your audience. This means that you must gauge the level of information your audience already possesses. Provide too little information and you will fail to create the context in which your argument can best be understood, evaluated, and accepted. Provide too much and you may lose people's attention, or they may feel that they are being patronized or talked down to. Provide an inappropriate level of information, whether too much or too little, and you broadcast the message that you have no real connection with your listeners or readers. If they sense this, they will surely question why they should invest time and attention in your argument.

As we'll discuss in a moment, two additional elements are required to achieve lucidity. The first is an orderly presentation. In many cases, chronological order is the simplest, most natural, and most comprehensible scheme. In other cases, you may want to move from the general to the specific or from the specific to the general, from the familiar to the less familiar or from the old to the new. Or you could simply proceed by breaking the information into discrete steps.

The Greek rhetoricians added a final element to lucidity: *enargeia*. This may be translated as "aliveness" or "vividness" or even "palpability." Abstract information (for example, general statements of principle, legal or technical jargon) or raw, undigested information (long lists of dates and numbers) often induces in listeners and readers alike a condition sometimes called MEGO, which is an acronym for "my eyes glaze over." If your audience zones out, your argument will almost certainly fail to persuade. Provide all necessary information in as vivid, palpable, concrete, and comprehensible a form as you possibly can.

"Brevity," wrote Shakespeare in *Hamlet*, "is the soul of wit." An argument shouldn't be longer than it absolutely needs to be. Cut it too short and you risk leaving out some important part of your appeal. But drag it out and you will lose your audience. Successful sales professionals know when to stop selling. The time to quit talking is as soon as you have sensed that the sale has been made.

Plausibility is an essential feature of the information you provide. If your facts and figures ring hollow or fail to ring true, your argument will almost surely be rejected. Plausible facts come from demonstrably plausible sources, and they tend to be corroborated by the experience of your audience. However, it is also the case that, sometimes, implausible facts are absolutely true.

> "Although we sold more widgets this past quarter than ever before in our company's history, we lost more money than in any other quarter in our history."

This statement is implausible but true. To prevent losing the trust of your audience, acknowledge the implausibility:

> "*As hard as it is to believe*, although we sold more widgets this past quarter than ever before in our company's history, we lost more money than in any other quarter in our history."

Generalize

One way to provide new information effectively is to begin by stating some general concept or principle, then proceed to more specific details.

> "Our department's policy has always been to evaluate equipment purchases in terms of value rather than cost. Among the three widgets available to us,

costs vary relatively little, but differences in value are extremely significant. Here are the specifics. . . ."

Beginning with a generalization is also useful for creating the context in which to view a specific circumstance or the case specifically relevant to your argument:

"Generally, you get what you pay for in a widget. The more you spend, the greater the array of features."

From here, you could continue this way:

"Among the three widget choices we are considering, this general principle certainly holds true."

Or this way:

"But, remarkably enough, this is not the case with the three widget choices we are considering."

Particularize

In some cases, with some subjects and some audiences, beginning with general principles will create confusion or fail to capture interest and attention. In such instances, begin with the particular and proceed to a generalization.

"When Jane Hawthorne stayed on the phone with ABC Shipping for six hours last Wednesday, working to overcome a software roadblock without compromising vital security, working that problem until it was 100 percent solved— *that* is what I mean by customer service. When you tackle a customer's problem, you own that problem. It's yours until it is resolved."

Move from the Familiar to the Strange

Teachers have long organized the contents of their courses by beginning with a familiar subject before introducing students to material of an increasingly unfamiliar or novel nature. Knowledge of the unfamiliar may be built upon a foundation of the familiar; or put another way, the unknown is built upon the known. When your argument requires acquainting your audience with new concepts, it is often most effective to introduce them in relation to concepts that are more familiar.

Move Step by Step . . .

A juicy T-bone steak is most appetizing, unless you are expected to take it down in a single gulp. In such a case, no matter how hungry you are, you will not go near it. Of course, such a notion is absurd. We may devour the whole steak, but we will do so one bite at a time. Similarly, even the largest, most complex subjects can be conveyed in bite-size steps.

. . . And Move Through Time

Just as you may divide a complex subject into steps, you may present an entire history—often helpful as the background context of an argument—in its most logical sequence: chronologically, through time, from beginning to end or from the start to the present. Unless you have some overwhelming reason for doing otherwise, historical background is always best presented in simple chronological order. In some cases, it is true, you may need to divide your story. If Joe was doing A, B, and C while Mary, elsewhere, was doing D, E, and F, you may want to tell Joe's story first and Mary's second, since it could be confusing to jump back and forth between these two characters. When you need to split the narrative in this way, make it clear that you are doing so:

> "While Joe was completing the widget receiver, Mary was hard at work on the transmitter. She began by gathering the necessary parts. . . ."

Feel It

Novelists are experts at what the Greek rhetoricians called *enargeia,* or what we call vividness or palpability.

> Instead of telling us that "Rowena was sad," a novelist will paint a word picture: "Pushing back her chestnut hair with her trembling fingers, Rowena sank into the chair beside the window with its pale light and began to sob, softly at first, then with heaving shoulders."

Most arguments do not require anything quite so melodramatic, but providing specific, real-world examples and anecdotes instead of rough abstractions can make your discourse more exciting, more comprehensible, more memorable, and ultimately, more persuasive.

> "When Jane saw Mr. Smith's face brighten into a broad, toothy smile, she knew that she had done a very good job of customer service that afternoon."

Keep It Real

Plausibility is not just a function of the likelihood of the facts presented, it is also the result of the tone of your argument and the perception your readers or listeners form concerning your character, trustworthiness, and authority. It may be helpful to present your credentials and demonstrate your motives; that is, to include an ethical appeal as part of your argument. You can also enhance the credibility of the information you present by doing the following:

• *Introduce nothing contrary to natural or historical fact.* Arguing that "this is the greatest achievement since Napoleon triumphed at Waterloo" will not enhance the perception of your authority.

• *Use words accurately and correctly, and maintain a tone suitable to the discourse and your audience.* "You guys ain't heard nothin' yet" will not persuade the hiring committee to give you that endowed chair in the English department.

• *Avoid hype.* It is better to risk understatement than to venture into exaggeration. Most people resist a hard sell.

Cut It Short

Give your readers or listeners just enough information to persuade them. In some instances, just enough may be no more than two or three sentences. Other arguments may require the expanse of an entire book—and still not be too long. Brevity in an argument is not an absolute matter. It is relative to the subject and the audience. Observe these general rules:

- Don't feel obliged to start at the beginning. Start at the point where the facts are of concern to your readers or listeners.

- Examine your presentation for irrelevant or extraneous information, then cut it out.

- Even if certain facts are relevant to the subject, delete them if they contribute nothing to an appreciation of your argument or if they are likely to fail to make your readers or listeners receptive to your point of view. A competent car salesman trying to sell you Model X will discuss neither the price of kumquats nor the virtues of Model Y. The former is irrelevant, and the latter, though relevant (Model Y is another car, after all), will not help make the sale.

THE PROOF AT THE CORE

What the Romans called the *confirmatio,* the confirmation or proof, is the core of the argument. Or, to use a more appropriately dynamic image, it is the fulcrum on which the weight of your persuasive message is successfully lifted.

At its most basic, this is the point at which you gather and present the evidence and reasons that support your thesis. You therefore face three tasks:

1. Gathering your evidence or reasons
2. Editing your evidence or reasons
3. Arranging your evidence or reasons

Add . . .

Sometimes it is easy to marshal the evidence and reasons that support your position. Sometimes, however, it takes considerable thought. Many writers prepare an argument by formulating a thesis, then, skipping over the statement of facts (at least for the present), they make a list of items that support the thesis. Compiling such a deliberate inventory can be useful for three reasons. First, it makes it easier for you to get everything out on the table. Second, it helps to ensure that you leave nothing important out. Third, it makes completing the three tasks simpler because a list is an efficient way to gather items, to cull out items you don't need (evidence and reasons that don't contribute effectively to supporting your thesis), and to arrange items. It's easier to move things around in a list than it is to edit things after they have been worked into a narrative.

. . . Subtract

Successful painters will tell you that what's left out of a picture is at least as important as what's put in. Effective writers say the same thing. When you construct an argument, your natural tendency is to throw absolutely every possible supporting item into the mix. Sometimes this is not a bad idea, especially if your inventory list of supporting items is brief. In most cases, however, editing your inventory is an important step. It is more persuasive to give someone three good reasons for agreeing with you than it is to bury your reader or listener under ten reasons of varying strength. In fact, it is more persuasive to offer just three *very good reasons* than ten good reasons or even three very good reasons plus seven pretty good reasons.

Not that three is the magic number. The number of support items you include in the confirmation or proof portion of your argument depends on the demands of your subject. Complex subjects may require many, many supporting items, whereas simpler subjects call for just a few. The point is to avoid overloading your audience with information. Your objective is not to overwhelm them. It is to persuade them, to move them to assent and action. Therefore, offer just enough evidence and reasons to support your thesis persuasively.

Include the Weak

Cull supporting items down to the most effective ones, but don't reject out of hand all of the weaker reasons. When should you include the weak ones?

• *Include weaker reasons and evidence along with the strongest when supporting items are generally in short supply.* In these cases, inclusiveness is a virtue.

• *Include weaker reasons when they are more commonly held than the stronger reasons.* Let's say you are arguing in front of a citizens' meeting that your town should install new streetlights on inadequately lit streets. You understand that the most commonly held reason for investing in the lighting is that it will reduce crime. This is what most people believe, and this is why many people will likely support spending money on new streetlights. At the same time, through your own research, you have learned that crime prevention comes behind traffic and pedestrian safety and increased evening retail activity as statistically supported benefits of adequate street lighting. Bearing in mind that your objective is to obtain backing from the citizen group to finance the lighting, you wisely decide not to tell your audience that crime prevention is a "weak" reason for installing more streetlights. Nor will you leave this reason out of your argument. On the other hand, you also decide not to falsify your argument by pandering to your audience's belief that crime prevention is the most important reason for investing in street lighting. Instead, you decide to construct an argument that employs all three support items.

• *Include weaker reasons for dramatic effect.* Persuasive arguments usually build a powerful case, much as a skillful composer uses such devices as increasing volume (crescendo), accelerating tempo, and making orchestration increasingly elaborate to build a powerful passage in a piece of music. Beginning with a relatively weak reason or two throws into more dramatic relief the stronger reasons that follow. Just make certain that the weaker reasons do not outnumber or overshadow the stronger—and, of course, make certain that your strongest reasons really are compelling.

Conclude with the Strong

Notwithstanding what we've just discussed about the appropriateness of using weak reasons (if they are commonly held reasons or for dramatic effect), it is important never to conclude the confirmation section with anything other than your strongest supporting item. Logic might tend to suggest that strong reasons should precede weak ones; however, in any sequence, people remember best what comes last. For that reason, end strong.

Usually, when relatively strong and weak reasons are included, speakers and writers begin with the weaker and end with the stronger. Sometimes, this pattern can be varied to achieve the freshness of surprise. You might begin with a relatively strong reason, go to a somewhat weaker one, then conclude with the strongest reason of all. Even in this departure from the usual pattern, however, the strongest reason ends the confirmation section of your argument.

In the case of reasons of roughly equal strength, consider other organizational strategies, as discussed in "Matters of Fact" earlier in this chapter.

DEMOLITION DERBY

Classical rhetoricians prescribed a *refutatio*—refutation—to follow the *confirmatio*, or confirmation. Their assumption was that every point of view engenders an opposing point of view; therefore, it is always necessary to refute the opposition in order to lend further support to your point of view. Modern writers and speakers do not always feel it necessary to refute the opposition, at least not explicitly. They point out that including a refutation in an argument runs the risk of inadvertently promoting the opposition, just by giving it an airing. They also point out that many people respond unfavorably to what they perceive as a negative appeal—criticizing or attacking an opponent.

It is true: Unintentionally promoting the opposition and leaving your readers or listeners with a negative message are significant risks of refutation. But failing to acknowledge and adequately refute opposition can also be a risky strategy. Your audience may conclude that you are ignorant of important opposing points of view. Or they may conclude that you are aware of them, but are ignoring or evading them in the hope that they will go away. They may conclude that you are incapable of refuting the opposition. Even if people do not draw these conclusions, they may feel unsatisfied by your failure to compare your proposal to those that compete with it. You may successfully argue that your proposal is *good*, but your audience may want to know how it is *better* than a competing proposal. Remember, somewhere in the back of the minds of most people is the well-worn mechanic's adage: "If it ain't broke, don't fix it."

The Art of Refutation

Refutation is an art rather than a science. It has few set rules.

First, as we have just discussed, there is no hard-and-fast requirement that every argument must include a section of refutation. Decide whether it is riskier to omit or to include the refutation, based on your sense of the pervasiveness and strength of the opposition. If you believe that your argument is far superior to that of the opposition, including a refutation will actually make your position appear all the stronger. Just about everyone interested in automobiles would agree that a Porsche 911 is a beautiful car. Put it in a group of econoboxes from the 1970s and it will seem even more magnificent. Ideally, you should not treat the refutation as a grim necessity in your argument—a grudging issuance of "equal time" to your opponent or a required rhetorical exercise—but as a major asset to your argument. A horse race run alone is pretty dull. Add a few more horses as competition, and it becomes exciting, compelling, and meaningful.

Another matter of art rather than science is the location of the refutation. The classical rhetoricians always put it after the confirmation—the presentation of the core of your case. Most of the time, this is indeed a very good place for it; however, if you are facing opposing points of view you know to be popularly held and well received, it makes sense to consider beginning your argument by refuting them. Think of the situation this way: A popularly held opposing argument is a building that occupies the same lot on which you want to build your argument. Elementary physics tells us that two objects cannot occupy the same space at the same time. Your first task, therefore, is to knock down the existing structure so that you can build your own.

If you believe that the opposing arguments are weak and not widely held, it is an outright mistake to begin with the refutation. In these cases, put the refutation in its classically ordained place, fully presenting your case before refuting anyone else's.

Similarly, you may want to delay the introduction of opposing arguments as long as possible if you perceive or believe that your audience is hostile to your point of view. It is a mistake to show red meat to a hungry dog, only to offer him oatmeal instead. Similarly, if you begin by reminding people of the position they embrace, you can end up reinforcing their bias against whatever you have to offer, thereby stopping their ears and closing their minds. When facing what you believe will be strong bias or outright hostility, get your thesis and proofs out as quickly and as forcefully as you can. That done, tackle the refutation.

Despite the absence of absolute rules, refutation generally relies on one or more of the following: an appeal to reason, to ethics, or to emotion, or the use of wit.

The Appeal to Reason

Exposing the flaws in the logic of an opposing argument is a powerful form of refutation. If possible, identify a statement that contradicts a premise of the opposition and demonstrate that the contradiction is true. Deductive logic tells us that if one of a pair of contradictories is true, the other must be false.

> "Joe argues that, under his plan, sales have increased by 6 percent; therefore, we should continue to follow his plan. In fact, because customer returns have increased by 8 percent under Joe's plan, sales have actually declined by 2 percent; therefore, it's time to try a different plan."

The statement "Sales have increased by 6 percent" is directly contradicted by the statement "Sales have declined by 2 percent."

Of course, it is not always possible to refute opposition by finding and presenting direct contradictions. Usually, the best we can do is to offer contrary propositions. There are two ways to do this:

1. *Deny the truth of an opposition premise by proving the premise to be false.* This can be done effectively through evidence or testimony: "Joe argues that, under his plan, sales have increased by 6 percent; therefore, we should continue to follow his plan. But either Joe's figures or his math is in error. Sales are actually flat; therefore, it's time to try a different plan."

2. *Attack the inferences or conclusions drawn from the premises.* "Joe argues that sales have increased by 6 percent under his plan; therefore, the company should continue to follow his plan." This time you refute him by saying, "While it is true that sales are up by this amount, the increase has nothing to do with Joe's plan. During the period in question, forty new businesses moved into our region. Sales increased because the market increased. Had we been operating under my plan, sales would have increased by some 10 percent in this expanded market."

The Appeal to Ethics

In refutation, the ethical appeal pits your character or authority against that of someone who holds an opposing view. If you are a grocery clerk promoting a new diet over the opposition of an eminent physician, you are not likely to have much success with the ethical appeal. On the other hand, if you are a professor of ecological biology at a major university promoting a wetlands policy in opposition to the arguments of a local real estate developer, you may well have a strong platform from which to make an ethical appeal.

The Appeal to Emotion

In refutation, this mode of appeal can be quite effective, but it suffers from a questionable reputation and requires thorough knowledge of the sentiments likely to prevail among your audience. The Reverend Martin Luther King Jr.'s "I Have a Dream" speech, made in Washington, D.C., on August 28, 1963, is a stunning example of an appeal to emotion. The greatest of such appeals rise to the level of vision and share the vision with the audience. Who could fail to be moved by King's speech? Well, he knew better than to deliver it to an audience of Ku Klux Klan members.

It is important to remember that the appeal to emotion is not incompatible with the appeal to reason, and both of these approaches can be combined with the ethical appeal. Although it relies mainly on an appeal to emotion, King's speech also appeals to reason (arguing that racism and segregation are harmful to the entire nation, black and white alike) and is made all the more compelling by King's reputation as a clergyman and civil rights leader. Indeed, an appeal to emotion is rarely effective when employed entirely on its own.

The Role of Wit

Using wit—typically ridicule or sarcasm—to refute your opposition is a very risky strategy. Ronald Reagan was a master at this. Famously, during a televised debate with Jimmy Carter during the 1980 presidential campaign, Carter challenged candidate Reagan to defend his opposition to a pending Medicare bill. Instead of offering an appeal to reason, Reagan responded with the phrase "There you go again." Reagan's tone and body language converted this innocuous sentence into devastatingly effective ridicule, which deftly deflated the challenge. Few speakers could have pulled it off. Ronald Reagan did, although it would be very easy to see this response as a dodge rather than a refutation.

Despite the risks involved in refutation by wit, ridicule, or sarcasm, there are some instances of opposition that hardly merit any other response. During the Civil War, John Pope, a pompously unpopular Union general, habitually closed the orders and official messages he wrote with the phrase "Headquarters in the Saddle." This was, in effect, an argument intended to support the conclusion that Pope was a dynamic general who maintained his headquarters in the field, wherever he happened to be. Instead, the phrase set off an avalanche of jokes in both the Union and Confederate armies to the effect that Pope (in Robert E. Lee's words) "had his headquarters where his hindquarters should be." The ridicule created by these jokes remains attached to Pope's memory to this day.

THE FINISH LINE

After going through an introduction, including a statement of your thesis, then a statement of fact, then its proof in the confirmation, followed by the refutation of opposing arguments, you may be left wondering: What's left? And the fact is that many arguments just peter out, falling flat at the finish line.

The classical rhetoricians often referred to the last section of the argument as the *recapitulatio*, the recapitulation, which really is not a very exciting prescription for a conclusion. It implies mere summary and repetition. The better way to think of the end is as a call to action. This may require some form of recapitulation, which Quintilian called *enumeratio*, an enumeration or listing of the main points, but the recapitulation is followed by what Quintilian called *affectus*: eliciting the desired emotional response in the audience. To shift from the classical age to more modern times, think of the entire argument as a sales pitch (you are trying to sell your point of view) and the end of the argument as closing the sale. You need to point your audience in the direction of the action you desire: voting a certain way, supporting your proposal, accepting your point of view, and so on. Until action is taken, the sale remains unconsummated.

Close the Sale—Aristotle Style

Aristotle wrote that the concluding portion of an argument should accomplish four things:

1. It should leave the audience with a favorable opinion of the speaker and an unfavorable opinion of those who oppose him.
2. It should summarize the argument.
3. It should amplify the proposals, positions, or opinions made in the body of the argument while simultaneously destroying or at least mitigating the force of opposing proposals, positions, or opinions.
4. It should stir desirable emotions in the audience members, emotions that make them eager to act as the speaker wants them to act.

This list of requirements is helpful, although (except for the last requirement) you may find it desirable to vary the order, and you may also find it difficult and even unnecessary to separate the first three steps in any rigorous manner.

Inspire

You may find it most useful to interpret Aristotle's first requirement as simply an injunction to inspire your readers or listeners. Inspire them with your authority and trustworthiness, as well as with the compelling cogency of your argument. Inspire them, that is, with the confidence to accept your argument and to act on it.

Sum It Up

Recapitulate, briefly, the highlights of your argument, the points you want your audience to take away with them. Concentrate on those aspects of your argument most likely to motivate the action you seek.

Amplify

Think of this as an amplification of your recapitulation, an opportunity to add final extra emphasis to your most important points. Combined with the recapitulation, this step should lead directly into the concluding call to action.

Call to Action

End by giving your audience an explicit direction:

> "The decision is clear and urgent. Adopt my plan so that we can get started pushing sales to the level we all deserve to enjoy."

Be Reasonable

How to use logic to make your case airtight
and move people your way.

As hard as it may be to believe, especially when in the middle of a football game, a clearance sale, or a war, human beings are rational creatures much of the time. Even when people fail to be reasonable, they tout rationality as a lofty virtue of great value. If you were to ask the question "Why on earth did you make *that* decision?" most people, most of the time, will say that "Because it made logical sense" is a better reply than "It felt good" or "Because he told me to do it."

EXERCISE THE AUTHORITY OF LOGIC

The appeal to reason is not inherently superior (in a moral sense) to the appeal to ethics or to emotion, but it is almost always more reliably persuasive. And that is what this book is about. Whereas the ethical and emotional appeals are perceived to have a strong element of relativity and subjectivity, the appeal to reason seems (and in some ways is) far more objective and free from bias. Present someone with logical reasons for doing what you want them to do and they are more likely to feel that the decision is theirs rather than yours. Lay out a rational argument and people "see for themselves" why what you propose is "a good idea." With the other modes of appeal, there is a stronger possibility of a *he-tried-to-talk-me-into-it* response and a commensurate resistance to persuasion. Perhaps even worse, if your listener or reader *is* persuaded, she may be overcome later with a form of buyer's remorse, complaining bitterly, "Why did I let *him* talk *me* into *this*?"

USE THE POWER OF DEFINITION

All rational argument proceeds by explanation, and explanation, ultimately, relies on definition. An explanation is, really, a form of extended definition. To argue rationally is to explain, and to explain is to tell what a thing is, to describe it, to break it down into its constituents, or to demonstrate how it operates. All of these operations require definitions, and the explanation itself may be regarded as a compound definition, an extended definition made up of subordinate definitions.

Aristotle, who thought about so many things, thought hard about the principle of definition. He argued that a definition that truly defines a thing is a definition of that thing's essence—an "essential definition." An essential definition identifies and presents that which makes a thing what it is, while also distinguishing the thing from all other things. As examples:

> "The human being is a two-legged animal" reasonably describes a human being, but it is not an essential definition, if only because one could also describe a bird this way.

> "The human being is a rational animal" has been accepted by many generations of philosophers as an essential definition, because it seems to describe our essence and differentiates us from all other animals.

Obviously, there is no need to begin a philosophical dissertation every time you need to define something. But the Aristotelian ideal of an essential definition gives you a clear target to aim for.

In a sound and solid definition, one that at least approaches the essential target, the subject and predicate are equivalent, much like the material on either side of an equals sign in a mathematical expression.

> "The human being is a rational animal" can be converted to "A rational animal is a human being" and still be valid, much as $1 + 2 = 3$ can be written $3 = 1 + 2$ with the same validity.

> In contrast, "The human being is a two-legged animal" cannot be converted to "A two-legged animal is a human being" because this definition leaves out birds.

In an essential definition, the thing to be defined (which Aristotle called the *definiendum*) has to be in the same general category (*genus*, Aristotle called it) as the specific differences (*differentiae*) that distinguish it from everything else in the same genus.

> In our example, "animal" is the *genus* and "rational" is the *differentia*, the thing that distinguishes the human being from every other member of the *genus* (that is, from every other animal).

In formulating definitions, you may find it useful to pursue Aristotelian logic even further. Aristotle wrote that the *differentiae* in a given definition usually specify one or more of what he called the four "causes" of a thing: the material cause, the formal cause, the efficient cause, or the final cause. In this scheme:

> A chair may be defined a member of the *genus* furniture. Its *material cause* is wood. Its *efficient cause* is the fact that it has been made by a carpenter.

Its *formal cause* is that it consists of a horizontal seat resting on four vertical legs with a vertical back rising from the seat. Its *final cause* is that it is used for sitting.

Do you need to go through an exercise in Aristotelian logic every time you want to define or describe something? Of course not. But you can use this approach as a kind of informal checklist to ensure that you are creating complete, clear, and valid definitions and explanations.

The Aristotelian approach is by no means the only valid method for creating sound definitions. You can also use synonyms, etymology, description, and example to define terms and concepts, and you can use them in combination or individually.

Definition by *synonym* is a straightforward method that can be greatly aided by a dictionary. Just be aware that synonyms are not mathematical equivalents. For instance:

> *Destroy* and *demolish* are synonymous, yet they also possess different connotations. To clear a lot for new construction, you demolish the existing building. True, that means you destroy it, but the word *demolish* implies more purpose, planning, intention, and precision than the word *destroy*.

Definition by synonym is a useful shortcut for getting your meaning across, but it carries the risk of intellectual sloppiness. Shades of meaning—connotation—are important, and in some situations, connotation is downright critical.

Etymology—the study of the origin of words—can serve as a fascinating and illuminating adjunct to definition or as the definition itself.

> "When I say that we, the members of this council, must at all cost avoid becoming idiots, I don't mean to be merely insulting. The word is Greek in origin. In the early Athenian democracy of Pericles, the *idiotes* were people who did not take part in public life. They were the purposely uninformed—the nonvoters. We must not become nonparticipants, the uninformed nonvoters. We of the council must become engaged in the public debate so that we can ensure that our organization has a voice, a clear and influential voice, in this community."

Description is an extended form of definition and is appropriate for more complex terms and concepts.

The final form of definition is the *example*. Although this form consumes space in a written argument and time in a speech, it can be dramatically effective. It is one thing to provide a concise dictionary-style definition of the word *courage*, say, and quite another to define it by telling the kinds of stories John F. Kennedy included in his famous 1956 book *Profiles in Courage*. Each of the profiles in that volume was presented, in effect, as a definition-by-example of courage, and the book earned the author a Pulitzer Prize.

Whatever method you employ to create a definition, one cardinal rule must be observed. You cannot define a word in terms of itself. For example:

"A human being is a being that is human" is not a valid definition. You must define a thing in terms other than itself. Failure to do this is called a *tautology*, which means repetition—that is, double-talk.

Ask someone, "How do you know that?" and you'll often receive this tautology in response: "I know what I know." This answer purports to define "what I know," but it simply tells us that "what I know" means "what I know." And that is about as useful as the equation $1 = 1$.

INDUCE PERSUASION

Two powerful engines are available to drive arguments: inductive reasoning and deductive reasoning. In most arguments concerning complex, real-life issues and situations, induction plays a larger role than deduction, although both are important. Induction reaches conclusions (or formulates theses) by generalizing from the observation of a series of particulars. In its most rigorous form, induction is familiar to us as scientific reasoning.

Drug X is administered to one patient who is afflicted with disease Y. The patient recovers. The scientist formulates a thesis that drug X is a cure for disease Y. To test this thesis, drug X must be administered to a significant number of patients afflicted with disease Y.

In scientific reasoning, the more particular instances that can be accumulated in support of a thesis, the more likely a thesis is considered to be valid.

In most arguments, induction is less rigid than it is in scientific reasoning and, really, inductive arguments are nothing more than arguments by example. To support the thesis that employees who are given two weeks of paid vacation are more productive than employees who are given only one week, either you would have to conduct an experiment at your place of business, giving one group of employees two weeks of vacation and another one week over a period of a year or more, or you would have to gather other exemplary evidence, perhaps from other firms. If you picked just one or two employees who had worked in situations offering one week and two weeks of vacation and asked them whether they believed they were more productive with one week or two, you might get some interesting responses, but these would be mere individual anecdotes. One or two employees is an insufficient number to base your argument on.

Tommy is an eight-year-old boy. He sees a robin *walking* with a worm in its beak. He sees a sparrow *hopping* while picking up seeds from the ground. He concludes by induction that walking birds eat worms and hopping birds eat seeds. Then he thinks nothing more of it. As a grown man now thirty years old, Tom is strolling down the sidewalk. He sees a brown bird that is neither a sparrow nor a robin *hopping* with a worm in its beak. Another childhood belief shattered. The moral of this story? Conclusions arrived at through induction require multiple examples.

One of the most frequent uses of inductive reasoning, or argument by example, is the application of historical precedent to support an argument:

> One of the arguments frequently used in attempts to dissuade the administration of President George W. Bush from committing to Operation Iraqi Freedom was the example of the Vietnam War. One could object that this single example is insufficient to support the thesis that invading Iraq was a bad idea; however, those who used the example skillfully in effect divided it into many examples, suggesting that the proposed Iraq venture was in several ways similar to Vietnam and suggesting that it, like the Vietnam War, it would fail for similar reasons.

While often compelling, argument from historical examples or precedent does not guarantee success. Indeed, Operation Iraqi Freedom went forward.

Beyond the general proposition that the more examples you can bring to bear in support of your thesis, the more compelling your inductive argument will be, there are no hard-and-fast rules about arguing from example. The success of the argument will depend in large part on your good judgment and common sense. You need to avoid the impression that you are jumping to conclusions based on an example or two. You need to be persuasive in the generalizations you make from the examples you do present. And you need to avoid giving the impression that you are cherry-picking your examples, identifying only those that support your thesis and ignoring or suppressing those that do not.

BE DEDUCTIVE

In contrast to induction, deduction is all about rules, the rules of logic, which are as absolute as the laws of basic mathematics. You will rarely encounter situations in which full, formal logic is required to create a persuasive argument. This said, some familiarity with deductive logic is a useful aid to constructing sound arguments—and to refuting arguments that exhibit faulty logic.

The Syllogism

The heart of deduction is the syllogism, yet another invention from Aristotle. The syllogism is a scheme that is useful in analyzing and testing deductive reasoning. The syllogism consists of *premises*, which are propositions, and a final proposition, the *conclusion*, which follows logically (that is, necessarily) from the premises. The form of the syllogism is simple:

If A is true

and B is true,

then C must be true.

For example:

All men are mortal. (A is true.)

Socrates is a man. (B is true.)

Therefore, Socrates is mortal. (C must be true.)

The syllogism has three propositions, the first two of which are the premises and the last, the conclusion. The syllogism also includes three terms: a major, minor, and middle term. The major term is the predicate term of the conclusion. In this case, it consists of the word *mortal*. The minor term is the subject term of the conclusion. Here, it is *Socrates*. The middle term is the term that appears in both premises, but not in the conclusion: *men/man*.

The proposition that contains the major term is the *major premise*: *All men are mortal*. The proposition that contains the minor term is the *minor premise*: *Socrates is a man*. The conclusion is the proposition deduced from the major and minor premises. If that definition strikes you as too vague, then define the conclusion as the proposition that contains both the major term and the minor term, but not the middle term.

The Square of Opposition

The propositions of an Aristotelian syllogism are most properly called categorical propositions because they assert or deny something categorically, without conditions or alternatives attached. Logicians schematize the four possible categorical propositions in a diagram, called the "square of opposition," as shown here:

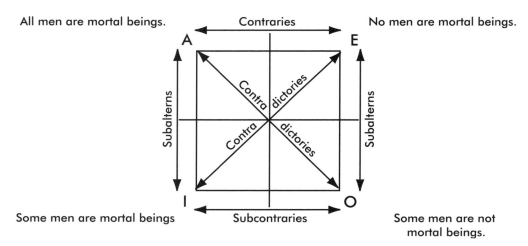

In the diagram:

- The A proposition is known as a universal affirmative. "All men are mortal" is an example of a universal affirmative.
- The E proposition is a universal negative: "No men are mortal."
- The I proposition is a particular affirmative: "Some men are mortal."
- The O proposition is a particular negative: "Some men are not mortal."

Why the *A*, *E*, *I*, and *O* labels? The square of opposition is intended as a mnemonic device, an aid to memory. The *A* and *I* appear in the Latin word *AFFIRMO*, meaning "I affirm," and are associated with the two possible categorical affirmative propositions, whereas the *E* and *O* appear in the word *NEGO*, meaning "I deny." These are associated with the two possible categorical negative propositions.

Logicians analyze categorical propositions in two dimensions: quantity and quality. "Quantity" refers to whether the proposition is universal or particular. "Quality" refers to whether the proposition is affirmative or negative. On the square of opposition, the *A* and *E* propositions are above the horizontal line drawn through the middle of the square. These are the universal propositions, whereas those below this line, the *I* and *O* propositions, are the particular propositions. The *A* and *I* propositions, which are to the left of the vertical line drawn through the center of the square, are the affirmative propositions, whereas the *E* and the *O* propositions, to the right of the vertical line, are the negative propositions.

So far, the diagram is very useful. But difficulties can sometimes develop when you try to translate concepts of quantity into actual English words. It's easy and always unambiguous to express quality: A statement is either affirmative (*is*) or negative (*is not*). Quantity is another matter. Qualifiers such as *all* and *every*, or *none* and *not any*, are easy and specific. In terms of logic, so are words such as *some* or *few* or *many*. Although they are vague as far as precise numbers are concerned, logically they are all the equivalent of *some*. But what about the proposition that states "Dogs are friendlier than cats"? Is this intended as a universal affirmative or a particular affirmative? Even more difficult is a statement like this: "This black paint chip is the opposite of white." On the face of it, this would seem a particular affirmative, because we are apparently considering only one black paint chip. But because the proposition is predicated on an unspoken universal affirmative, "Black is the opposite of white," most logicians would identify this apparently particular affirmative as a universal affirmative. The only way to avoid these ambiguities is to be as precise as possible in your use of language, always including words that specify quantity.

Now that you have been warned about an area in which logic and language may conflict, let's return to the square of opposition diagram. It reduces to schematic form the possible courses deductive reasoning can take:

1. If A is true, I must be true. And if E is true, O must be true. If all men are mortal, some men must be mortal. If no men are mortal, some men must not be mortal.

2. If I is true, no deduction can be made concerning A. If O is true, no deduction can be made about E. If some men are mortal, we cannot deduce (infer) that all men are mortal. The truth of the universal proposition cannot be inferred from the particular proposition.

3. If A is true, then E is false. And if E is true, then A is false. If all men are mortal, the proposition that no men are mortal must be false.

4. If A is false, no deduction can be made concerning E. And if E is false, no deduction can be made concerning A. Whereas contrary propositions cannot both be true (see item 3), they *can* both be false. If the proposition that no men are mortal is false, we may not conclude that all men are mortal. It is logically possible that this is false as well.

5. In the case of the contradictories (A and O; E and I), one must be true and one false. Collectively, these relationships represent the Law of Contradictions, which holds that a thing cannot both be and not be. This being the case, the following deductions may be made concerning propositions opposed diagonally on the diagram:

> If A is true, O must be false.
>
> If A is false, O must be true.
>
> If O is true, A must be false.
>
> If O is false, A must be true.
>
> If E is true, I must be false.
>
> If E is false, I must be true.
>
> If I is true, E must be false.
>
> If I is false, E must be true.

6. If I is true, no deduction can be made concerning O. And if O is true, no deduction can be made about I.

7. If I is false, O must be true. And if O is false, I must be true.

Note that the subcontraries (the I and O propositions, which are below the horizontal line) can both be true, but they cannot both be false. The statements that "Some women are Catholics" and "Some women are not Catholics" can both be true, but both cannot be false. Moreover, while we can infer the truth of one statement from the falsity of the other, we cannot deduce the truth of one from the truth of the other.

Pitfalls

Much of what Aristotle systematized in the syllogism, and what the logicians following from him schematized in the square of opposition, is merely common sense and quite simple. Nevertheless, things can go wrong in deductive argument.

The first pitfall to be aware of is failing to distinguish between validity and truth. A syllogism is valid if it is formally correct.

> "All men are mortal; Socrates is a man; therefore, Socrates is mortal" is a valid syllogism. But so is this statement: "No men are mortal; Socrates is a man; therefore, Socrates is not mortal." Whereas the first syllogism is both valid and true, the second is valid but untrue.

Validity concerns form, whereas truth concerns matter. It is all too possible to begin with false premises and create from them a perfectly valid syllogism, which, because of its validity, has the unwarranted air of truth. Be prepared to evaluate an argument for its validity as well as its truth. Do not mistake one for the other.

The other common pitfall in the application of deductive reasoning is a failure to understand the concept of *distribution*. According to logicians, distribution means the extension of a term to apply to all of the objects or individuals of a class. In the syllogism about Socrates, the term "men" is said to be distributed because "all" covers the entire class of that term. In the case of "some men," the term "men" is said to be undistributed because "some" designates a quantity less than the total number of members of the class.

It is easy to see that deciding whether a term is distributed or undistributed presents no difficulty in the subject of a syllogism. However, it is not always easy to recognize this distinction in the predicate term because of ambiguities of language. Here is a rule to serve as a guide:

> The predicate terms of affirmative propositions (A or I propositions) are undistributed, whereas the predicate terms of all negative propositions (E or O propositions) are distributed.

Bearing these pitfalls in mind, we need no more than six criteria to judge the validity (but not the truth) of a syllogism:

1. There must be three terms, no more, no fewer.
2. The middle term must be distributed at least once.
3. If a term is not distributed in the premise, it cannot be distributed in the conclusion.
4. No conclusion can be drawn from two particular premises.
5. No conclusion can be drawn from two negative premises.
6. If one premise is negative, the conclusion must be negative.

Let's reexamine the Socrates syllogism—"All men are mortal; Socrates is a man; therefore, Socrates is mortal"—according to these six criteria:

1. It has three terms and only three terms.
2. The middle term *men* (the term that occurs in both premises, but not the conclusion) is distributed.

3. *Socrates*, the term in the conclusion, is also distributed. (As a proper noun, Socrates may be regarded as a universal term.)

4. The conclusion is properly drawn from one universal and one particular premise.

5. The premises are affirmative, not negative, so a conclusion may be drawn.

6. Neither conclusion is negative, so it is not necessary to draw a negative conclusion.

A syllogism that fails to meet these six criteria is not a valid syllogism.

Other deductive pitfalls are also possible. Remember, these are flaws in form, not content. They render the syllogism invalid, even if the premises are true in content. One of the most common logical flaws is the fallacy of the undistributed middle. Consider:

> All men are mortal.
>
> All women are mortal.
>
> Therefore, all women are men.

Whenever the middle term (*mortal*) is the predicate term of two affirmative premises, the middle term is undistributed; therefore, no conclusion can validly follow from it.

In dealing with hypotheses, the most common flaw is the fallacy of affirming the consequent. Consider this valid syllogism:

> If he is a Democrat, he will vote for a liberal candidate.
>
> He is a Democrat.
>
> Therefore, he will vote for a liberal candidate.

In a hypothesis, we propose that the truth of the *if* clause (called the *antecedent*) implies the truth of the main clause (called the *consequent*): If he is a Democrat (antecedent), he will vote for a liberal candidate (consequent). However, the truth of the consequent (he voted for a liberal candidate) does not necessarily imply the truth of the antecedent (he is a Democrat):

> If he is a Democrat, he will vote for a liberal candidate.
>
> He voted for a liberal candidate.
>
> Therefore, he is a Democrat.

Even if we assume that the hypothesis "If he is a Democrat, he will vote for a liberal candidate" is true, we cannot conclude that voting for a liberal candidate necessarily means that the voter is a Democrat. Yet certain biases would certainly tempt some people to accept the second syllogism as both true and valid. Consider another pair of hypothetical syllogisms that take the same form:

If he has a helmet, he won't hurt his head.

He has a helmet.

Therefore, he won't hurt his head.

But:

If he has a helmet, he won't hurt his head.

He did not hurt his head.

Therefore, he has (or had) a helmet.

What if he fell on his rear end?

Another common fallacy involving the hypothetical syllogism is denying the antecedent:

If he has a helmet, he won't hurt his head.

He does not have a helmet.

Therefore, he (will) hurt his head.

Again, what if he fell (or falls) on his rear end?

You can test the validity of hypothetical syllogisms by looking carefully at the minor (the second) premise:

- If it affirms the antecedent, the conclusion is valid.
- If it affirms the consequent, the conclusion is invalid.
- If it denies the consequent, the conclusion is valid.
- If it denies the antecedent, the conclusion is invalid.

THE ENTHYMEME

The syllogism is a good tool for working through the deductive logic of an argument; however, most real-world arguments do not move through the full three-course logic of the syllogism. Instead, they use the enthymeme, an abbreviated syllogism, which contains a conclusion and one of the premises—the other premise being implied.

"Socrates is mortal because he is a man" is an enthymeme. The premise "All men are mortal" is implied, but the equivalents of "Socrates is a man" and "therefore, Socrates is mortal" are both present.

A Probability Tool

As Aristotle defined it, the enthymeme is also more than an abbreviated syllogism. It is a means of drawing tentative conclusions from probable premises. Whereas the syllogism occupies the realm of pure logic, the enthymeme is suited to the messy realm of human activity, which is always contingent and rarely yields the certainty of absolute truth. Thus, the enthymeme is the perfect tool for persuasion, which deals with contingency and probability far more often than it does with certainty.

Consider the difference between these two examples:

> *Statement 1:* All men are mortal. Socrates is a man. Therefore, Socrates is mortal.
>
> *Statement 2:* We will not make our sales quota next quarter because we've spent next to nothing on advertising.

The first is a syllogism based on as near to absolute truth as is possible. As far as we know, in all human experience, all men have been mortal. Let's assume we know Socrates. We have no reason to believe that he is anything other than a man. Therefore, the conclusion approaches absolute certainty: Socrates is mortal. The second example is an enthymeme based on informed experience. It is reasonable to perceive a correlation between advertising and sales. Assuming that the sales quota for next quarter was based on past experience, in which advertising was used, then it is reasonable to argue that the absence of advertising will keep us from attaining our sales goal. Is this an absolute certainty? By no means. Is it a probable outcome? Yes. Therefore, within the limits of what is knowable, this enthymeme is valid and as true as it *can* be; that is, while it may not be absolutely convincing, it is highly persuasive.

The Importance of What Isn't There

The fact that one of the premises in an enthymeme is implied rather than actually present does not mean that this implied premise is unimportant. It is just as critical as if it were clearly spelled out. In fact, it is often the implied premise we go after when we want to attack an argument that's in the form of an enthymeme. Consider this example:

> "He must be a Democrat because he wants to expand welfare programs." The implied premise is that "all who advocate expanding welfare programs are Democrats."

If you believe this is true, don't attack the enthymeme. If you think it is an unwarranted thesis, attack the enthymeme by attacking this implied thesis.

But is it worth attacking?

In the realm of pure logic, the world of certainties and absolutes, the deductive reasoning here is certainly vulnerable. Demonstrating the truth of the implied premise, "All who advocate expanding welfare programs are Democrats," would be impossible, because one could certainly find at least one registered Republican who favored expanding welfare programs. But we don't dwell in the realm of pure logic and the world of certainties and absolutes. Our arena is a place of relative truth, contingency, and probability. You might therefore deem it fruitless in any practical sense to attack the implied premise because, most of the time, you believe it to be true. In your mind, you may change the "all" to "most," and then the enthymeme rings with *probable* truth.

Signs

In addition to dealing with probabilities, enthymemes, according to Aristotle, also deal with what he called *signs*. "Where there's smoke, there's fire" is an old saying that is also an enthymeme. Its implied and unstated premise is "Smoke accompanies fire," or more to the point, "Smoke is a sign of fire." The smoke is not a cause or a reason for fire, but it is a sign, an indication of it.

Aristotle distinguished between what he called infallible and fallible signs. *Infallible signs* invariably accompany a certain thing, whereas *fallible signs* sometimes accompany that certain thing. Both have value in arguments, although, naturally, infallible signs are more persuasive than fallible signs. You may not be able to prove your thesis with fallible signs, but you may still present a persuasive argument. Suppose you want to persuade your investment partners to buy a certain empty lot in a down-at-the-heels neighborhood for the purpose of building a new condominium. You argue:

> "Yes, the neighborhood is rough at the moment. That's why the price is so low. But look down the block—the lawns are being trimmed, the houses are being painted, and I just read that the ABC chain is going to build a new ABC Home Furnishings store on Baker Street. These are all clear signs that the neighborhood is reviving. Let's get in while the price is right."

These are not infallible signs, but they are strong signs of a reviving neighborhood, the implied premise here being, "People who cannot afford the nicest established neighborhoods are willing to pay good money to live in a neighborhood that is improving and seems to have a bright future."

How to Win with Enthymemes

The enthymeme is the ideal vehicle for persuasive discourse based on an appeal to reason. It streamlines the logical form of the syllogism so that it can be used in ordinary speech, yet it retains the strong backbone of systematic logic. At its best, the result is a compelling clarity of thought and expression.

Logical arguments are winning arguments; however, logical discourse does not require ponderous phrases beginning with *if*, *then*, and *therefore*. The deductive flow of your argument can be made apparent without them. Logical arguments do, however, require an awareness of how the deductive process works, with particular awareness of the difference between truth and validity as well as the necessity of both.

Logical arguments do not require that you possess absolute certainty or truth, but they do call for sufficient judgment to determine probability and likelihood. In contrast to the universe of mathematics, you are rarely required or expected to prove your theses. You are merely expected to present a persuasive case for the likely truth or value of what you propose or recommend. Experience and common sense generally count for a great deal in the appeal to reason. While you should be aware of the logical pitfalls that arguments can easily fall into and that can be fatal to what you advocate, be aware that merely avoiding them does not necessarily make your argument persuasive. Persuasion requires empathy and understanding in addition to unimpeachable logic. As you devote time to the logical structure of your argument, also try to see the issues from the point of view of your readers or listeners. Make certain that you reach a level of probability that will persuade *them* by addressing their concerns, interests, worries, problems, and desires.

Although the appeal to reason rests on a foundation of logic, never forget that it is an appeal to *human* reason. It will do you no good to construct a formally admirable argument if it lacks content that appeals directly to the concerns of your audience. The appeal to reason has the great force of objectivity. A well-reasoned argument "makes sense." Yet, ultimately, it is up to you to make that apparently objective truth compelling to people who are pushed and pulled by many subjective considerations as well. Put yourself in the place of those you want to persuade. Logic should help you to persuade your audience, but it should never be presented as a force somehow superior to their wants and needs. Logic is a wonderful vehicle of persuasive discourse. But don't make the mistake of thinking of it as the destination. That, as always, is the action you desire to persuade others to take.

Be Ethical, Be Emotional

*Two alternative and complementary approaches
to persuasion: the ethical appeal and the
appeal to emotion.*

The classical rhetoricians believed that, in an ideal world, reason would reign, and the appeal to reason would be the only necessary mode of argument. However, they understood that they did not live in an ideal world and, accordingly, developed the ethical and emotional appeals as persuasive alternatives.

ALTERNATIVES TO REASON

The alternatives to reason have always been a bit suspect, as if they were both inferior to, and less legitimate than, the appeal to reason. In fact, there is nothing irrational or unreasonable about appealing to your own character or to the emotions of your audience. Decisions are rarely made on the basis of pure reason. People commonly rely on trust or confidence and feelings when deciding what to do, and in many contexts, these sentiments are no less legitimate than logic. Moreover, few people can neatly separate their "logical selves" from their "trusting selves" or "emotional selves." Nor is it necessarily desirable to do so. Generally speaking, the most persuasive arguments partake of all three modes of appeal: They "make sense" logically, they are advocated by someone worthy of confidence, and they are agreeable to the sentiments of the audience.

THE FORCE OF CHARACTER AND IMAGE

What the classical rhetoricians called the appeal to ethics, or the ethical appeal, is really a pleading of one's own character and authority. The ethical appeal can be a strong positive force or an even stronger negative one. The most rational, logical argument about the humaneness of letting barnyard chickens freely roam in and out of the henhouse will fail to persuade if the speaker is a fox. A bad reputation

61

will undermine the most rational of appeals to reason, whereas an especially fine reputation may well compensate for holes in the logic of an argument.

Who You Are

You possess a great advantage when you attempt to persuade a close friend of something. Your friend knows and trusts you, valuing your character and judgment. Similarly, if you are a public figure with a good reputation that extends throughout your department, throughout the city you serve, or throughout the nation, your arguments will automatically be endowed with a certain persuasive force. "If it's good enough for John, it's good enough for me!"

Know who you are. Make a realistic assessment of your reputation by asking yourself these questions:

• *Do you have good reason to believe that your audience regards you as trustworthy because you have demonstrated this quality to them?*

• *Do you have good reason to believe that your audience regards you as an authority in the field in which you are speaking or writing?*

Who You Say You Are

If you are not confident that people know who you are, tell them. Make certain that your audience is aware of your qualifications, in terms of both your integrity and relevant technical expertise. Often, you need only to introduce yourself. In a speech, you might say something like:

> "Good evening. I'm Jane Jones. For those of you who don't know what I do here, I am the director of information technology and have been in our IT department for seven years."

In a written document, you may want to include a separate biographical blurb to accompany your argument:

> "Jane Jones is the director of information technology for ABC Corporation. A graduate of XYZ Institute of Technology, she has worked in the corporate IT field for more than a decade."

Merely introducing yourself does not constitute an adequate ethical appeal. Your entire argument should convey your integrity and authority, creating a favorable image of who you are and why *you*, of all people, are worthy of favorable consideration.

Creating an Image

When you get up in the morning to prepare for a day at the office, you shower and otherwise groom yourself, then you dress. Perhaps you have laid out your clothes the night before. Perhaps you put together your outfit in the morning. Either way, you select your clothing with some sense (or perhaps an acute consciousness) of what is appropriate to your line of work and your particular workplace, as well as what conveys an image of who you are. You prepare yourself in the morning to meet the world, especially your particular segment of the world. You prepare the image you wish to project to others.

You should prepare at least as thoughtfully when you sit down to compose an argument. Think about the image of yourself you want to convey. This image, which is the essence of the ethical appeal, must be consistent and must pervade the entire argument. You cannot use language that suggests calm, cool rationality in one part of the argument, then suddenly slip into an extravagant claim or lapse into name-calling. Your audience will remember the slip, the single thoughtless word, the lone nasty comment far more vividly than they will recall what you intended as the substance of your message.

Think, then, of who you are or who you wish to be. Use your imagination to find words that grow naturally out of that image. When you review your argument, test your words against the image. Modify or delete any words that do not contribute to it.

> "If you want to project the image of a competent IT professional, use language appropriate to the role."

This, however, brings up another aspect of image. When you dress for the office, you dress, of course, to please yourself, but you also dress with an eye toward pleasing others. You might be most comfortable with denim cutoffs and a T-shirt, but as an investment banker, you wear a suit, shirt, and necktie, which, while not especially comfortable, convey an image of professionalism, good taste, and good sense. The costume is at least as much for the benefit of your customers and colleagues as it is for yourself. Similarly, the language you use also creates your image, so you must choose words with your audience, not just yourself, in mind.

> "If, as an IT professional, you are speaking to a group of other IT profession-als, you will want to use the professional vocabulary at its most advanced level. If, however, you are speaking to a more general audience, you will want to modify that vocabulary. It must remain at a professional level, but you must take care that it is comprehensible to your listeners."

Using specialized jargon on a general audience will not convey an image of professional competence. Quite the contrary, it will suggest that you are unable to function outside of your narrow area of specialization.

Selling the Image

Although the ethical appeal is a function of sustained image, there are two places in the argument where more explicit attempts to sell the image may be made: the introduction and the conclusion.

We have already mentioned the necessity of introducing yourself. The opening of your argument is also the place to extend this introduction to an explanation of your motive.

> "My name is Mary Smith. I am a pediatrician who has practiced in this city for twenty-five years."

So far, this is a good basic introduction that briefly and effectively establishes the speaker's credentials. She continues:

> "In my work with children, I sometimes see evidence of abuse: the kinds of bruises, abrasions, and lacerations that don't come about through normal play. Of course, I routinely report any such observations to child protective services. But, recently, I began to feel that just following the law was not enough. My profession is dedicated to helping children get well and stay well. I no longer believe that my professional responsibility ends with writing up a report. That is why I have come to speak with you. I want to get your support for a new child-endangerment law. . . ."

This introduction makes a strong ethical appeal. We are informed not only of the speaker's professional qualifications, but we also learn something of her moral character. It is difficult to turn your back on an earnest person.

Our physician might close her argument in the same spirit:

> "I have no political ambitions myself. I love being a doctor, but my colleagues and I need the support of strong legislation to do what we love to do and what we must do: help children get well and stay well. If this means I must step out of my office to make a political appeal, well, so be it. That is what I have done this evening. What I ask of you is . . . ."

Here is another ethical appeal, based on the speaker's image, her authority, and her motives. From this point, she will proceed to call her audience to action by telling them just what they must do to support the legislation she is arguing for.

Creating a Favorable Light

The next time you walk into an elegant shop or an upscale department store, take your eyes off the merchandise for a few moments and look instead at how the merchandise is lit. The designers of retail spaces devote a great deal of thought to lighting, because they appreciate the importance of showing merchandise in what is quite literally the best possible light—a favorable light.

At the very least, this is the goal of the ethical appeal: to present yourself in a favorable light, the best possible light. In most cases, the ethical appeal by itself is not sufficient to create a persuasive argument; however, it is very effective in putting other appeals, including the appeal to reason and the appeal to emotion, in the best possible light by presenting you in a favorable light. If people feel confident in you and believe you to be intelligent and possessed of good judgment and integrity, they will be receptive to your argument and ready to receive your reasons. Having listened to or read your argument, they will be all the more inclined to act in the way that you, a person of demonstrated character and authority, ask them to.

THE FORCE OF EMOTION

Many people, especially those in leadership positions, deny that emotion plays any part in the decisions they make. Often, such denials are made with considerable emotion.

By the end of the eighteenth century, rhetoricians made attempts to rehabilitate the appeal to emotion, arguing not only that it was legitimate, but that no attempt at persuasion could be expected to work without it. Some rhetoricians even attempted to analyze persuasion, showing which part could be accomplished through an appeal to reason and which part required an appeal to emotion. They argued that people are moved to a particular action by two things: the apparent desirability of the object of the action, and the conviction that the proposed action will attain the object. It is by an appeal to emotion that the object is made to appear desirable, but it is by an appeal to reason that the proposed means are made to appear feasible, the best way of achieving the proposed object. While it is doubtful that the psychology of persuasion can, in practical application, be broken down so mechanically and neatly, thinking in these terms may be helpful in guiding the composition of a persuasive argument. After all, from childhood we are taught to think very much in these terms:

> "Billy, if you really want that toy, you can get it by doing two things: Save your allowance and do some extra chores around the house, for which I'll pay you." Billy is driven by a strong emotion: desire for a certain toy. Recognizing that emotion, his mother makes an appeal to reason, showing him the means by which he may attain his desired object.

Danger! Humanity Ahead!

With his eye on the prize, Billy may well start to save his pennies and dutifully perform the chores his mother gives him. Then, in a month or two, cash in hand, he may gratify his desire with the cherished toy. However, it is also possible that his mother's appeal to reason will provoke the outburst of pure emotion known as the tantrum. Emotion cannot always be subordinated to reason or be made to work in productive concert with it. Knowing this, legions of the unscrupulous and the downright evil have employed the appeal to emotion to move masses to war, persecutions, pogroms, and genocide. This is one of the reasons that most people are wary of the appeal to emotion. And it is a very good reason. Nevertheless, that a tool can be abused does not mean that the tool should be banished. A screwdriver can be a deadly weapon of destruction or an indispensable instrument of construction.

Yet we must be aware of the suspicion people have when they hear an appeal to emotion. Think of the last time some salesman used the emotional appeal on you. Chances are that your guard went up. You became especially wary. That's what happens when people sense that their emotions are being deliberately manipulated. It is important, therefore, to use the emotional appeal with skill and discretion. If you wield it in a clumsy fashion, if you, in effect, telegraph or announce to your audience that you are going to play on their emotions or "tug at their heartstrings," their defenses will go up like the shields on an embattled science fiction spaceship. People know that they can control their intellect, but they cannot fully control their emotions. We can't help being angry, happy, sad, or scared. Tell somebody that you intend to control his emotions and he will exercise his will to resist you—because if *you* control *his* emotions, you control *him*. Although it is a perfectly sound persuasive tactic to begin an argument by announcing your intention to reason with your audience, to appeal to their intellect, it is an almost invariably fatal tactic to announce your intention to appeal to their emotions.

The objective in making an appeal to emotion, then, is to do so indirectly. Instead of *telling* your audience what to feel, *show* them the object or objects likely to stir the appropriate reaction.

> If you are making a charitable appeal, for example, do not, on the one hand, tell people that they should feel sad about the plight of homeless children and then, on the other hand, expect them to listen to you recite a long list of statistics. Instead, tell the story of a single homeless child. Describe what a single day of the child's life is like. Present a real and realistic picture. That picture, not you, will create the desired emotion in your audience. That done, you can reinforce the emotion with an appeal to reason—"Little Sarah's story is multiplied more than 5,000 times in our community"—and then extend that appeal to reason by telling your audience exactly what they can do to help. Having outlined the means of helping, you might end by recapitulating the emotional appeal: "You will be giving Sarah—all those Sarahs—a real chance at life, a chance she—they—won't have without your help."

Evoking Empathy

The Roman poet Horace (65–8 B.C.) wrote that if you want your reader or listener to feel something, you must first feel that thing yourself. The Russian theatrical director and acting teacher Konstantin Stanislavski (1863–1938) created an entire acting "method" (as he called it) around a similar concept. In the Stanislavski method, to evoke emotion in his audience, an actor should not merely counterfeit or simulate the desired emotion; he must actually feel it himself in order to externalize it and convey it to the audience. Similarly, to create an effective emotional appeal, you cannot simply tell your listeners or readers what to feel or even what you are feeling. You must externalize your emotions, embodying them in an object that will evoke these same emotions in your audience.

This is not as difficult as it sounds, and we do it every day. It is called storytelling. Consider these three accounts of the same incident:

Storyteller 1: A dog chased me. I was terrified.

Storyteller 2: I'm walking along when, all of a sudden, this big, black dog comes running around the corner, showing its sharp, white teeth and growling. I was terrified.

Storyteller 3: I was walking as usual down Greenfield Lane, past the house with that big, black Doberman. I noticed that the Doberman wasn't in the yard as he usually is.

Strange, I thought.

Then I looked away from the yard and straight ahead. There was the Doberman. It was standing there, tail straight down, lips drawn back over those sharp, white teeth. It growled this low, rumbling sort of growl.

For—well, I don't know how long—I just plain couldn't move. The two of us stood looking at each other, the dog's lips drawing tighter and higher over his teeth, the growling getting lower and lower.

I turned, ever so slowly, and slowly began walking away. For some reason I decided it would be dangerous to look back, that it would just provoke the dog to attack. So I forced myself to look straight ahead as I walked, slowly. My feet felt like lead, and my knees were so weak I didn't know if I could keep lifting my heavy feet and putting them back down.

Then I heard claws scuttling across the sidewalk, and I knew he was coming my way—fast.

Suddenly, my knees and feet worked just fine. I tore out of there as fast as I could. What I saw ahead of me was Joe's Grocery. That became my goal. I ran, pumping legs and arms as if I were eighteen again, let me tell you. And now I could hear *him* breathing behind me. Well, I swung to my right and jumped over the three stairs up to the grocery door, pulled the door open, and shut it right behind me. Then, *bang!* That dog goes right into the glass door. For a second, I thought the glass might shatter. But, no . . . .

Storyteller 3's account is longer than the other two accounts, but it is missing one thing both of those have: the word *terrified*. And what we find is that this third account is the stronger, the more compelling, and the more persuasive for leaving out that word. The story does not tell us how to feel. It shows us the object that creates the feeling, and it embellishes the incident by making us see, feel, and hear the actions produced by that feeling.

The emotional appeal requires you to tell a story, to show rather than just tell. Done well, this type of appeal will not merely acquaint others with your point of view, it will produce in them the very feelings associated with your point of view, the feelings created by your point of view, and the feelings your point of view creates. "Put yourself in my shoes," we often say. That is precisely the objective of the emotional appeal.

Arousing Anger

The appeal to emotion is often used to arouse anger in an audience, in order to motivate change or reform. When this is your objective, it may not be sufficient to tell a story. You may need to guide your audience more firmly through the careful use of emotionally loaded language. For example, you want to persuade your neighbors to support an initiative to clean up a vacant lot in your part of the city and convert it into a playground. You intend, in your argument, to make a solid case, showing with relevant statistics the need for the playground, how a playground will increase the value of nearby homes, how it can be expected to reduce juvenile crime, and what clearing the lot and building the playground will cost. But, after introducing yourself as a parent and longtime neighborhood resident (part of an ethical appeal), you wisely decide to continue with an appeal to emotion. You want to make your audience angry about the existence of an unsightly, filthy, rodent-infested empty lot in the middle of your neighborhood. You describe the condition of the place. You talk about how children play in this empty lot, among rats, broken glass, and who knows what else. But you need to intensify and to shape the outrage you want to stir so that you can point it in the productive direction of reform. You want to make your audience receptive to your call to action:

> "What I have just described is a shame, a *shame* we all share. This *disgrace* will remain in our neighborhood until we decide to work together to do something about it. The city, whose government is *burdened by an outmoded bureaucracy, cronyism, and old-boy politics*, is not about to *stir itself* to help us. We can choose to continue as *helpless victims of politics as usual* or we can *take matters into our own hands*."

The italicized words and phrases are emotionally loaded and designed to direct productive anger not at the empty lot, but at those responsible for perpetuating the blight. Moreover, the language specifically defines the empty lot as a "shame" and a "disgrace." This passage does not tell people what to feel, but it provides an interpretation of the anger that has been stirred in them. It puts a label on it. Without such guidance, you may simply have produced an angry crowd, whose rage will dissipate over the course of a day or a week. But by using a few emotionally loaded terms, you give direction to the anger. You have prepared your audience to receive a call to action.

Motivating Action

It is one thing to whip up emotion in an audience and another to make productive use of it. Don't leave people in a state of directionless agitation. Consider their stirred emotions not as an end but as a means to an end, that end being the decision or action you want to persuade them to take or perform.

Make a transition from the appeal to emotion to the appeal to reason:

> "We can choose to continue as helpless victims of politics as usual or we can take matters into our own hands. I have prepared a petition to the city council, demanding that a resolution be voted up immediately to reserve the lot for development as a playground. What I ask you to do, right now, tonight, is sign the petition. . . ."

Give your audience specific instructions for action, then close by assuring them that their action will be effective in achieving what has now been transformed into a shared objective.

> "Ladies and gentlemen, this petition is the necessary first step toward providing our children with the playground they need and deserve. In three other neighborhoods, similar petitions have secured action from the council. While I cannot absolutely guarantee that ours will produce the same result, the odds are on our side. More important, I *can* guarantee that absolutely nothing will happen if we fail to present at least 3,000 signatures. The welfare of our children is our responsibility, and we are now in a position to do something about it."

From here, the argument can proceed to reinforce the appeal to emotion with an appeal to reason, including relevant statistics. It can also detail the political and administrative machinery the petition will set into motion and, perhaps, how the neighborhood can have a voice in the design of the playground. The objective always is to move forward from the emotional appeal so that the energy it creates is channeled in the direction you want it to move.

Stay Out of the Palace of Fallacy

A little handbook of logical errors, faulty thinking,
and illegitimate argument that will help you avoid
these mistakes and give you ammunition against
the shoddy reasoning of others.

Many arguments fail to persuade us. Often, we find them factually wrong. It is easy, for example, to poke holes in the pitch of the car salesman who touts the virtues of an automobile on the basis of specs you know to be incorrect: "Three hundred horsepower? The manufacturer's brochure says 225!" But we also often encounter arguments based on correct facts, or on facts that we are not in a position either to refute or to verify, that just somehow *seem* wrong. The chain of reasoning seems faulty, yet we may not be able to put our finger on the error.

WHY ARGUMENTS FAIL

The classical rhetoricians paid almost as much attention to the fallacies of inductive and deductive reasoning as they did to the methods of persuasion. Fallacies that involve false or erroneous statements, errors, or inaccuracies of fact, are called *fallacies of matter*. Those involving specious, invalid, or even deceptive reasoning are called *fallacies of reasoning*. The latter fall into two categories: fallacies of *deductive reasoning* and fallacies of *inductive reasoning*.

THE FALLACIES OF MATTER

Arguments based on fallacies of matter are often the easiest to identify and refute—provided that you happen to know what the truth is. The proposition that the chair is white can be refuted by pointing to the black chair. Of course, the truth is not always readily available. In such cases, you must do the research necessary to find the truth. In the meantime, you may have to defer refuting a suspect argument by saying something like "I can't dispute your conclusion because I don't have the necessary figures. I need to look them up for last year and the year before. Then I'd like to take this matter up again."

To make it easier for you to recognize fallacies of matter, let's divide them into seven broad categories.

Mere Assertion

Some arguments are based on mere assertion: "My dog is smarter than your dog." To which the obvious response is "No, he isn't." Such disputes can go on forever—or until the disputants come to blows or both sides give up in mutual exhaustion.

If an assertion is liable to proof or refutation (perhaps some sort of meaningful contest might be arranged between the two dogs in question), then there is the possibility of resolving the dispute. If not, the dispute will be futile.

Some assertions relate to matters of taste. "Brand X mayonnaise tastes better than Brand Y" might be partly resolved in a taste test involving an adequate number of consumers, but it will never be definitive. More complex questions of taste— "Rembrandt was a better painter than Rubens"—cannot be resolved, although they can sometimes be argued more illuminatingly if, in the course of the argument, you fully explain the reasons for your assertion. Art and literary critics do this all the time. The results cannot be deemed conclusive in any absolute sense of truth or falsity, but they can be illuminating in terms of whatever criteria the critic articulates.

Factual Error or Deception

A common fallacy of matter is factual error or purposeful deception. The only counter to these fallacies is the truth, which can be ascertained by research.

Common sense is important here, not only in detecting errors and deceptions, but also in drawing the line between statements that require factual substantiation and those that do not require proof. Self-evident statements require no special support. A self-evident proposition is one that all (or at least almost all) people would immediately and automatically acknowledge as true:

> "It is better to be rich than poor" is almost certainly self-evident, as is "Freedom is preferable to slavery."

Another self-evident type of statement is the statement that is true by definition:

> "A triangle is a closed figure of three sides" does not require proof, because it is the definition of a triangle.

Of course, if the definition is in error, the statement is untrue.

Another category of statement that requires no proof is common knowledge.

This is the pool of information that any reasonably or even minimally informed person can be expected to know:

> "The president is the chief executive of the United States federal government." This statement doesn't need to be proved because it is common knowledge—unless you are talking to a man from Mars.

Common sense should guide us in the degree of precision we use or demand in an argument. For example:

> You say, "About 35,000 customers used our service last fiscal year." Someone objects: "You're wrong. The number was 34,998!"

The objection, even if the figure is true, is, in most contexts, silly. However, it would be quite pertinent to offer the 34,998 figure to counter an inflated assertion that "last fiscal year, nearly 40,000 customers used our service" or the vague assertion that "some 20,000 to 50,000 customers used our service." It is one thing to round off awkward numbers and quite another to deliberately distort figures or to blur them in hopeless vagueness.

There are also many contexts that cry out for accuracy:

> "More than 50,000 U.S. military personnel were killed in the Vietnam War" is true, but it is far more effective, meaningful, and morally sound to declare that "58,226 U.S. military personnel were killed in the Vietnam War."

The Half-Truth

A half-truth is a fallacy of matter that is almost always used deliberately to deceive. Everything that is said in the half-truth is true (verifiable fact), but material is omitted in order to conceal or distort the total picture.

> "John Smith has been seen in the company of known drug addicts for the past five years. He is not to be trusted."

On the face of it, this is a reasonable assertion—until we dig deeper and find out that, for the past five years, John Smith has been a professional drug rehabilitation counselor.

Misuse of Example

Examples are important means of supporting generalizations and explaining various elements on an argument. People naturally respond more readily to concrete examples than to abstract assertions. Indeed, when we challenge an assertion, we often demand an example.

Someone: "Jane habitually lies."

You: "Does she? Give me an example."

Examples are invaluable to many arguments, but they are subject to abuse. In evaluating (or using) examples, consider the following:

• *Is the example true and accurate?* Someone asserts, "Brahms *did* write opera. What about *Fidelio,* for example?" Problem here is that *Fidelio* is by Ludwig van Beethoven, not Johannes Brahms, who, in fact, wrote no operas.

• *Is one example sufficient?* Sometimes, a single example will serve to illustrate or clarify a point, but a single example is almost never adequate to provide full support for a generalization. "The aftermath of most revolutions is relatively peaceful. There was not much violence after the American Revolution." True, but what about the French Revolution, the Russian Revolution of 1917, and any number of revolutions in Central and South America during the nineteenth century? There is strong evidence that a period of violence follows most revolutions and that the relative peace following the American Revolution was the exception rather than the rule.

• *Can you offer or evaluate counterexamples?* "All revolutions are followed by periods of intense violence. Just consider, for example, the French Revolution, the Russian Revolution, and any number of revolutions in Central and South America during the nineteenth century." To which you might counter: "But what about the American Revolution?" The counterexample suggests that the universal quality of the generalization ("all revolutions . . .") is inaccurate and should be revised by substituting "most" for "all." The counterexample by no means negates the examples cited, however, and it might be interpreted as "the exception that proves the rule"—a lone example that stands in such stark contrast to the majority of examples and thereby tends to emphasize the validity of the majority of the examples.

• *What is the context of the examples that are offered?* "We have dozens of satisfied customers in your area." On the face of it, this statement offers strong exemplary support for the assertion "You can trust us to do the job right." But what happens if you investigate the context of the example and discover that the company in question has served 1,000 customers in your area, of whom two dozen are satisfied and the rest are considering a class-action lawsuit?

Misuse of Analogy

Properly used, analogies explain or clarify an unfamiliar concept by comparing it to a familiar one, or they persuade the reader or listener to a novel point of view by likening it to a familiar or readily accepted point of view.

> "Automobiles require inspection and maintenance by a qualified mechanic. Like cars, people require routine examination by a qualified physician."

In this case, the assumption is that most people would agree that automobiles require inspection and maintenance by someone with expertise in auto mechanics; therefore, this situation can be used as an analogy to persuade people to get regular medical checkups.

While analogies are useful, they are easily misused in arguments. Evaluate them in light of two dimensions:

1. *An argument by analogy always includes a first premise that makes a claim about the example used as an analogy.* In the example just given, the first premise is that cars require regular servicing by a knowledgeable person. The premise is true. Contrast: "Modern automobiles are essentially self-maintaining. Like them, people are better off avoiding routine visits to the doctor." The premise that modern automobiles are essentially self-maintaining is false; therefore, any analogy based on it is suspect at best and wrong at worst.

2. *Analogy requires a reasonably similar example.* This does not mean that the analogy in the premise has to be exactly, point for point, the same as the example in the conclusion, but the fit has to be reasonably good. To be sure, cars and people are very different from one another; nevertheless, there is enough similarity—both are complex systems subject to various malfunctions—to make the analogy valid.

It is always wise to view argument by analogy with a great deal of caution and skepticism. The function of analogy is primarily illustrative. It is rarely sufficient proof.

Misuse of Authority

Authority is a common means by which matters of fact are validated. For instance:

> "John designed our computer system. If he says that we need to upgrade the hard drives, we should not hesitate to spend the money on them."

The impact of this use of authority is very different from saying:

> "George used to repair computers—oh, ten or fifteen years ago. If he says that we need to upgrade the hard drives on our computers, we should not hesitate to spend the money on them."

Whereas John's authority may be taken as solid, the fact that George repaired computers a long time ago (ten or fifteen years is an epoch where the fast-moving technology of computers is concerned) does not make him a very persuasive authority when it comes to deciding whether to invest in an expensive hardware upgrade.

In evaluating arguments based on authority, consider the authority cited very thoroughly:

• *Are sources cited? Just who is the authority?* Saying "I read somewhere that doctors make a lot less money these days" is a far less persuasive than saying, "A survey in last month's *Journal of the American Medical Association* reported that internists, on average, made X percent less salary than they did just five years earlier."

• *Is the authority qualified, reliable, and free from obvious bias?* A well-published modern historian is more qualified to evaluate the performance of the sitting Republican president of the United States than either 1) the local bartender or 2) the Democratic candidate the sitting president defeated.

• *Is the authority representative of prevailing opinion?* "Creationism must be correct, and the theory of evolution wrong, because Professor X, a biologist, supports creationism." This may be true, and Dr. X may have perfectly good professional credentials; however, do some cross-checking and you will find that the overwhelming majority of biologists endorse evolution. Does this prove that the theory of evolution is correct and creationism wrong? By no means. But it does demonstrate that most scientists reject creationism and favor evolution; therefore, citing an authority who is out of the mainstream of professional opinion makes for a weak argument. Of course, the majority is not always right. There was a time when most well-educated people thought the sun orbited the earth, and people like Copernicus and, later, Galileo were in the minority in arguing that the earth orbited the sun. It can be persuasive to cite authorities who hold a minority opinion if you can convincingly demonstrate that their opinion is superior to that held by the majority—perhaps because it is based on new research. It is also true that all authorities are not created equal. If ten high school science majors argue that gravity is a physical *force*, but one Albert Einstein argues that it is a *field*, it would be a mistake to cite the majority opinion against the minority.

Be intolerant of so-called authorities who rely on ad hominem arguments:

"Nothing Dr. Smith says about human sexuality is worth listening to. He's gay."

Or:

"Jane Doe may be a distinguished professor of sociology, but nothing she says about living below the poverty line is of any value. She has never been poor herself."

Such personal attacks and name-calling almost always betray a prejudice sufficient to disqualify the source as a reliable authority.

Misuse of Causation

Arguments concerning cause and effect are among the most important we make, since they are all about taking action that influences the world about us.

"Spend our discretionary fund on X, because it will create Y. I know this to be the case because X always causes Y."

Some cause-and-effect relationships are well established. Others are more speculative. In most cases, the speculative propositions are based on a correlation between two events:

"People who subscribe to *XYZ Magazine* buy more widgets than nonsubscribers do. Therefore, we should buy ad space in *XYZ Magazine*."

The unstated conclusion is that advertising in this magazine will *cause* an increase in widget sales.

A perceived correlation between events may prompt false conclusions about cause and effect. In Latin, this is known as the *post hoc, ergo propter hoc* fallacy: "after this, therefore because of this."

You go to Las Vegas and lose a bundle. You tell yourself, "I knew I should have turned back the minute I realized I'd left my lucky rabbit's foot at home."

Superstitious beliefs are a common form of the *post hoc* fallacy. To avoid being misled by—or misleading others with—false cause-and-effect arguments, always ask the following questions of any cause-and-effect proposition:

1. *Can you explain how the cause leads to the effect?* If you cannot, odds are that the correlation of events is not a true cause-and-effect relationship.

2. *Is the proposed cause the likely cause?* It is not sufficient for an argument to propose a possible cause of an effect. It should propose the most likely cause. "It is possible that you failed your algebra exam because Mr. Smith doesn't like you, but it is far more likely that you failed because you haven't opened your algebra book in two weeks."

3. *Could the correlation of events be a coincidence?* Years ago, a favorite amusement of financial journalists was to point out that the rise and fall of the Dow Jones Industrial Average over a long period could be correlated with the rise and fall of women's hemlines. Do you conclude from this assertion that the one causes the other? And, if you do, which one causes which? Or is the whole thing a coincidence?

4. *Could apparently correlated events share a common cause?* "Violent video games have created a violent society. The evidence is all around us." Maybe. But it is more likely that the violence in society and the violence in video games have some common sources, perhaps in a breakdown of traditional values, the economic inequality of our society, or some other causes.

5. *Which event is the cause? Which event is the effect?* The mere fact of correlation does not establish the direction of cause and effect. The great American psychologist William James wrote, "We do not run because we are afraid, we are

afraid because we run." Do violent video games cause violence in children? Or do software makers create violent video games to satisfy a market that demands them?

6. *Is there a reciprocal relationship of cause and effect?* Often, a cause creates an effect, which then creates the cause. In William James's example, the fear created by running probably causes us to run faster, and the faster we run, the more frightened we become. One could also argue that violent video games create a demand for more violent video games, which, in turn, create an even greater demand for them.

7. *Is the correlation of events more complex than the cause-and-effect conclusion?* Many things we do create simple effects that can readily be accounted for. However, there is usually little need to create arguments about simple cause-and-effect relationships. As the old joke goes: A man visits his doctor and, raising his arms above his head, complains, "Doc, it hurts when I do this. What do you recommend?" The doctor, raising his arms above his head, replies: "Stop doing this." The cause-and-effect relationships usually worth arguing about are more complex. Make certain that the argument offered accounts for this complexity.

> "People who eat a good breakfast are healthier than people who skip breakfast. Therefore, eat a good breakfast."

It may be true that eating a good breakfast "causes" good health. But it may also be true that healthy people tend to eat a good breakfast because they are healthy—their good health being derived from a complex of other causes, including genetics, exercise, a low-stress lifestyle, and so on. Yet before you reject this argument as valueless, consider that it may identify *one* cause that contributes to good health; therefore, while eating a good breakfast does not cause good health, it may contribute to it. That a particular cause is not fully sufficient to account for a particular effect does not necessarily render it valueless.

THE FALLACIES OF DEDUCTIVE REASONING

Logical fallacies, whether in deductive or inductive reasoning, do not relate to the truth or falsity of the material in question, but are failures of coherence, breaks in the chain of reasoning.

Doesn't Follow

We commonly use the term *non sequitur* to describe a statement that is out of place in a series of statements. The literal meaning of this Latin phrase is more precise. It means "does not follow," and it is a good general description of all errors of reasoning. The quality they all have in common is that they do not follow in the chain of reasoning.

Doublethink, Doublespeak

Politicians and used-car salesmen are notorious for double-talk, the technical term for which is *equivocation*. In this deductive fallacy, the speaker or writer uses the same term with two or more referents so that, in effect, a fourth term is introduced into the syllogism or enthymeme. It is impossible to draw a valid conclusion from premises that have four terms.

> A wise judge carries weight.
>
> A fat man carries weight.
>
> Therefore, a fat man is a wise judge.

The phrase "carries weight" is used equivocally here; no conclusion drawn from these premises is valid.

Missing Links

Some arguments fail to supply the necessary link in the chain of reasoning between the major and minor term. Therefore, no valid conclusion can be drawn from them. The following example fails to demonstrate any connection between the first and second premise; therefore, the conclusion drawn from them is invalid.

> All Republicans are people.
>
> All Democrats are people.
>
> Therefore, all Democrats are Republicans.

It is easy to detect arguments that suffer from missing links when they are not only invalid but obviously untrue. We know that "all Democrats are Republicans" is false; it's nonsense. Detecting this kind of fallacy is more difficult when we don't know the truth or falsity of the premises:

> All Brand X microchips are made of super silicon.
>
> All Type 2 microchips are made of super silicon.
>
> Therefore, all Brand X microchips are Type 2 microchips.

This may be true, but you cannot determine truth from the argument, because it is invalid.

The *middle term* in a syllogism appears in both the premises, but not the conclusion. In the first syllogism, "people" is the middle term; in the second, the middle term is "super silicon." The *major term* in the first syllogism is "Republicans," the *minor term* "Democrats." In the second syllogism, the major term is "Brand X microchips," and the minor term is "Type 2 microchips." It may help you to recognize a syllogism that suffers from a broken link by visualizing the middle term as occupying a large circle in which the major and minor terms exist side by side (that is, neither *concentric* nor *intersecting*). Although both the major and minor terms lie within the middle term, they are not connected with one another.

Illicit Process

No conclusion can be drawn from two particular premises. Look at the classic example of a valid syllogism:

> All men are mortal.
>
> Socrates is a man.
>
> Therefore, Socrates is mortal.

The major premise, "All men are mortal," is universal because it applies to all men. The minor premise, "Socrates is a man," is particular, because it applies to Socrates. Because one of the premises is universal, we can draw a conclusion from the premises. However, contrast the following:

> Plato is a man.
>
> Socrates is a man.
>
> Therefore, Socrates is mortal.

While the conclusion is true, it cannot be validly derived from the premises because both are particular. In short, the conclusion simply does not follow from the premises. It is a non sequitur, and all arguments that attempt to draw a conclusion from two particular premises are examples of illicit process.

Conclusion from Two Negative Premises

Two negative premises cannot establish a relationship among all three terms of a syllogism. For this reason, no conclusion can be drawn from them.

> No men are mortal.
>
> Socrates is not a man.
>
> Therefore, Socrates is not mortal.

Aside from the truth or falsity of the matter in this syllogism, it is invalid because it attempts to draw a conclusion from two negative premises. Suppose no men are mortal, and suppose Socrates is not a man. These do not guarantee that Socrates is not mortal. Although we are told that Socrates is not a man, for all we know—and the point is that we *do not know*—Socrates could be a member of some other mortal species. A conclusion from two negative premises is impossible.

Negative Premise, Affirmative Conclusion

If one of the premises in a syllogism is negative, then the conclusion must also be negative. An affirmative conclusion is invalid. Consider:

> No men are mortal.
>
> Socrates is a man.

The only valid conclusion that can be drawn from this is a negative one:

> Therefore, Socrates is not mortal.

The affirmative alternative, "Therefore, Socrates is mortal," while we know it to be true, is invalid—a non sequitur.

Perched Atop the Dilemma's Horns

Many arguments attempt to force an either/or conclusion where none is logically possible. Some situations in life are in fact binary: "Either she is pregnant or not." Logically, there is no third possibility because the alternatives presented are mutually exclusive. Being pregnant excludes not being pregnant, and not being pregnant excludes being pregnant.

However, some arguments attempt, invalidly, to put the audience on the horns of a dilemma by offering alternatives that are not necessarily mutually exclusive. "Either you are for us or against us" is a classic instance of what logicians call the *disjunctive fallacy* (a *disjunctive proposition* is the technical name for an either/or proposition). The proposition refuses to acknowledge a third alternative: neutrality. Even worse, it fails to recognize shades of assent or alliance.

Beware the Hypothetical

Arguments that begin with a hypothetical proposition (one that starts with "if") are vulnerable to the fallacy of affirming the consequent.

> **Joe:** If the shop steward caves in to management on the question of salary, the power of the union will diminish.
>
> **Jack:** The power of the union has diminished.
>
> **Joe:** Well, the shop steward must have caved.

Jack has affirmed the consequent—the "then" part of an if/then hypothesis: "[Then] the power of the union will diminish." Joe commits the fallacy of affirming the consequent by drawing the conclusion: "Well, the shop steward must have caved."

Note that the hypothesis is quite reasonable, and we can assume that it is a fact that "the power of the union has diminished." Nevertheless, while the conclusion is also plausible, it is not logically valid. It does not logically and necessarily follow from the hypothetical proposition and the affirmed consequent. It is possible that the shop steward stood up valiantly to management, but that management was unimpressed. That is, the diminishment of the union's power might have some other cause, despite the best efforts of the shop steward. The point is that we just do not know and can draw no valid conclusion from this argument.

Denying the Antecedent

As affirming the antecedent leads to an invalid conclusion in arguments based on a hypothetical proposition, so denying the antecedent will also yield a logically invalid conclusion.

> **Joe:** If the shop steward stands strong against management on the question of salary, the power of the union will grow.
> **Jack:** The shop steward did not stand strong.
> **Joe:** The power of the union will diminish.

The antecedent is the "if" part of an if/then, or hypothetical, proposition. Jack denies the antecedent, asserting that "the shop steward did not stand strong." Joe draws an invalid conclusion from this: "The power of the union will diminish."

Yet again, this exchange is plausible. It is a reasonable interpretation of events. Nevertheless, it has no necessary logical weight. We cannot *conclude* that the power of the union *will* diminish. We can *predict* that it *may*. But it is also possible that it will be unaffected or even increase—perhaps as a result of some cause not even contemplated in this argument. We do not know, and based on this hypothetical argument, we cannot know.

THE FALLACIES OF INDUCTIVE REASONING

Whereas in deductive reasoning valid conclusions follow necessarily from valid premises, in inductive reasoning, conclusions are derived from generalization based on particular facts or instances. Three major fallacies commonly afflict inductive reasoning.

Conclusion Jumping and Faulty Generalization

It is all too easy to jump to a false conclusion or to make generalizations that prove to be unwarranted. Typically, this fallacy is caused by one or more of the following:

1. The evidence on which we base our generalization may be irrelevant.

> "Carrying a rabbit's foot brings good luck. Joe won the lottery, and he carries a rabbit's foot. Clara, who carries a rabbit's foot, was almost hit by a bus, but it missed her."

2. The evidence may not be representative.

"Plenty of people win the lottery. I know someone who knows someone who has a friend whose cousin remembers a person who won $100."

3. The evidence may be inadequate.

"Our new drug is very effective. We have tested it on three patients."

Generalizations based on the statements of authorities are also subject to fallacy. The authority cited may be biased, insufficiently competent, or outmoded. It is also possible to use the evidence of a perfectly reliable authority poorly. The authority's opinion may be misunderstood (this is a pitfall in highly technical fields), misquoted, deliberately distorted, or taken out of context.

After This, Therefore Because of This

Fallacies of causation abound. The most common is the *post hoc, ergo propter hoc* ("after this, therefore because of this") fallacy, which results when event B follows event A, prompting the conclusion that event A caused event B.

"It never fails. Every time I leave my umbrella at home, it rains."

Other fallacies of causation include:

1. Assigning an inadequate cause to an effect:

"My wheel wouldn't have fallen off if someone hadn't dinged my car door in the parking lot. " (Contrast: "My wheel wouldn't have fallen off if I had remembered to tighten the lug nuts when I changed my flat tire.")

2. Failing to consider the possibility of more than a single cause of an effect:

"I wouldn't have had that accident if I had gotten enough sleep the night before." (We happen to know that the speaker also downed three pints of very good ale before he got behind the wheel.)

These first two fallacies apply to arguments from effect to cause. When we go in the other direction, arguing from cause to effect, we can also err in the following ways:

1. Failing to establish that a potential cause of an effect could and did operate in a particular situation:

"I won; therefore, carrying a rabbit's foot brings good luck." (No evidence of causation is offered.)

2. Failing to consider that the same cause can produce other effects:

"I failed that calculus exam. The professor hates me." (We happen to know that the speaker has never been within ten feet of his calculus textbook.)

Bludgeoned by Analogy

Analogies prove nothing. They can be very useful in helping to explain unfamiliar concepts by comparing the unfamiliar to something familiar, and they can be a powerful adjunct to persuasion, but they carry no logical force. (Review "Misuse of Analogy," covered previously in this chapter.)

FALLACY GRAB BAG

Some common fallacies apply to both deductive and inductive reasoning because they are formal fallacies as well as fallacies of matter.

Begging the Question

Called by medieval logicians *petitio principii*, this is a fallacy of circular logic. In deductive reasoning, begging the question occurs when the conclusion we are trying to prove is subsumed into a premise. For example:

"I am right because I am an authority on the subject."

That this enthymeme begs the question becomes quite apparent when we expand it into a full-blown syllogism:

All authorities on the subject are right.

I am an authority on the subject.

Therefore, I am right.

Even setting aside for the moment the fact that the speaker makes no effort to prove his authority, the reasoning is circular. The second premise and the conclusion say the same thing using different words because the first premise sets up a tautological definition of authority, defining it in terms of itself. (In effect, it says, "I am right because I am right.") Thus, the argument simply moves in a circle and cannot get anywhere.

Various stock phrases are red flags signaling the approach of a begged question: "As all intelligent people know." "It goes without saying that . . . ." "Obviously." "There can be no denying that . . . ." "Unquestionably." "Without doubt." These and similar formulas are all attempted substitutes for genuine argument. They ask you to accept a conclusion without proof.

Poisoning the Well

A special form of begging the question is often called "poisoning the well." It goes like this: "Only a traitor would protest this war." Without offering an argument, the speaker tries to preempt an opposing position by tainting it. If only a traitor would protest this war, and you protest this war, then you must be a traitor.

Attacking the Man

The *ad hominem* ("to the man") argument does not attempt to refute an opponent's argument but instead attacks the opponent's character. Almost always, this is a fallacious approach, which, because it is an alternative to argument, should not even be called a flawed argument. The ad hominem attack avoids the issues: "Don't be impressed by the facts and the argument of my opponent. He is a wife beater."

Usually, it is a good policy to reject out of hand ad hominem appeals; however, there are instances in which character is as relevant as the issues, facts, and logical quality of an argument.

> Two political candidates each take laudable stands on issues important to you. Candidate A has been a lawyer for the poor and a much-admired county judge. Candidate B was recently disbarred for mishandling a client's funds but presents a somewhat more impressive argument than Candidate A on issues of importance to you. Whom do you vote for?

Popular Pandering

Another substitute for a real argument, one that grapples with the issues, is called the appeal *ad populum* ("to the people") fallacy. Politicians are sometimes guilty of pandering to the irrational fears and prejudices of their audience by using such emotionally loaded terms as "the American way," "patriotism," "traditional values," "evildoers," "communism," "atheism," and the like.

Dragging the Red Herring

Yet another attempted substitute for a solid argument is the red herring. Competing hunters would sometimes drag a herring across a trail in order to lead the opponent's hounds on a false scent and away from the prey. Similarly, in an argument, a disputant may try to dodge, rather than address, the issue at hand:

> **Opponent:** You claim that I made a mistake in investing the firm's money in widget futures. But what about all those times I put our money in productive investments?
>
> **You:** The issue is not the past, but the present. We need to talk about the consequences of having put our money in those widget futures and how we're going to make up the shortfall.

Loading the Question

The *loaded question*, also called the *complex question*, may be seen as a subset of begging the question, because it subsumes the conclusion in the question. The classic example is this: "Tell me, when did you stop beating your wife?" Any attempt to offer a simple answer to the question will result in self-incrimination. The question is loaded or complex because it combines two questions: "Do you beat your wife?" and "When did you stop beating her?" Moreover, the second question in effect answers the first even as it asks it.

Just as you should not allow yourself to be bullied into climbing onto the horns of an illegitimate either/or proposition, you should not fall into the trap of giving a simple answer to a complex question. Divide it into its constituent parts, then answer them.

> "First, you are asking whether I beat my wife. The answer is no. Second, you are asking when I stopped beating her. Obviously, if I never beat my wife, there was no beating to stop."

Just because you receive an invitation to engage in a fallacy, you are not required to accept.

Welcome to the House of Style

How to use the most effective style to make your communication more persuasive.

The classical rhetoricians were concerned, in the first place, with "discovering" arguments, then, in the second place, with arranging the argument in an appeal to reason, to emotion, to character, or to some combination of these. The third concern of the classical rhetoricians was *style*, by which they meant the process of putting thought into words. The Greek rhetoricians called style *lexis*, a single word in which the ideas of thought, word, and speech were combined. The Latin rhetoricians used the term *elocutio*, which means "speaking out." In both cases, style is presented as the necessary bridge between a would-be persuader and an audience to be persuaded. Style, therefore, is not a synonym for fancy or flowery language, but for *effective* language—language that succeeds in communicating thought persuasively.

DEFINING *STYLE*

As the classical rhetoricians use the word, *style* is at the very heart of writing and speaking. Style requires, at minimum, a command of grammar and an adequacy of vocabulary. *Persuasive* style requires even more: an ability to fit style to the matter of your argument and to the nature of your audience, which means that an effective speaker or writer must be able to summon up a variety of styles as the particular occasion demands. Fitting the style to the matter is, in part, a function of diction, which, in turn, relies on a well-stocked arsenal of vocabulary. It is also a function of the composition of words in sentences of appropriate length and rhythm.

DICTION AND DICTIONARY

Persuasive writers and speakers need to possess a rich general vocabulary. We need to be good all-round persuaders; therefore, we need a command of language adequate for expression in a variety of contexts and degrees of complexity. A rich vocabulary is *not* a collection of superfluous verbiage. Expression is a vehicle that should be adequate to convey meaning; however, the vehicle should never appear as more important than meaning.

> You are expecting an eagerly anticipated guest for dinner. His vehicle drives up. Do you announce, "Joe's car is here," or "Joe is here"? Which is more important to you?

How do you build a good general vocabulary?

The most effective method is by reading as much as you can whenever you can. Any reasonably well educated adult can figure out the meaning of most words by the context in which they occur; however, keep a dictionary handy, and look up any unfamiliar words *when* you encounter them. This habit will expand your vocabulary quickly and accurately.

If a dictionary is so helpful, why not simply read the dictionary?

In fact, some people derive a great deal of pleasure from perusing the pages of a dictionary. There is nothing wrong with this, but it is not a good way to build vocabulary. For words to be truly useful, we must encounter them in context, not on isolated exhibit in the dictionary. Looking at a stuffed tiger in the glass case of a museum is no substitute for seeing the animal in the wild. So it is with words.

Combing the dictionary for new or unusual words may result in the inappropriate use of words for the sake of their novelty. Consider:

> "This is a very competitive market. We need to get our product out the door fast."

Or:

> "This is a very competitive market. We need to get our product out the door with alacrity."

Both sets of sentences are perfectly correct, but which of them makes the important point more effectively? *Alacrity* is a good word, but is it the right word here? Is it a more effective word than *fast*? Would the writer have even used *alacrity* had he not happened to come upon it in the dictionary? Like any other tool, a dictionary, then, may be used well or misused.

THE RIGHT WORDS

Taking the time and effort to find and use just the right words to say what you mean goes a long way toward creating clarity—the single most important quality of effective verbal expression.

But what is the right word?

It is the word that, in a given context and for a given audience, promises to perform most adequately in three dimensions:

1. Purity of diction
2. Propriety of diction
3. Precision of diction

Purity of Diction

By "purity of diction," rhetoricians mean that the words you use should be the same words generally in use in your time and place. They should not be conspicuously old-fashioned words, foreign words, inappropriately technical words, or coinages known to very few or to you alone. Although contemporary colloquial speech is appropriate in many situations, outright slang usually is not.

Propriety of Diction

Words are appropriate—that is, they meet the test of what rhetoricians call *propriety*—when they suit the subject, purpose, occasion, and audience of a particular argument. Consider these examples:

"My opponent is mistaken . . ."

"My opponent is wrong . . ."

"My opponent is dead wrong . . ."

"My opponent, as usual, is dead wrong . . ."

"My opponent is lying . . ."

"My opponent is an idiot . . ."

"My opponent is stupid . . . "

"My opponent is retarded . . ."

In the context of most debates, only the first phrase exhibits acceptable propriety of diction.

Tuning your diction to a level appropriate to a particular subject, purpose, occasion, and audience is a lot like deciding how to dress for a given event. No one has to tell you not to wear jeans and a T-shirt to a formal wedding reception or a tuxedo when you're going out to play tennis. You have naturally developed a sense of what dress is appropriate to a variety of occasions. Similarly, it behooves you to devote thought to what level of diction is appropriate in a given context.

Ideally, writers or speakers develop a good sense of how to pitch their discourse for their target audience level, speaking neither up nor down to them. It is, however, better to err on side of talking up to them, rather than talking down. If your discourse flies slightly above their heads, people are likely to regard it as a sign of your respect. If, however, people sense that you have dumbed down your discourse, they will, quite rightly, resent it.

Let us borrow once again from the analogy of appropriate dress. Most dress-for-success gurus advise you to look around your workplace, notice how most people dress, then try to dress just a notch above the rest. Observe a similar rule of thumb in adjusting your vocabulary. Aim just a notch above what you perceive to be the vocabulary level of your audience.

Precision of Diction

The meaning of most words has two dimensions: denotation and connotation. *Denotation* is the dictionary definition of a word. *Connotation* is the cluster of emotion and tone that surrounds a word. If denotation is a word's meaning, connotation consists of its shades of meaning.

Since considerations of connotation can be related to issues of propriety of diction, which we have just discussed, let's begin with connotation.

> You want to praise a guitar maker you greatly admire. Do you say, "He is a consummate *craftsman*" or "He is a consummate *artist*"? Both statements are judgments of high praise, but the second, because of its connotation, raises the assessment to a higher level. It also invites disagreement. Some people would argue that a guitar maker must be a craftsman because he's obliged to follow certain acoustic rules and woodworking traditions that preclude him from the greater imaginative freedom the word *artist* connotes.

Because connotation is usually emotional in content, it can be a very potent element of a word. *Attorney*, *counselor*, *lawyer*, and *mouthpiece* all denote someone who practices the law, but they present a variety of connotations and, depending on the audience, carry a variety of emotional power.

With respect to denotation, if it is not always possible to make certain that you are suggesting what you want to suggest, it is possible to make certain that you are saying what you mean. However, depending on your command of vocabulary, this may require extra caution. For instance:

> "I received fulsome praise from the senator" sounds like a very good thing indeed—until you actually look up the word *fulsome*, which means "offensively flattering or insincere."

Or:

> "Late! What do you mean? I'm always absolutely punctilious"—which means a person who lavishes excessive attention on matters of protocol and etiquette.

THE RIGHT RHYTHMS

Everyone is familiar with the idea of rhythm in music. Lyrics—words intended to be sung—also have a rhythm, even if they are spoken rather than set to music.

Traditional poetry, also unsung, likewise has a regular rhythm. Less obvious are the rhythms of effective prose. Yet good writers are always aware of creating a rhythm to their words. This does not mean a sing-song quality or something you could tap your foot to, but rather, fashioning sentences and paragraphs that flow naturally, carrying the reader along, and, in so doing, enhancing the reader's appreciation of the writer's meaning and message.

The most effective way to develop a rhythmical prose sense is to read plenty of good literature and begin to take note of how writers use repetition of words and sounds and how they manage varying sentence length to establish rhythms that aid effective communication. Once you become conscious of rhythm, you will begin to employ it in your own writing. Specific examples of adding rhythm to speech and writing are discussed in the section "Got Rhythm?" toward the end of this chapter.

SPICE O' LIFE

Generally speaking, the best style for persuasive discourse is a style adequate to your subject and appropriate to your audience, a style sufficiently flexible and complex to convey persuasively what you need to convey, but a style that does not obscure meaning with unnecessary ornament. Just as the clothes you wear should focus attention on you—rather than on themselves—the words and sentences you employ should focus attention on your meaning rather than on themselves. Style should be more or less transparent. Your ideas, more than your expression of them, are what you should put on display.

This said, it is important to introduce a generous amount of variety of language as well as sentence structure and length. If you repeat the same dull language, you will surely lose your readers or your listeners. If you string together nothing but simple sentences, you will end up creating a laundry list rather than an effective argument. On the other hand, if you work with nothing but long, complex sentences, you will induce fatigue in your readers or listeners. A good strategy is to set up major points with longer sentences, then drive home those points with something shorter.

SPEAKING FIGURATIVELY

Six-year-old Johnnie wants to be taken to the park as soon as his parent drags home from the office. "I'm sorry, Johnnie. I need to rest. Today was a real bear," says his parent. "What? How? A bear?" the boy asks. "Oh, it's just a figure of speech."

And that, really, is the way many of us think when it comes to the similes, metaphors, and images that enter into even our everyday speech. We tend to dismiss these figures of speech as decorations or embellishments, add-ons that are not strictly necessary to get our point across. Actually, this is not such a bad way to treat figures of speech. If they are used indiscriminately, they can detract from style and obscure meaning. Ornamental speech for its own sake is of little practical value.

But consider that the classical rhetoricians—the writers, speakers, and philosophers who thought so hard about the art and science of persuasion—did not regard figures of speech as merely the icing on the cake. Aristotle wrote that metaphor gave "charm and distinction" to expression; even more important, he believed that metaphor gave "clearness" and "liveliness" to what we had to say. The Greek rhetorician, philosopher, and critic Longinus wrote that "imagery" could "infuse vehemence and passion into spoken words." Combined with argument, Longinus wrote, images are so persuasive that they virtually enslave a hearer or reader. This may be a stretch, but another rhetorician, the Roman Quintilian, did believe that figures of speech lend "credibility to our arguments" by "exciting the emotions."

Appropriately used, figures of speech are powerful aids to persuasion because they enhance the directness of language. "One picture is worth a thousand words," the old saying goes. But we cannot always communicate through pictures. When you are describing how to change the battery in a cell phone, for example, you are best off avoiding vague abstraction and using the most concrete words you can find: "Take the phone in your left hand and, with your right, press and hold the button on the back of the phone. Then, while pressing this button, slide the cover back toward you until you hear a click. . . ."

But not every subject is concrete. Many things we talk or write about concern abstractions—ideas, concepts, values, principles, and so on. The further away we are from pictures and concrete reality, the more difficult it is to convey meaning powerfully and persuasively. The function of figures of speech is to return the abstract to the realm of the visual (or to some other physical sense) and to the realm of the concrete. A good figure of speech helps us not merely to understand a thought, but to see, hear, and feel it. Human beings respond more powerfully to immediate reality than to language removed from reality. Figures of speech can go a long way to reuniting language with reality, thereby making language more appealing and persuasive.

Don't be afraid to use figures of speech, but use them only when you are certain that they help you to convey your meaning. For now, consider this example:

> You want to convey the speed and accuracy with which a defense attorney attacked a point made by the prosecutor. You could simply say: "The defense attorney attacked the prosecution's point with speed and accuracy." Nothing wrong here, except that it is dull and therefore does not describe the defense attorney in persuasive terms. So you use a figure of speech: "The defense attorney shot through the prosecutor's point like an arrow." This figure of speech creates a physical image in the reader's or hearer's mind. We *see* the swift and accurate arrow, and maybe we even hear the twang of the bowstring, followed by the sharp thwack of impact. The result? We *feel* the sense of what the writer or speaker says.

Some cautions are in order, however. The best figures of speech are generally the simplest and the freshest. Overly complicated figures of speech stumble all over themselves and get in the way of meaning, while stale figures of speech—that is, clichés—are just plain tired and tiring.

Compare the vivid statement that "the defense attorney shot through the prosecutor's point like an arrow" with this cliché: "The defense attorney had a mind like a steel trap." In and of itself, this figure of speech is a good one, but we've heard it so often that it has lost its power. For this reason alone, it is best to avoid clichés. Perhaps even worse, the use of clichés suggests that you lack originality and that you are therefore obliged to get your thoughts secondhand.

Another pitfall to avoid is the figure of speech that works against itself—the so-called mixed metaphor. Remember, a figure of speech is essentially a substitute for a picture or for concrete reality. If it does not present a clear picture, the figure of speech merely adds to the confusion instead of creating greater clarity.

"The defense attorney shot through the prosecutor's point with a mind like a steel trap." The effect of this figure of speech, this mixed metaphor, is to create nonsense. Be certain that the figures of speech you use make sense rather than nonsense, creating meaning rather than unintended comedy.

A TOOL KIT OF STYLE

Trope is the classical term for the figurative use of a word. The classical rhetoricians recognized and classified a variety of tropes, the most important of which are those that speakers and writers find most useful today.

Hyperbole

The word *hyperbole* is sometimes used to criticize a speaker or writer who exaggerates: "You have a *million* things to do? You are guilty of hyperbole, my friend." But hyperbole is also a legitimate trope, useful when you want to make a very emphatic point:

"His ignorance is a bottomless pit."

"I would sell my firstborn to get an opportunity like that."

"I'd vote for a baloney sandwich before I'd vote for that candidate."

"I'd walk a million miles for one of your smiles."

Hyperbole can be a great deal of fun to invent, but it is not without pitfalls:

• Hyperbole is strewn with clichés: "You look like a million bucks." "This thing weighs a ton!" "I'm so hungry, I could eat a horse." "He's as strong as an ox."

- Truly witty hyperbole requires an exercise of imagination. It is easy to end up just sounding silly or childish: "You have more troubles than a bird has feathers."

- In some contexts, hyperbole may trivialize a serious matter: "He had more wounds than a Swiss cheese has holes. That is why they gave him the Medal of Honor."

- The figurative use of hyperbole may be mistaken for mere exaggeration. For example, "I'm exhausted. I feel as if I've just finished running a marathon" is so unimaginative that it might be misinterpreted as an attempt at a realistic description of your fatigue, which may lead to accusations such as "Oh, please! You're just trying to get sympathy."

Understatement

The opposite of hyperbole, understatement deliberately minimizes a description or a proposition for rhetorical effect.

> "My house had just burned down, my wife left me, my business partner was wanted for embezzlement, and I had a telephone message saying that my doctor wanted to 'talk to me.' The message was marked *urgent*. You can say I was a bit upset."

Like hyperbole, understatement is exaggeration—except that it moves in the opposite direction. As with hyperbole, understatement requires judicious application. It is less subject to cliché than hyperbole and rarely sounds childish, but used inappropriately, an understatement may trivialize important matters, and it may be mistaken for a genuine absence of feeling or emotion.

Irony

As a trope, irony may used in two ways. The first way is to make a statement that implies a meaning opposite to the literal meaning. The second is to speak or write in derision or mockery. Examples of the first sense of irony include:

> "That was haute cuisine, indeed," he said, after choking down a stale peanut butter and jelly sandwich.

> Benedict Arnold was very loyal—most of all to himself.

> Who *doesn't* enjoy eight straight hours of French opera?

Examples of the second sense, using mocking irony, include:

> Martha may not have been very pretty, but she had a personality to match.

> Lady Astor, the first woman MP in the British House of Commons, said to Winston Churchill, "Sir, you're drunk!" Churchill replied, "Yes, madam, I am drunk. But in the morning I will be sober and you will still be ugly."

Asked to comment on *4:33*, a composition by avant-garde music composer John Cage, which consists of exactly four minutes and thirty-three seconds of silence, Igor Stravinsky replied: "I look forward to a work of major length from this composer."

Both forms of irony can be used to add a dash of wit to an argument, but the operative words are *dash* and *wit*. It is all too easy to fall into the trap of overusing irony and applying it with a heavy hand. The result is leaden and tends to undermine your authority, thereby making your argument less persuasive. Avoid irony unless it is both genuinely amusing and genuinely helpful to your argument.

Another danger of either type of irony is that it may make you look sarcastic, frivolous, lightweight, or even mean-spirited, thereby blackening your character. This can sabotage any ethical appeal you may be inclined to make.

The first type of irony has an additional danger. The ironic statement might sail over the head of your audience, who may take your statement at face value so that your ironic criticism of the president—"Oh, he's a great one, all right"—might be interpreted as sincere praise. Be certain that your irony will be correctly understood as ironic.

Personification

Classical rhetoricians called personification *prosopopoeia*. It is the attribution of human qualities or faculties to inanimate objects or even abstractions. Personification is present in many common words, phrases, and sayings: *fatherland, Mother Nature, mother tongue, necessity is the mother of invention, time heals all wounds, a friendly-looking street, an angry storm*, and so on.

Personification is useful for stirring the emotions, as long as you avoid the implication that inanimate objects and abstractions really do have human characteristics. At the very least, this kind of trope can sound hackneyed or even childish. At the worst, it can lead to dangerous and unwarranted assumptions.

"Luck is a lady I know just how to handle," said the habitual gambler as he unfolded his last hundred-dollar bill.

Substitution

Sometimes we substitute a descriptive word or phrase for a proper name, or we substitute a proper name for a quality or attribute associated with that name. For instance:

"The Great Navigator first glimpsed the New World on October 12, 1492." ("Great Navigator" equals Columbus.)

"Art Tatum was one of the most innovative pianists in jazz. This Columbus of the keyboard took the music to places it had never been before." ("Columbus of the keyboard" is Art Tatum.)

Classical rhetoricians called this kind of substitution *periphrasis*. It can be very helpful and may even stimulate thought. Take time to choose an appropriate and illuminating substitution so that you avoid absurdities like this one: "The Mercedes is the Cadillac of automobiles."

Metaphor and Simile

Metaphors and similes are basic tools of verbal communication, and used thoughtfully but sparingly, they are powerfully persuasive.

A metaphor is an *implied* comparison between two unlike things that nevertheless have something in common. A simile is an *explicit* comparison between two unlike things that nevertheless have something in common. Another way to think of these two tropes is that a metaphor describes one thing in terms of something else, whereas a simile says one thing is *like* another. If you declare "My love is a red, red rose," you are using metaphor. If you say instead, "My love is like a red, red rose," you are employing simile. Because a metaphor in effect swaps the identity of two things, it is rhetorically more forceful than the simile, which merely likens one thing with another. Simile, however, is especially useful if you want to qualify the comparison you make. For example:

> Joe is courageous but also clever. Instead of saying, "Joe is a lion and a fox," you might want to be more subtle: "In some ways, Joe is like a lion, but he is also like a fox."

Use metaphor and simile sparingly. If you transform everything into something else or compare everything to something else, not only will your meaning become obscure, you will begin to sound silly, as if you are parodying yourself. Also, as noted previously in introducing figures of speech, avoid mixed metaphors.

> "Don't despair! There is always light at the end of the rainbow!"

Be aware that metaphor and simile call for freshness of imagination. It is very easy to fall back on comfortably dull clichés:

> "He was hard as nails."

Before we leave metaphor and simile, we should take note of a special case of extended metaphor—the allegory. An allegory is a narrative, a story, in which one reality implies (or "stands for") another. Entire books have been written as allegory, perhaps the most famous being John Bunyan's *Pilgrim's Progress*, published in 1678. When the purpose of allegory is to teach a moral lesson, it is called *parable*. Parables are familiar from childhood fables:

> "Remember the story of the grasshopper and the ant? The grasshopper worked hard during the pleasant days of summer, gathering and storing food

for the long winter. In contrast, the ant played all summer. Come winter, of course, the grasshopper had plenty and the ant suffered mightily. The moral? Don't be deceived by the comfortable present. Plan for the hard future."

Wholes and Parts

Two figures of speech may be thought of as specialized metaphors. They are the *synecdoche* and the *metonymy*. Both deal with the relationship between wholes and parts.

In the synecdoche, the part stands for the whole:

> Probably the most familiar example is from the Lord's Prayer. When we ask, "Give us this day our daily bread," we intend the word *bread* to stand for all form of physical sustenance—including, but not limited to, bread.

> When sending the infantry to attack, the military commander talks about "putting boots on the ground," the word *boots* functioning as a metaphor for soldiers or ground forces of all kinds.

Closely associated with synecdoche is metonymy, the substitution of an attributive or suggestive word for what is actually meant. If synecdoche substitutes the part for whole, metonymy substitutes for the thing actually meant something closely associated with it.

> The most familiar instance of metonymy is the use of *crown* to mean royalty or a royal government. Apprehending a suspect, the king's policeman might declare, "I arrest you in the name of the crown," meaning "in the name of the king" or "by authority of the royal government."

> In the United States, we often say something like "Washington responded with mixed signals," meaning that the United States government responded ambiguously. The metonymy here is Washington, D.C., the nation's capital and center of the U.S. government.

Synecdoche and metonymy are so similar that taking the trouble to distinguish between them is mostly of academic interest rather than practical value. Certainly, they both serve the same poetic purpose and can add a rhetorical punch to an argument. Anything that makes your reader or listener sit up and take notice aids in the reception of your message and, therefore, in carrying your argument persuasively.

Oxymoron and Paradox

Ask a soldier for an oxymoron and, quick as a salute, he will respond, "Military intelligence." An oxymoron joins together two terms that are ordinarily contradictory:

"Parting is such sweet sorrow."

Or:

"Alfred Hitchcock creates the painful pleasure of suspense."

The great power of the oxymoron is that, in combining contradictions, the effect can be arresting and startling, forcing a reader or listener to stop, think, and consider.

Paradox is closely related to oxymoron, but whereas the punch of an oxymoron derives entirely from the meaning of the two contradictory terms yoked together, the force of the paradox derives from the entire statement. A paradox is more complex than an oxymoron.

The French saying, *Plus ça change, plus c'est la même chose* ("The more things change, the more they remain the same"), is a paradox, whereas the phrase *changeless change* is an oxymoron.

Like the oxymoron, the paradox is a puzzle and, as such, can be a highly effective way to engage the interest of your audience.

Rhetorical Questions

The rhetorical question is a question asked not to elicit an answer but to make a statement, albeit obliquely rather than directly.

Any good salesman knows the value of a rhetorical question. It engages the prospect by putting him in the position of reaching (apparently for himself) the conclusion that the salesman wants him to reach. "A car that goes from 0 to 60 mph in under six seconds and gets thirty miles to the gallon. Is that a good value?" There is only one possible answer, because the question is really a statement: "This is a good value." However, by framing it as a rhetorical question, the salesman puts the answer—the statement—in the mind of the prospect. And we all know that the very best ideas are those that come from ourselves.

The rhetorical question can be useful in shaping the response you want to elicit from your readers or listeners. It makes your argument interactive by requiring the audience to respond—yet it leaves room only for the response you desire.

Puns and Other Wordplay

Puns are fun, but they do not enjoy a lofty reputation among rhetoricians. They rely on the multiple meaning that many English words have:

"If we don't hang together," Benjamin Franklin told his fellow revolutionary conspirators, "then surely we will hang separately."

A really clever pun can underscore an important point in an argument, but the operative word here is *clever*. A pun that falls flat makes your argument look feeble.

Other types of wordplay from classical rhetoric that are worth knowing about include:

- *Paronomasia*, which is the use of words with similar sound that have different meaning. "A friend *in deed* is a friend *indeed*."
- *Syllepsis*, the use of a word understood differently in relation to two or more other words, which it modifies. "Sometimes I *take* heed of your wise advice, and sometimes I just *take* two aspirin."
- *Anthimeria*, which is substituting one part of speech for another. This is more common than its unfamiliar technical name would suggest. For example, "Book a reservation" transforms the noun *book* into a verb. "Un*hand* me!" is shorthand (yes, this is a pun) for "Take your *hands* off me!"

HERE'S THE SCHEME

Up to this point, we have been dealing with figures of speech centered on the meaning of individual words. These are tropes. The other important category of figurative speech is the *scheme*, which puts the emphasis on patterns of word usage within sentences or paragraphs. Schemes are effective building blocks for persuasive arguments.

Joining Opposites

Juxtaposing contrasting ideas in a sentence or paragraph is called *antithesis*. This scheme is effective when the antithetical elements are in balance:

"General Patton was profane yet religious; steeped in military tradition, yet an advocate of the most modern technology; fierce yet compassionate when it came to the welfare of his men."

Antithesis projects a balanced outlook and gives the impression of judgment, objectivity, and justness in presenting an argument. Done well, the balanced sentences produced by antithesis create the effect of an aphorism (a terse statement of truth—an adage) and invites people to quote your words.

Apposition and Parallelism

Apposition places side by side two elements, the second of which explains or modifies the first:

"John Doe, the chief executive officer, was on vacation at the time." The clause set off by the commas is an appositive, which explains who John Doe is.

Broader than apposition is *parallelism,* in which there is a marked similarity in a pair or series of words, phrases, or clauses, all of which are related. The simplest kind of parallelism attaches a series of attributes to a concept:

"Einstein's equation was brilliant, precise, profound, and revelatory."

Now, contrast this version of the sentence, which does not exhibit parallelism, so the elements do not exhibit a similarity of structure:

"Einstein's equation was brilliant, showed great precision, exhibited profundity, and came as a revelation."

More complex parallelism uses entire clauses or phrases with similarity of structure:

"I, Abraham Lincoln, do solemnly swear that I will faithfully execute the office of President of the United States, and will, to the best of my ability, preserve, protect, and defend the Constitution of the United States."

Or:

"I will not pay my taxes, pay your taxes, or pay anyone's taxes."

Parallelism is the mark of careful thought and, done well, speaks volumes for the author's ability to reason well and express herself with maturity. In this way, parallelism is an aid to the ethical appeal, suggesting that the writer or speaker is worth devoting time and attention to.

Parenthesis

In contrast to apposition and parallelism, *parenthesis* forcefully inserts an element into a position that interrupts the expected syntax of the sentence.

"When I first proposed the new sales program—and I did so against vigorous objection—we were at the end of a fifth year of declining sales."

The parenthesis gives to written discourse the feeling of spoken speech, enlivening it and making it more immediate. It also deliberately sets the thought behind the sentence on a tangent, which can be very useful for putting the reader's or listener's thoughts in a desired frame; however, if the parenthesis merely distracts attention or misdirects your audience, it should be avoided.

The parenthesis is an effective means of editorializing, of nudging your audience in the direction you want it to go.

"Today, sales are up—the doubting majority should take note—by 10 percent."

Expressive Economy

Two schemes introduce elements of economy into expression. The *ellipsis* is the purposeful omission of a word or words that are readily implied by the context of the sentence. For example:

"In war, George Washington was fearless and decisive; in peace, decisive and judicious."

Omitted here, after "in peace," is repetition of the phrase "Washington was," which would have been ponderous to include. Of course, we could have inserted "he was" to avoid repeating "Washington," but even this would have sounded, well, clunky.

In rhetoric, ellipsis moves your sentences along, saving your reader or your listeners time and effort. Ellipsis also adds elegance to your expression, making it appear lean and trim instead of bloated and overweight.

Another, even more striking form of economy is the *asyndeton*. The most spectacular instance of this scheme was written by Julius Caesar:

Veni, vidi, vici. "I came, I saw, I conquered."

The asyndeton purposefully omits conjunctions between a series of related clauses. Who can deny that "I came, I saw, I conquered" is a far more powerful statement than "I came, and I saw, then I conquered"? Asyndeton imparts energy to the statement of a series of events, making their progression seem inevitable—which, in some contexts, means that the sentence will be more compelling, more persuasive. Consider these two proposals for increasing sales. Which is more persuasive?

"Spend 15 percent more on advertising, spend 5 percent less on distribution, hire three more sales reps, increase quarterly sales by 25 percent."

"If we spend 15 percent more on advertising, cut distribution costs by 5 percent, and hire three more sales reps, we will increase quarterly sales by 25 percent."

There is nothing wrong with the second sentence, but the first, employing asyndeton, has the inevitability of a mathematical equation. It rolls along, seeming unstoppable.

Got Rhythm?

All good writing has a certain rhythmic sense, whereas poor writing jerks and halts and is therefore difficult to read or listen to. There are some devices that can be used to add a special element of rhythm for the purpose of emphasizing a portion of your speech or writing.

Alliteration is the repetition of consonants in two or more adjacent words:

> In *The Raven*, Edgar Allan Poe wrote of "the silken, sad, uncertain rustling of each purple curtain," showering the reader with a cascade of *s* sounds that imitate the sound of the curtain's rustling.

> President Richard Nixon's vice president, Spiro T. Agnew, memorably lambasted critics of the embattled administration as the "nattering nabobs of negativism."

Overused, alliteration is both unintentionally comic and fatiguing. Used in strategic bursts, however, it has the effect of underscoring an important point and making it all the more memorable.

What alliteration does with consonant sounds, *assonance* does with vowels.

> The British poet Percy Shelley called George III "an old, mad, blind, despised, and dying king," using assonance in the repetition of the long *i* sounds in *blind, despised,* and *dying.*

Assonance is harder to pull off than alliteration, but it serves much the same purpose in persuasive prose, which is to underscore the passage.

Alliteration and assonance involve repetition of sounds. The repetition of entire words or groups of words can also be a highly effective means of emphasizing key points of an argument. Mere repetition is usually a symptom of bad writing, but deliberately patterned repetition requires skill and can produce worthwhile results.

The simplest form of repetition was called *anaphora* by the classical rhetoricians. It simple repeats the same word or phrase at the beginning of successive clauses or sentences:

> "Jane Doe is the most experienced candidate. Jane Doe is the most trustworthy candidate. Jane Doe is the most intelligent candidate."

This type of repetition gets old fast, but it can be an instrument of the greatest eloquence:

> Winston Churchill stirred his countrymen to defend the British Isles against Nazi aggression with: "We shall fight on the beaches, we shall fight on the landing grounds, we shall fight in the fields and in the streets, we shall fight in the hills."

Whereas anaphora repeats words at the beginning of successive sentences or clauses, *epistrophe* repeats them at the ends of successive sentences or clauses:

"I am good, you are good, we are all good."

In rhetoric, epistrophe has one advantage over anaphora. The last word in a sentence or clause always enjoys a position of special prominence. By repeating it, epistrophe adds to the special emphasis the word or phrase already has.

Although the indefatigable Greek rhetoricians classified several additional schemes of repetition, only two are generally useful in persuasive writing or speaking.

Anadiplosis sounds like a dread disease, but is, more benignly, the repetition of the last word of one clause at the beginning of the next. The effect is to produce a kind of chain of events:

"The fire made smoke, the smoke produced soot, the soot contaminated the alarm sensors, and the alarm sensors failed."

Obviously, this scheme is useful when you need to illustrate a chain of causation or to narrate a series of events. The impression of clarity that anadiplosis produces can be highly persuasive in an argument. Anadiplosis can also be used for the purposes of special definition:

"In our company, maximum effort is routine, routine effort is underperformance, and underperformance is never acceptable."

Finally, there is *antimetabole*, a special form of repetition that, while relatively rare, can give forceful impact to a statement. This scheme consists of repeating words, in successive clauses, but in reverse grammatical order. For example:

"You can take the boy out of the country, but you can't take the country out of the boy."

"We do not run because we are afraid, we are afraid because we run," said the American psychologist William James.

"Ask not what your country can do for you; ask what you can do for your country," President Kennedy declared in his inaugural speech.

Not with a Whimper

In Chapter 3, we mentioned a rule of thumb for arranging the order of elements in an argument from least important to most important. This may seem counterintuitive, since the natural inclination for most people is to list items "in order of their importance," which means in order of *decreasing* importance; however, as any dramatist knows, it is always best to end with a bang and not a whimper. Just as you should arrange an argument so that it ends with your strongest point or most important issue, it is an effective strategy to arrange the words, phrases, or clauses within a given sentence in order of *increasing* importance. The Greek word for this survives in our own language: *climax*.

Here is an example:

> "This decision will affect employees in this department, in this division, throughout the company, and even across the entire industry."

Notice what happens if you alter the arrangement:

> "This decision will affect employees throughout the company, across the entire industry, and in this department and division."

The sentence still makes sense, but the effect is of random order rather than order that is the product of careful thought.

In the example given, the most desirable order is obvious from the nature of the material. It is natural to move from the smallest unit to the largest. Sometimes, however, the best order is not obvious, and, in fact, the decision you make concerning order is what tells your reader or listener which element is most important. Compare these two versions:

> "This decision will affect employees throughout the company, will affect the public's perception of our company, and will have great impact on each of our families."

> "This decision will affect employees throughout the company, will have great impact on each of our families, and will affect the public's perception of our company."

Climax may also be manipulated for special effect:

> "If you do not tell the truth in this matter, you will be in violation of the law, you will have committed a sin, and you will have disappointed me."

Here, the speaker wants to put extreme emphasis on his relationship with the person to whom he is speaking. The emphasis is achieved through the order of the elements of the sentence so that the most personal element is listed last and therefore indicated as the most important.

Go Beyond Words

*Classical (and modern) secrets of body
language and the nonverbal aspects of
verbal communication.*

The classical rhetoricians divided the art of rhetoric into five parts: *Inventio* (invention or discovery) concerns itself with finding arguments; *dispositio* (disposition or arrangement) is about organizing the argument effectively; the third part is *elocutio* (style); the fourth is *memoria* (concerned with memorizing speeches); and the fifth and final division is *pronuntiatio:* delivery.

The most famous of the early Greek orators, Demosthenes—the man famous for practicing speeches while holding pebbles in his mouth, to improve his pronunciation—was once asked, *What is the most important part of rhetoric?* His reply: "Delivery, delivery, delivery."

A PSYCHOLOGIST LOOKS AT COMMUNICATION

The Greeks and Romans thought that words and voice were very important, but they put even greater emphasis on the use of gestures (*actio*). Indeed, the classical orators probably more closely resembled actors than speechmakers.

In 1970, Julius Fast published a runaway bestseller called *Body Language.* Suddenly, the reading public discovered what Demosthenes and other orators had known long ago: Much of your message is nonverbal, a matter of gestures and glances. Just how much? A year later, in 1971, psychologist Albert Mehrabian published a study in which he concluded that listeners evaluate the "emotional content"—the persuasive power—of a speech primarily on the basis of facial expressions and body movement. Visual cues accounted for 55 percent of the weight listeners put into the evaluative balance, vocal qualities such as tone and pitch of voice made up 38 percent, and the verbal content—the actual words—counted only 7 percent.

If you find this hard to believe, think of the last time you bought a car or some other big-ticket item. How much of your decision was based on the salesman's presentation? Was he "shifty-eyed" or straightforward? Was he confident in expression and tone, or evasive? Or look back into history. The famous televised debates between John F. Kennedy and Richard M. Nixon during the 1960 presidential campaign produced no clear winner. A majority of people who listened to the debates on the radio thought Nixon was the more effective of the two. However, most people who watched the debates on television judged Kennedy to have come out on top. The reason? Nixon *looked* nervous. His body language was shifty and evasive, and (to his misfortune) he sweated visibly and profusely. JFK, in contrast, was cool, collected, yet intense. He made a visual connection with his audience. Of course, whether broadcast on the radio or TV, the words were identical.

CONSIDER THE AUDIENCE

We will discuss some general delivery and body language rules in a moment, but among your very first considerations concerning the visual presentation of yourself should be your audience.

There is no mystery about scoping out your audience. You do it every day. To your boss you speak one way, to Joe Client another, and to Jane Client, another way still. You say different things and present yourself differently to different people. Naturally, knowledge of your audience *should* influence your choice of topic (vacuum cleaner manufacturers don't want to hear about parking regulation reform) and your choice of language: In discussing a given subject, you use one set of vocabulary with an audience of specialists and another with the uninitiated. Your audience should also influence how you present yourself visually.

Dress

Different audiences and occasions call for different wardrobe choices. A speaking engagement at a formal banquet may require a tuxedo or a formal gown, and an address to investment bankers calls for a conservative suit, whereas a talk to the sales force at a corporate retreat is best delivered in neat casual clothes.

Your clothing should not speak louder than you do. The goal is to get people to devote their attention to you, not to your attire. This means you should gauge the level of your audience and dress just a notch above that. Of course, whatever you decide to wear should be in impeccable repair and neatly dry-cleaned or laundered.

Two practical notes: Avoid tight-fitting or uncomfortable clothing. Public speaking creates enough nervous tension without your adding an unnecessary additional degree of physical discomfort. Avoid large, dangling jewelry, which tends to make very irritating noises through most public address systems. You want your audience hanging on your words, not cringing at the sound of tinkling metal.

Grooming

As with clothing, your personal grooming should be impeccable and suited to your audience. The close-cropped, clean-shaven look may go over well with the investment bankers, who will see in you one of themselves, whereas a mullet and beard are likely to set up a formidable nonverbal obstacle to persuasion for that group. Conversely, a spiky coif and flamboyant makeup may be right on pitch for a young woman speaking to a conference of hip home furnishings buyers, but it will not be well received by the investment bankers.

Are such considerations shallow? Absolutely. Do such considerations affect persuasion? Profoundly.

Persona

"I gotta be me!" Sammy Davis Jr. proclaimed in his signature song. For the persuasive speaker, the proper response to this sentiment is "Not necessarily."

Remember, the classical orators were more like actors than speechmakers. They were not hesitant about playing a role suited to the audience before whom they appeared. As Supreme Allied Commander, Europe, during World War II, as a candidate for president of the United States in the 1950s, and as president, Ike Eisenhower was celebrated for his trademark smile, which radiated a combination of warmth and confidence. Those who knew him in more private settings, however, remember him as a rather sour man with a hair-trigger temper. Does this mean he was a phony? No. Does it mean he was putting on an act? Yes—but for the good of the war effort and (he must have believed) the nation. Eisenhower created a smiling persona he knew his audience would find more palatable and persuasive than a dour and angry old man.

Gauge your audience and style your demeanor accordingly. Talking to the sales force? Better rev up the energy, and don't be afraid of making big, even somewhat exaggerated gestures. Speaking to a group of fellow economists? Nothing wrong with a smile, but don't given them your impression of a circus ringmaster.

Lying is, at the very least, unethical. Telling the truth in ways that appeal to your audience, even if doing so requires some conscious acting on your part, is not only ethical, it is of positive value to both you and your listeners. What you have to say is beneficial and important.

ENTRANCE AND EXIT

"She sure makes a great entrance!"

It's a common observation about people who come on as anything but common. Your mother always told you how important first impressions are. Well, the entrance you make is the ultimate first impression. It shapes how the audience sees you, and how the audience sees you lingers well into your speech, contributing to or subtracting from the persuasive force of your message. Entering a room or walking onstage makes a powerful statement about who you are and who you think you are.

No matter how tall or short you are, walk tall. It is a fact that tall people tend to command greater authority than short people. Unfair? Yes. But it's the way things are. This doesn't mean that it is impossible for short folks to be persuasive, but it is undeniable that height makes a positive impact, especially as a first impression. This applies to men as well as women.

If you're shy a few inches, what should you do? Wear elevator shoes? Short men might think of thicker soles and heels, and short women may want to wear a higher heel, but if you go overboard here, you are only going to draw attention to your absence of stature. A far more effective way of adding height is to walk tall. Stride. Do not cringe, stoop, or slouch. Whether you are five-four or six-four, focus on maintaining an erect posture as you approach the podium. Move without hesitation. This is your first message to the audience. It says: *I know how to carry myself.*

GIVE GOOD VOICE

The musical qualities of your voice are its pitch and tone. They go together. One piece of advice is almost universally applicable: Lower the pitch of your voice.

• Most people perceive a lower-pitched voice as more authoritative than a higher-pitched voice. This holds true whether a man or a woman is the speaker.

• Anxiety tends to raise the pitch of your voice. If you reveal your anxiety to your audience, you will undercut the persuasive impact of your message. Moreover, consciously lowering pitch will not only disguise your nervousness, it may actually help relieve your nervousness. You'll no longer sound scared—*to yourself.*

• Pitching your voice lower gives it a more pleasing tone. It is easier on the ear. Lowering pitch also slows you down and encourages the more precise articulation of each word. You won't speed, and you won't mumble.

Here are two more tweaks you can make to pitch and tone:

• Avoid ending declarative sentences on a rising note. This verbal tic is more common in women than men, but, in either case, audiences find it annoying and distracting. Worse, the rising inflection makes each statement sound like a question—tentative, even doubtful. It is as if the speaker is unconvinced and is looking to the audience for assurance. Your job is to persuade. That requires sounding as if you yourself are already persuaded.

• A nasal voice makes audiences uncomfortable. They tend to think you are unwell and perhaps in discomfort. Lowering the pitch of your voice will help minimize the nasal quality of your voice, but if you have persistent allergies or chronic breathing problems that contribute to this voice quality, you should consider consulting a physician.

INHALE, EXHALE

Effective public speaking begins with effective breathing. This is not always easy. Anxiety produces shortness of breath, and shortness of breath makes it that much more difficult to speak. The difficulty and discomfort of speaking when we are anxious serves to increase anxiety. It is the most vicious of vicious circles.

With practice, the anxiety of public speaking is reduced. There are other little tricks you can try while you are waiting to speak:

- Pull up on the bottom of your chair and silently count to five. Repeat as often as you like.

- Put your hands together at right angles to one another, the thumbs gently interlocking. Now press your palms together as tightly as you can. Repeat as necessary.

- If you can do so out of the view of your audience, close your eyes and deliberately concentrate on relaxing each muscle in your body. Start with your toes and work your way up, moving on to the next set of muscles only after the previous set is relaxed. When you get to your chest, inhale deeply and slowly. Then focus on your back. Relax it. Lay your head back and relax your neck muscles.

- Prepare by visualizing a peaceful natural scene: a waterfall, waves lapping a beach, tall pines waving in a breeze against a blue, blue sky.

- Take the focus off yourself. Think about your audience and how you are about to delight them by offering words of great value and interest.

Much of the anxiety you may feel in speaking before an audience does not come from the event, but from the unpleasant feelings associated with anxiety itself. The faster the heart beats, the tenser the muscles, the more we fear—and the more we fear, the faster the heart beats, the tenser the muscles become, and the more the butterflies beget butterflies.

In addition to the five exercises just mentioned, concentrate on your breathing. Don't let it come fast and shallow. Make it deep and slow. Breathe as if you have never felt better—and you may soon find that you do, in fact, feel better. Moreover, by concentrating on your breathing, you will have more breath to give your voice. You will sound more authoritative and confident. As you hear yourself speak with authority and confidence, you will continue to *feel* increasingly authoritative and confident.

ADJUST VOLUME AND TIMING

Public speech is louder than private speech. That is the nature of the beast. Even if you use a microphone, speak up. Consciously project your voice, but never shout or strain.

How loud is loud enough? When you find yourself enjoying the full, resonant sound of your own voice, you are probably speaking loudly enough.

As you must speak up, so you must slow down. Normal conversation proceeds at about 200 words per minute. Public speech should not exceed 150 words per minute. Of course, you aren't going to be counting your words as you speak. A more practical rule of thumb is to adjust your rate of speech so that it takes you a full two minutes to read a double-spaced page of text set in 12-point type.

Most of us talk too fast to be heard comfortably in a public-speaking setting. Try writing in the upper left-hand corner of each page of your typescript the words Slow Down.

LEARN THE GRAMMAR OF BODY LANGUAGE

Tall people with deep voices have a natural edge over shorter folk with higher voices. Unfair, perhaps, but true. It's also true that people who are body language "naturals"—who instinctively know how to move persuasively—have an advantage over the rest of us. Fortunately, although there is only so much you can do to appear taller and to lower the pitch of your voice, there is a great deal you can do to improve your body language. With a little awareness and a little practice, anyone can develop an effective body-language vocabulary.

Overall, the goal is to project an image of relaxed energy. We are all familiar with the phrase "nervous energy." That is not what you want to convey. Evidence of nervous energy includes rapid-fire speech, a tapping foot, darting eyes, fingers drummed on the tabletop, a knee pumping up and down while you are seated, a foot shuffling while you are seated, and so on. In contrast, the signs of relaxed energy are a bright expression, a smile, erect but not rigid posture, a sitting position that is slightly forward. The object is to create an impression of enthusiasm and confidence—what you could sum up in the single word: *poise*.

Breathing—Again

Relaxed energy begins with something we have already mentioned: breathing. Whereas anxiety tends to produce short, fast breaths, consciously breathing more deeply and more slowly not only masks this symptom of anxiety, it actually reduces the level of anxiety—and it makes you a more persuasively sonorous speaker. Rapid, shallow breathing conveys nervous energy, whereas measured, deep breathing both suggests and promotes relaxed energy.

Of the Eyes

After the simple act of breathing, nothing conveys relaxed energy more powerfully than your eyes. Whether you are speaking to one person or to an audience of hundreds or thousands, make and maintain eye contact. There is a good reason why someone challenging the honesty of a statement says, "Look me in the eye and tell me that." Eye contact is an unfailing token of openness and honesty.

Eye contact does even more. We've all heard people talk about the "sparkle" in someone's eye. It is, to be sure, a kind of cliché, but if you think beyond the cliché, it is really a judgment that a certain person has a special quality, an almost magical energy. Remarkable? Yes. Rare? Not really. In truth, we all have a sparkle in our eyes, but this is rarely seen because so few of us are comfortable making full eye contact when we meet or speak to others. Consciously strive to make and maintain eye contact, and the other person will see that sparkle in *your* eyes.

It is not always easy to maintain eye contact in a public-speaking context, especially if you are reading from a script at a lectern. Thoroughly rehearse even a written speech so that you can look up from the text frequently. Be certain to direct your glance to different sections of the audience. Give everyone a look at your eyes. Avoid the following mannerisms:

- *Narrowing the eyes* communicates hostility, disagreement, resentment, or disapproval. Marked narrowing—squinting—suggests outright puzzlement (or maybe you just need to wear your glasses).
- *Marked avoidance of eye contact* conveys insincerity, fear, evasiveness, or, at the least, lack of interest.
- *Downcast eyes* convey shame.
- A *steady stare* suggests an arrogant need to control the situation. Even worse, this gesture can make you look just plain weird.
- *Raising the eyebrows* indicates surprise or disbelief. This habit may or may not be a negative thing, but it is something to be aware of.
- *Peering over the top of your eyeglasses* suggests strong doubt or disbelief.

Of the Head

What you do with your head contributes in a major way to the impression of relaxed energy. Tilting your head to one side indicates interest, which is especially important when you have finished speaking and are listening to feedback, or when you are in a Q & A session. The head cocked slightly to one side conveys that you are listening very closely and with great interest. While this is a most desirable gesture, be certain that you vary it. No body language gesture is positive if it is maintained statically.

Thrusting your chin out slightly conveys confidence. Just don't go to excess. Thrust your chin out too boldly, and you run the risk of looking like an old newsreel of Benito Mussolini: strutting, pompous, and arrogant.

Nodding up and down conveys agreement. This gesture can be very useful during a Q & A exchange. Contrarily, it comes as no surprise that shaking the head from side to side conveys disagreement. Try to avoid this during Q & A, even if you disagree. Express your differences verbally rather than through body language. Most dangerous of all is the mixed signal. We have all seen someone do something like this:

> Question: "Are you telling the truth?" Answer: "Of course I am," but the person is shaking his head ever so slightly even as he is answering. Beware of saying *yes* as you shake your head *no*.

Be conscious of your body language so that you can avoid such garbled transmissions. They are sure ways to undercut your credibility and your persuasiveness. Some other negative body language habits to avoid:

- *Scratching your head* indicates confusion or disbelief.
- *Rubbing the back of your neck* suggests disbelief or anxiety.
- *Lowering your chin* conveys defensiveness and insecurity.
- *Rubbing the forehead* indicates confusion.
- *Putting your hands anywhere near your mouth or nose* conveys extreme nervousness or evasiveness.

Of the Expression

The single most powerful positive aspect of facial expression is the smile. A smile suggests that you have nothing to hide, that you are confident and open to communication and suggestion. It suggests that you enjoy speaking to your audience. Smile as often as you can, unless, of course, the content of your speech makes a smile inappropriate: "This is a major crisis, ladies and gentlemen." Even if the subject of your discourse does not call for a smiling delivery, avoid giving in to expressions of sadness or despair. Also avoid:

- *Sighing,* which is a strong sign of distress or even hopelessness.
- *Yawning.* If you can't keep yourself awake, how can you hope to interest your audience? To yawn is simply insulting. You cannot recover from it.
- *Lip biting,* which is a powerful signal of great anxiety.
- *Pursing your lips,* which conveys strong resistance to suggestion or great skepticism—a closed mind.

Of the Hands

Many speakers are overly self-conscious about their hands. For a variety of reasons, many people believe that "talking with your hands" is distracting or somehow suggests an absence of class. In fact, hand gestures are powerful nonverbal aids to persuasion. Yes, it is better to avoid exaggerated, big gestures—they are distracting—but don't put your hands in your pockets or otherwise hide them.

Feel free to gesture naturally with your hands to drive home a point. Open hands, palms up, suggest honesty and openness. Rubbing the hands together communicates positive expectation. Putting the fingertips of both hands together steeple-fashion conveys confidence.

Avoid, however, the following movements:

- Overuse of big, theatrical gestures
- Fist pounding or making a fist
- Stabbing the air with your finger
- Crossing your arms in front of your chest, which conveys defiance, defensiveness, resistance, aggressiveness, or a closed mind
- Hand-wringing, which is a strong signal of worry verging on terror

As mentioned in "Of the Head," do not put your hands to your face, mouth, forehead, or the back of your neck. Do not run your fingers through your hair. All of these gestures convey anxiety or evasion.

Of the Stance

In a public-speaking context, walk upright and stand at the podium in an upright but relaxed posture. Do not lean on the podium—although it can be highly effective to lean forward from time to time to make a strong point. Soldiers standing at attention for extended periods quickly learn to appear rigid without actually standing rigidly. The secret is to avoid locking your knees. Instead, flex them slightly. This relaxes you without putting you into a slouch.

HOW TO LISTEN—AND WIN

In most business contexts, the public presentation of an argument is not a simple lecture. It involves a degree of give-and-take, sometimes a great deal of it. The ability to speak persuasively is, of course, central to making an effective argument. In most real-world situations, however, the ability to listen skillfully and effectively is just as important.

The first requirement for effective listening is *to listen*. Remember the superstudent in grade school who simply couldn't resist raising her hand to answer each and every question or to make a comment whenever the teacher paused to take a breath? Don't be that way. No matter how eager you are to respond or to interject, exercise self-control. Hear the other person out fully. Only after the other person's lips stop moving should your reply come.

This does not mean that you should bite your tongue and sit on your hands. Try to look as if you are enjoying the conversation and that you are, in fact, intensely interested in what the other person has to say. Smile. Nod when appropriate. React. Indeed, transform yourself into a mirror. Demonstrate that you are listening—really listening—by mirroring the other person's message.

If the person is excited about something, get excited, too. If she expresses delight, smile in return. If he raises an issue that is clearly of critical importance to him, *show* that the subject is of critical importance to you, too.

Maintaining an attitude of lively restraint as you listen to the other person does not mean keeping silent. Respond to important points in the interviewer's conversation with words and phrases that add fuel to the dialogue.

Words and Phrases to Use

accurate	explain that further	I understand	take into account
additional	extraordinary	it's an issue we face	tell me more
agree	fertile	opportunity	that's a concern of mine, too
consider	I agree	positive	that's interesting
correct	I appreciate that	productive	thought
discuss further	I hadn't thought of it that way	pursue that further	we should discuss
evaluate	I see	right	yes

If some well-chosen words can productively perpetuate the conversation, others may kill it.

Negative Expressions to Avoid

absolutely not	no	that can't be done	that's settled	you're mistaken
couldn't possibly	no way	that's not the way I do it	wrongheaded	you're wrong

Obviously, receptive listening does not require you to agree with everything the other person says, but the listening portion of your presentation is an opportunity to focus your message on the needs of the audience. You now have an opportunity to demonstrate, explicitly, how your ideas and opinions are directly relevant to the needs and concerns of the people you are addressing.

Listen for clues to, or outright statements of, what interests the other person, then pounce on the idea and discuss it in terms of your argument or proposition.

To achieve skillful listening and productive give-and-take, avoid transforming the Q & A into a monologue, but do not restrain yourself so much that you appear to be a passive listener, without any ideas or opinions of your own.

Perpetuating productive give-and-take is both a verbal and nonverbal exercise. Just as you should project a positive body language vocabulary, you would do well to become sensitive to the nonverbal cues of the person or people to whom you are speaking. For instance:

• If the other person tilts his head to one side, you can assume that he is listening intently to what you are saying and is interested. Sales professionals call this gesture a "buy signal," something that suggests that you should continue speaking in the current vein.

• Head scratching indicates confusion or disbelief. Don't be afraid that you are losing this person. Take this signal as your cue to pause and ask a question: "Am I making myself clear enough here?" Or, "I'm not sure I'm making myself clear. Let me put it another way. . . ."

• Lip biting indicates anxiety and may suggest that an issue you have brought up has touched a nerve. Respond by expressing your understanding of the sensitive nature of the hot-button issue: "I realize that this is an area that causes anxiety, but I think it's an important issue to explore."

• If the person to whom you are speaking rubs the back of her head or neck, she may be getting frustrated or impatient. If possible, move on to another topic as gracefully as possible: "But, of course, this isn't as important as XYZ." Another good response is to ask the other person where *she* wants to go: "If you like, we can continue on this subject or move on to ABC."

• If the other person lowers his chin markedly, he may be conveying a degree of defensiveness. Perhaps he has interpreted something you've said as a criticism. If you did not intend to be critical, make a soothing remark: "Of course, I recognize that everyone has his own style in such matters. We need to be flexible and use what works."

• When the other person nods up and down, accept the gesture as a strong buy signal. Keep the conversation going in the current vein.

• If something you say provokes a head shake from side to side, be aware that what you have said is being rejected. Respond to it directly: "I sense that you don't agree with me on this point. What part of my position gives you trouble?"

• If the other person narrows her eyes, it usually means the same thing as a head shake from side to side, so again, respond directly: "I feel that we're not in agreement on this point. Can you tell me what disturbs you about what I've said?"

• A pronounced narrowing of the eyes into a squint suggests puzzlement rather than disagreement. Pause, then offer a remark such as "I'd like to be very clear on this point. Let me put what I've said another way."

• Raised eyebrows indicate surprise or outright disbelief. Respond directly: "I know this is hard to believe, but . . ."

• It is difficult to interpret the meaning when someone avoids eye contact. Perhaps the other person is just shy. The best response is to be friendly or friendlier. The more serious situation is when eye contact noticeably drops off *during* the conversation. This suggests that you are losing the other person's interest. Take quick action: "I can say more about ABC, but perhaps you want to move on to XYZ. Yes?"

• The person who stares intently at you is probably trying to be intimidating. Ignore it as best you can. Do not respond.

Another cue to how you are coming across in a conversation is how the other person is breathing. Look for signs of breathlessness: the shallow, rapid breathing patterns typical of anxiety. Respond with reassurance: "Of course, that's a problem we can solve." Look for the caught breath, a sudden intake of air that indicates the other person's eagerness to say something. Invite a comment at once.

The most alarming signal to watch for is the sigh, which always suggests frustration or a high degree of boredom. Don't panic, but do move on to another topic.

All good things must come to an end. Be sensitive to the verbal and nonverbal signs that the conversation is coming to a close. These include:

- Phrases beginning with "Well, it's been . . ." Or, "I want to thank you . . ."
- The other person rising from her chair
- The person setting his eyes on the door

Of course, it is always possible that the person to whom you are speaking will say something like, "Well, I have to go now." Whatever the signal, do not seek to prolong the conversation. You might close with, "Have I answered all of your question?" just to make certain that you are not leaving anything important unsaid or unasked. But now is the time to assume that you have made the sale, and as any good salesman knows, once you've made the sale, it's time to shut your mouth. The conversation is at an end.

PART II

Make Your Case and Get Your Way

CHAPTER 9

Talk Yourself into the Job You Want

How to apply the tools and tactics of classical rhetoric to create effective cover letters and ace job interviews.

No argument is more important than the one you make to win the job you want. Writing a letter in the language of Aristotle or speaking in an interview in the manner of Cicero won't get you hired, but expressing what *you* have to offer with the persuasive emotion and logic of the best and the brightest rhetoricians puts you in a most powerful position. Present yourself with persuasive clarity and you become what every employer wants—namely, exactly the person he needs.

WORDS TO USE

Words are the elements of any argument. Naturally, your choice of words has a great deal to do with the particulars of the subject at hand—the job you are trying to get, your qualifications, what you perceive as the employer's needs, and so on—but there are some words that are powerfully persuasive in virtually any context, resume, cover letter, or interview. These are words that tend to trigger a positive perception in a target employer. Include as many of the following words as you can in your communications with the prospective employer.

accomplishments	consult	goal	proactive	self-starter
achievements	cooperate	improved	profit	service
advise	coordinate	information	reevaluated	started
alert	created	initiated	responsive	success
awake	earned	leadership	results	successfully
aware	efficiency	motivated	revitalized	team
build	energetic	open	seek	teamwork
committed	evaluation	positive		

WORDS TO AVOID

Just as some words create positive feelings in your prospect and build rapport with him, so others set off alarm bells and tend to wreck rapport. The sound of one of these words is to a prospective employer what a paint scratch is to the owner of a brand-new car: a small imperfection grossly magnified. All of the following words have one thing in common. They are negative rather than positive. Whereas positive words invite a conversation to continue, negative words bring the process to a halt—and, generally, that means you don't get the job. Avoid these words in your communication with prospective employers:

annoying	depressing	hard	slow
bad	difficult	incompetent	tired
boring	frustrating	problem	trouble

AT STAKE

The classic recipe for rabbit stew begins, "First, catch your rabbit." The classical rhetoricians advised would-be orators to begin with "discovery," the identification and selection of your subject. In any argument that really matters, this is the same as asking before you begin, *What's at stake?* When you're looking for a job, the question is quite easy to answer. The job you want is at stake.

Think of it this way: Your every act of communication with the prospective employer is an argument on the subject of why she should give you a job. That is your subject, and everything you write or say should, in some way, focus on that subject.

YOUR GOAL

So far, so obvious. But, in arguing yourself into a job, there is also an angle beyond the obvious. For *you*, the job is at stake. But *for the employer*, the job is also at stake. She needs the position filled and the job done—and not just filled and done, but filled and done well, in a way that will reduce costs, increase sales, create customer satisfaction, generally enhance the bottom line, and ultimately make her—the boss, the person with the power to hire you—look good.

Like you, the potential employer has much at stake. Therefore, when you argue your subject—why she should give you the job—you have a twofold goal: 1) to persuade the target employer to give you the job, and 2) to persuade the target employer that giving you the job is the answer not to *your* need for a job but *her* need for the job to be done superbly.

Your goal is to get the job. You need to create an argument that persuades the prospective employer that her goal is to "get you into the job." The goals are different in terms of perspective, but they are identical in function. Getting you into the job will be a great benefit to you *and* the employer. Your argument, therefore, is that you have an interest in common: the job. Persuade her of that.

Successful salespeople understand that their goal is to persuade the customer that product X offers a valuable benefit, a benefit so worth possessing that the customer will part with something of value to obtain it. Salespeople are motivated by a need to make a living, so selling the product benefits them personally. But that, of course, is not the argument the salesperson makes. He does not say: "Please buy this car from me. I need the commission to pay my mortgage this month" (although if there were a comic-strip thought balloon above the salesperson's head, that's probably what he'd be thinking, but those words remain as they should, unspoken). Instead, the salesperson focuses his sales pitch on the benefit to the customer: "This car looks great, goes fast, and sips gas."

YOUR APPEAL

Classical rhetoricians recognized three basic approaches to persuasion: the appeal to reason, the appeal to emotion, and the ethical appeal. All three are important in arguing yourself into a job.

The Appeal to Reason

Most business people pride themselves on making reasonable decisions. In fact, business people, even very successful ones, are first and foremost people, and while logic is important to them, an appeal based exclusively on logical reasoning is not likely to succeed. In addition to making a logical case for getting the job, you will need to give the prospective employer the right feelings (in an appeal to emotion) and the right feelings about who you are (in an ethical appeal). This said, it is nevertheless supremely important to present your qualifications and experience in a manner that persuasively demonstrates that you are a logical fit for the job in question. If, for example, you are applying for a bookkeeping position, undue emphasis on your background as a nightclub comic is not logical. Emphasize your relevant experience—those aspects of yourself and your history that obviously apply to the job in question. This doesn't necessarily mean that your nightclub experience is irrelevant.

> If you did your own bookkeeping as a nightclub performer, you might be able to make a very persuasive argument about the value of this experience. For instance, let's say that your compensation was based on a "percentage of the house" and is proportional to the size of the audience in the club. This presents a bookkeeping challenge. How did you meet the challenge? What techniques did you use? How did you make certain that you were paid fairly? Do what you must to make as much of your experience and training appear logically relevant to the bookkeeping job for which you are applying.

While it is important *actually* to present yourself and your history logically, it is also critical that you create the *unmistakable impression* of logic throughout your entire presentation. You want the target employer to feel that you are appealing to his intellect and good judgment. You must make it possible for the target employer to believe that he can make the *logical* decision to hire you. He must feel confident that, if asked why he hired you, he won't have to answer, "I don't know. I just went with my gut," even if that is the truth. Instead, you want to enable him to respond: "She was the best-qualified candidate because of A, B, and C."

The two elements indispensable to a logical appeal are clarity and relevance. We will address clarity throughout the rest of this chapter. As for relevance, the important principle to bear in mind is this: You and your skills are portable, not stationary. Present them in ways that are most relevant to the needs of the target employer. This means, as we will see, that you must reject the notion that your resume is fixed, unalterable, and "is what it is." Don't rely on a boilerplate resume; instead, tailor the presentation as the occasion and the prospect require. Presenting the identical resume to prospects with differing needs is illogical. The logical approach is to create relevance.

The Appeal to Emotion

An emotional appeal cannot stand alone in the job-application situation, but it is an indispensable adjunct to both the appeal to reason and the ethical appeal. The idea is to appeal to the prospect's emotions as a way of highlighting and emphasizing key aspects of the logical and ethical appeals.

> You are applying for a position in customer service. The target employer has your resume, which makes clear your prior relevant education and experience. Logically, you are an appealing candidate. Your resume also lists your involvement in some community volunteer activity. This information helps to make you an appealing candidate on ethical grounds. Now, how can the emotional appeal be made to work to enhance these two other modes of appeal?
>
> You can say: "As you can see from my professional experience and the volunteer work I do in the community, I am committed to working with people. For me, that's what business—any business—is all about: people. Customers love to be treated like human beings. They see right through a phony and appreciate someone who is really passionate about helping them. But, then, I don't have to sell you on the benefits of having a people person in customer service."

Why let the logic of your resume speak for itself? Help it along. Highlight it. Color in the outlines of logic with feeling. *Committed, people, love, phony, passionate,* and *helping* are all highly effective emotional words in this context. They are aimed at giving the prospective employer the feeling that, in hiring you, she will be making the right choice.

Especially in the job-application context, there is a significant danger in relying too heavily on the emotional appeal. It should be distinctly subordinated to both the logical and ethical appeals, lest it seem empty. No one likes to feel emotionally manipulated—what old-time business folk called "soft-soaped" or "buttered up." Create this feeling and you will also generate suspicion, a negative emotion that instantly gets between you and the job.

Never begin with the emotional appeal. The foundation of a job application consists of training, experience, and other concrete and quantifiable elements of your personal history. The emotional appeal serves mainly to underscore these elements and to elaborate on them, allowing the target employer to acquire strong positive feelings about them. You are, in essence, building on the facts:

Fact: "I have four years' experience in customer service."

Feeling: "It sure would be great to feel confident in the experience of the customer service department."

Expression (building on fact)*:* "I am a seasoned customer service rep who will bring solid experience to your department. There won't be any learning curve, and you can rely on me from day one."

The Ethical Appeal

As we've seen, an *ad hominem* argument attacks the person who advocates a certain thesis rather than the thesis itself:

"The 'self-evident truths' in the Declaration of Independence must be false because the document's author, Thomas Jefferson, was a slave owner."

In most cases, the ad hominem approach is an evasion of argument rather than a valid argument. However, there are numerous contexts in which the character of the person who makes an argument does bear on the validity of the argument. For example, a speech on judicial reform by a disbarred attorney is not likely to be very persuasive, even if its logic is impeccable.

In no context is character more relevant than when you are arguing yourself into a job. A prospective employer wants logical reasons for hiring you, and she wants to feel good about her decision, too, but she is also quite properly concerned about bringing a person of high ethical character into her professional family. While an argument based on a strong ethical appeal will not compensate for a resume wholly deficient in relevant professional, vocational, or educational experience, any doubts about your character will tend to negate all other aspects of your background. For this reason, the ethical appeal should always be part of the argument you present to target employers.

The most effective ethical appeal is made from a basis of fact. It is not sufficient to declare that you are a good person of solid character. Your employer will want evidence. For that reason, it is always a good idea to include volunteer and charitable activities in your resume and present them as aspects of your life that are genuinely meaningful to you. It is also important to emphasize your commitment to professional ethics—ethics directly relevant to the job for which you applying and the industry at large. Don't be vague or general about this issue:

"Ethics are important to me."

Get as specific as you can:

"I don't believe that our business is about making sales. It's about making customers, and that means giving them good value that is also fair value. I want my customer to feel good about doing business with me and my firm, and I want to feel good about the business *I* do. Ethics are important to me, but they are also just good business. Sound ethics create trust, and that means they create customers—sources of business over the long term."

THE RESUME

Each communication with a prospective employer requires you to invent yourself and deliver yourself. This book is not about writing a resume. You can find plenty of model resumes and how-tos at your local bookstore. Major online resume sites, such as Monster.com, also have ready-made resume templates, complete with interactive tutorials. The point I want to make here is to think of *everything* you write or say to a prospective employer as an argument supporting the thesis that you are exactly the right person for the job that employer needs to fill. This means rejecting the idea of the resume as some sort of "objective" summary of given facts about yourself. The resume is an argument.

Invent Yourself

Before you sit down to write your resume, think about the job for which you are applying. It is always a good idea to keep a general "boilerplate" resume handy and up-to-date so that you can respond quickly to opportunities as they arise; however, do not make the mistake of assuming that you must send out this boilerplate version, unaltered, to each and every prospect. Edit and shape your resume to fit the needs of each employer you contact. Without falsifying any information, use your resume to invent and reinvent yourself to suit your prospect.

Consider this resume item:

Diadem Company, Eastwood, NY
Manufacturing Engineer, 2000–2004

I was responsible for all projects pertaining to assigned customers, including Westinghouse, General Electric, General Dynamics, and Biomed Industries. The scope of work ranged from the production of gas and turbine components to the fabrication of specialized items for biomedical applications.

This is a good, straightforward presentation of an important item of experience. Assume the applicant is addressing a biomedical manufacturer. Here is an appropriate reinvention:

Diadem Company, Eastwood, NY
Manufacturing Engineer, 2000–2004

I was responsible for all projects pertaining to assigned customers, including such leading designers of biomedical products as Biomed Industries.

There is no fiction here, just a reinvention based on the facts and aimed at a particular employer, a biomedical firm.

Consider this reinvention, aimed at an employer who is looking for a "Project Manager" with engineering experience:

Diadem Company, Eastwood, NY
Manufacturing Engineer, 2000–2004

As manufacturing engineer, I was a project manager responsible for all projects pertaining to assigned customers, including Westinghouse, General Electric, General Dynamics, and Biomed Industries. The scope of the projects I managed ranged from the production of gas and turbine components to the fabrication of specialized items for biomedical applications.

Use the words the prospective employer uses. Your job title might have been "manufacturing engineer," but that does not require you to chain yourself to that language. Within the bounds of truth, emphasize the aspects of your experience that dovetail with the requirements of the job. Here, the applicant reinvents himself as a project manager simply by emphasizing the project-management dimension of his engineering experience.

Deliver Yourself

Having invented yourself for a resume that targets a particular employer, you must now decide how to deliver yourself in that resume.

Most employers see hundreds, even thousands of resumes in any given hiring period. Obviously, most resumes fail to get their authors a job. There are any number of reasons for this failure, but the single most important reason is that customarily, job seekers deliver themselves as people with "experience." In fact, most resumes have a long section headed "Experience." The trouble with this delivery is that the target employer is really not interested in your experience. What she wants to know about are your *qualifications*.

"Experience" is nothing more or less than what you've done in the past, whereas "qualifications" include not just what you have done, but what you have achieved. They also take in qualities, skills, and abilities that make you *qualified—*

that is, possessed of the qualities and skills that make you suitable for a particular task.

So rethink the resume and deliver yourself in terms of qualifications instead of experience. Just what is it you want to present yourself as qualified for?

The obvious answer is the *job*. But think through what this means. It means understanding the job as a collection of what the target employer needs—and it is precisely these needs that traditional resumes fail to address. Instead, the traditional resume focuses on the needs of the applicant, which is something that's of little interest to the target employer.

To refocus the resume on the target employer's needs, move away from the traditional resume in three important directions:

1. Whereas the traditional resume inventories your duties, use your resume to describe abilities.
2. Include in your resume a persuasive indication of your level of performance—how well you do your job.
3. Whereas the traditional resume lists responsibilities, be sure that your resume presents accomplishments.

Start your rethinking of the resume from the very beginning. It is customary to begin a resume with a statement of your employment "objective," like this:

OBJECTIVE: Quality Assurance Engineer

This tells the prospective employer very little of interest (to her) or value (to her). It does convey the obvious: that the applicant wants a job. But it also diminishes opportunity by stating the objective so narrowly. Unless this particular target employer has an opening in a position with this precise title, it is not likely that she will pursue the applicant's candidacy. (Sadly, she may have an opening for the equivalent of a quality assurance engineer, but her firm may identify this position with a different title; therefore, she will take a pass on this applicant.)

Talk about stepping up to the plate with two strikes against you! This kind of conventional, narrow statement of objective is too specific, yet it provides too little information.

Some applicants move in the opposite direction, composing a statement of objective that is too broad and self-centered:

OBJECTIVE: Finding an opportunity to utilize my skills, education, and energy in a working environment that offers a good, solid career path.

Well, that's very nice—for the applicant. But what's in it for the prospective employer? Not only is this objective statement too broad—Who *doesn't* want "a good, solid career path"?—it is so narrowly focused on the self that it seems to offer a potential employer nothing.

Deliver your statement of objective—by definition, a statement about yourself—in a way that addresses the needs of the employer. Do this, and the target employer will behold a person whose leading objective seems to mesh almost miraculously with what she wants from the person who fills the position.

An effective statement of your objective motivates the target employer to read beyond the first line of your resume. Consider:

> OBJECTIVE: To obtain a position where my decade of material, production, and inventory control experience will be a company asset.

Not bad. This certainly says something about what the applicant wants as well as what he has to offer. We can make it even better by transforming the applicant's *experience* into *qualifications*:

> OBJECTIVE: To obtain a position where my decade of creating innovative and cost-effective systems for material, production, and inventory control will be a company asset.

The phrase "creating innovative and cost-effective systems" transforms passive experience into active qualifications. Pay particular attention to the use of the verb form: "creating." Verbs and verb forms tend to energize any description of qualifications by suggesting action and movement. Nevertheless, we can do still better:

> OBJECTIVE: To be a member of a team that needs my decade of experience creating innovative and cost-effective systems for material, production, and inventory control.

The words *team* and *needs* powerfully set this resume apart from the others the target employer may receive. Employers are accustomed to seeing such terms as *firm, company, employer, corporation,* and *organization.* Emphasizing the word *team* will catch her off-guard, making her stop to think and then propelling her through the rest of the resume. Moreover, the word *needs* shifts the focus from you to the employer. After encountering this word, the target employer finds that she is no longer reading a job application, but a possible answer to what her team needs.

Assuming your statement of objective has captured the interest of your target, don't count on holding that interest for long—but don't sell yourself short, either. There is a classic story about a neophyte Hollywood screenwriter who asked his seasoned and cynical agent how long the summary of his screenplay ("treatment" is what they call such a summary in the movie biz) should be. The agent answered, "No more than ten pages. Any longer and the producer's lips get tired." Most people who give advice about resume writing are like that agent. They will tell you never to write more than a single page or to devote no more than one page to each ten years of your experience.

Forget such stabs at formulaic quantification. Sure enough, a good rule of thumb is to be brief. But a better rule of thumb is to be as brief as you can be and still deliver your qualifications and abilities effectively. A laundry list is boring, but if your qualifications and abilities are such that they cannot be encompassed within a single page, go right on to another.

This said, you *can* productively delete the following items of dead weight from your resume:

• *Detailed descriptions of jobs held more than ten years ago.* You should mention these jobs, especially if they are relevant to the needs of your target employer; however, keep the descriptions to a single line each.

• *Reasons for leaving previous jobs.* This leads you into negative territory, which is better avoided. If a prospective employer is curious, she can always ask you about these matters during an interview.

• *Salary history and/or pay desired.* There is nothing to be gained by including this material, even if a want ad asks for it. To begin with, you should try never to be the first party in a negotiation to mention money. Elicit an offer from the prospective employer, then respond to it. If you include salary information in your resume, you may give the prospective employer a reason to pass you by: "Oh, he's out of our league," or, "Someone who's been paid that little can't be much good." You also tend to lock yourself into a salary level that may be lower than the prospective employer is actually prepared to offer—and there is no good way to negotiate up from a figure *you* have provided.

• *Your personal biography.* This information is of no interest to a prospective employer.

• *Date of availability.* This is more appropriately addressed in an interview. A resume that states your immediate availability suggests desperation. A resume that gives a specific date may provide the prospective employer with a reason to exclude you from further consideration.

• *Names of references.* Employers assume that you have references available. These can be provided during the interview. (However, there is nothing wrong with dropping key names in the resume, where appropriate. For example, if you are applying for a job as a graphic designer and you served an internship with a well-known and highly respected graphic designer, include this information as part of your qualifications.)

• *Letters of recommendation.* These should not come from you, but should be sent by your recommender directly to the target employer. They should be individually addressed to the specific target. General or boilerplate letters addressed "To whom it may concern" will make little impression.

If appropriate in your field or industry, you might include certain items of backup information along with your resume, such as a bibliography of professional articles you have written, a list of special courses you have taken, a list of special equipment with which you have competence, a list of clients, and so on.

Resume Don'ts

- Don't be sloppy.
- Don't be flashy.
- Don't go to a professional resume-writing house. They make your resume look just like it's been produced by a "professional" resume-writing house (which, of course, it has). Employers know this look well and are heartily sick of it. They will wonder: *Why can't this guy write his own resume?*

Resume Do's

- Opt for a neat, functional, and pleasant page layout.
- Write short paragraphs, separated by double spaces.
- Provide generous margins: one and one-quarter inches, left, right, top, bottom.
- Use appropriate highlighting devices, such as marginal descriptions and under-lining (or italics or boldface type—but not all three).
- Use centered headlines to stress positions held and achievements achieved.
- Choose a readable typeface. Avoid eccentric or novelty fonts and fonts that imitate handwriting.
- Feel free to include a photograph of yourself, an informal portrait that shows you in appropriate business attire.

THE COVER LETTER

Recall from Chapter 3 that the classical rhetoricians advised orators to begin any argument with an *exordium*, an introduction intended to lead the audience into the speaker's subject without unsettling, confusing, or disorienting them. This part of the argument often included the speaker introducing himself in an ingratiating manner. Think of the cover letter that you include with your resume as your exordium, your opportunity to introduce yourself, to make the prospective employer comfortable with you and receptive to you, to ingratiate yourself with her.

These days, the online submission of a resume does not always provide an opportunity for the inclusion of a separate cover document. Don't let this stop you from sending one. Even when you submit a resume online, you can make your e-mail a cover letter or, if you are restricted by an online form provided by the target employer, you may even send a hardcopy cover letter by snail mail or by separate e-mail.

But is the cover letter necessary? And was it *ever* really a necessary accompaniment to the resume? Wasn't the cover letter just a kind, pro forma thing, a bit of business etiquette? Why revive it now if you don't have to?

The answer is that, yes, the cover letter was pro forma—and that remains precisely the problem with 99 percent of cover letters. They succeed in being polite, but a well-coached five-year-old can also succeed in that. Rethink the cover letter. Whatever else it is, it is an opportunity to communicate with a prospective employer, and every such opportunity is infinitely precious. Don't waste it on mere etiquette.

Invent Yourself

As with the resume, the cover letter presents an opportunity to invent yourself to suit the needs of a particular prospect. Unfortunately, most cover letter writers not only fail to invent themselves, they actually "uninvent" themselves, at least a little bit. Consider this example:

> Dear Sirs:
>
> My current position no longer presents a challenge to me, so I am looking to move on to a more challenging position.
>
> I am the assistant customer service supervisor for XYZ Corporation, and I would like to be considered for a similar position with your firm. I want to work for a company that offers excellent opportunities for advancement. Your company has a reputation for offering this kind of work environment. I know I would be happy working for you, and I promise that you would be pleased with my work.
>
> Please find my resume enclosed. I look forward to hearing from you.
>
> Sincerely,

Mother always said when you're asked for your opinion, try to say something nice. The "nice" thing about this letter is that it is short. But aside from that virtue, the rest is pretty grim—and all too typical. Take a closer look.

First, what sensible reader would go beyond the salutation before committing the letter, together with its accompanying resume, to the circular file? The surest way to say "I don't really care about you" is to fail to address a person by name. As if the meat-grinder impersonality of the salutation weren't bad enough, forcing the wrong gender on your reader (this letter was delivered to a Ms. Mary Smith, as it turns out) is profoundly offensive.

Before you write a cover letter, get a name and use it. Nobody likes to read a form letter.

Assuming—and this assumption takes a big leap of faith—that the target employer gets beyond the salutation, she will find yet more to turn her off. This writer begins by saying, in so many words, that he is tired of his job. Starting off with a negative is never a good way to sell anything, especially yourself. Don't present yourself as history, over and done with. Invent yourself. Offer up your potential: your *future*. That, after all, is what the prospective employer is buying.

Our letter writer compounds his bad start by asking to be considered for a position "similar" to the one he is bored with. The implication is that he is in a rut of his own making. Who needs him? In essence, this cover letter says nothing beyond the following:

I am bored with my present job.

I am an assistant customer service supervisor.

I want to be an assistant customer service supervisor—or something "similar." (I can't think of just what that might be.)

Your company will do about as well as any other.

My resume is enclosed.

There is nothing much for the target employer to go on. But it's even worse than it looks at first glance. Of the 103 words in the body of the letter, eleven of them (10 percent of the letter) are either "I" or "my." The focus is on the writer of the letter, when it really needs to be on the reader of the letter. She is not interested in you per se, but she is intensely interested in what you will do for her and her firm. A cover letter is an opportunity to tell a target employer what you will do for her, but very few cover letters take advantage of this opportunity.

Deliver Yourself

Invent yourself in the cover letter as precisely the person the prospect needs, then deliver yourself as the answer to this target employer's problems. Do so by including the following five elements in the letter:

1. A strong opening
2. An appeal to the target employer's self-interest
3. Highlights of your qualifications and accomplishments
4. The creation of desire
5. A call to action

Open Strong

If the cover letter is the exordium of an argument aimed at getting you a job, the opening line of your cover letter is the *exordium of the exordium*. Start by saying nothing about yourself except in terms of what you can do for the target employer. Begin with a statement that equates your ambitions with the target employer's well-being, success, and prosperity. For example:

"I am a terrific assistant customer service supervisor, who will make a real difference to your operation."

This may propel your reader through the rest of the letter, but it is a general assertion rather than a statement of fact. Instead of making assertions, which rest on the ultimately shaky support of adjectives, dig into your experience and come back with strong verbs and nouns:

"As assistant customer service supervisor at XYZ Corporation, I have developed new techniques for upselling that I believe will interest you."

This example offers something concrete—something real—to the reader of the letter. You can be even more concrete by writing in the language of business, which is the language of dollars and cents:

"As assistant customer service supervisor at XYZ Corporation, I developed upselling techniques that were responsible for $64,300 in added revenue last quarter. I would like the opportunity to talk with you about this as well as some other revenue-generating ideas I believe will be of interest to you."

The principle is simple: Start by addressing your reader's needs rather than detailing your own.

Develop the Appeal by Highlighting Your Qualifications

Immediately after your strong opening, develop the appeal to the self-interest of your target employer. Be specific, but brief. Present a valuable revelation, then indicate your willingness to share it.

"As assistant customer service supervisor at XYZ Corporation, I developed upselling techniques that were responsible for $64,300 in added revenue last quarter. I'd like to talk with you about this as well as some other revenue-generating ideas I believe will be of interest to you. I discovered that XYZ, like many other firms, was not making the most of its customer service operation. Management regarded it strictly as a support service rather than as another center of profit. With surprisingly minor changes, I introduced upselling as a major customer service function."

Obviously, the more achievements you have under your belt, the more specific you can be about what you offer an employer. If you are a newcomer, just getting out of school, deliver as much specific material as you can. Perhaps you created an important project as part of your college course work. Maybe the subject and substance of your thesis or dissertation is relevant to the needs of the target employer. What about special experience as an intern or as a volunteer? Were you a leader in student government? Think about it, package it, and deliver it in your cover letter. Specifics set you apart.

Create Desire

If your qualifications and achievements are not extensive, integrate discussion of them into the first paragraph of your letter as part of your appeal to the target employer's self-interest. However, if you have a good deal of experience and an extensive record of qualifications and achievements, develop them in a separate paragraph or even two.

You are not obliged to list everything. Filter this section so that the achievements and qualifications you discuss directly appeal to the self-interest of the target employer. You don't want to create an argument in support of the thesis that you are a jack-of-all-trades, but you do want to say that you have—specifically—what your prospect needs. Use your cover letter to highlight those features of your qualifications and achievements that most obviously dovetail with the job in question.

Take another look at the first paragraph of our sample letter:

"As assistant customer service supervisor at XYZ Corporation, I developed upselling techniques that were responsible for $64,300 in added revenue last quarter. I'd like to talk with you about this as well as some other revenue-generating ideas I believe will be of interest to you. I discovered that XYZ, like many other firms, was not making the most of its customer service operation. Management regarded it strictly as a support service rather than as another center of profit. With surprisingly minor changes, I introduced upselling as a major customer service function."

Where to go next? Start a new paragraph that begins with another appeal to the employer's self-interest:

"You may also be interested in some of the cost-saving procedures I have implemented."

Continue:

"These procedures include supervising the installation of a customer-friendly automated call director and participating in the redesign of our customer service database. I estimate the quarterly overhead savings of these innovations to be in the neighborhood of $11,000."

At this point, the writer has commanded the attention and developed the interest of the reader. The next step is to take interest to the level of desire. Start a new paragraph suggesting that the wonderful things outlined in the opening two paragraphs are available—to the employer willing to pay for them:

"I made these innovations during the four years I spent with XYZ. You will find all of this detailed in the resume I have enclosed. My work has given me a keen appreciation of the problems as well as the great, untapped potential of customer service. I would greatly enjoy sharing some of my ideas with you."

Call to Action

Classical rhetoricians called the closing part of a persuasive oration the *peroration*. Think of it as a call to action—the part of the cover letter that makes it possible (and easy) for the target employer to take positive action on what you have delivered.

What action do you want the prospective employer to take? Ultimately, you want her to make a job offer. More immediately, however, you just want her to take the next step, which is to call you for an interview. Make that possible:

> "I will call you during the week of March 3 to learn when we might get together. If you will not be available during that week, please call me."

If you are writing to an out-of-town employer, be certain to mention the particulars of your availability for an interview:

> "I will be in Anytown during March 3–5. I will call you before then to learn when we might get together to talk. If you will not be available during that period, please call me."

THE INTERVIEW

Some people look upon the interview as an exciting opportunity to make a big hit and score a great job. Others—the vast majority—face the occasion with fear and loathing.

"I am what I am," Popeye the Sailor Man used to say. We've all been taught that we are who we are and, moreover, that you should always "just be yourself." True, nobody likes a phony, but when you're getting ready for an interview, you'd better make sure you bring along the right "self" for the job. As you've done with the resume and the cover letter, invent yourself.

As for the spontaneous, anything-can-happen nature of the interview situation, you don't really need to surrender completely to a random universe. It is possible—and essential—to prepare for spontaneity.

Invent Yourself

Most job hopefuls prepare themselves for an interview by doing nothing more than worrying intensely about it. It is much more useful—and a lot less uncomfortable—to spend that valuable preinterview time by inventing yourself. Here's how:

1. Learn about the company where you are applying for a job.
2. Learn about your target position within the company.
3. Anticipate the company's needs, goals, and problems; figure out some ways that you can answer the needs, help achieve the goals, and solve the problems.
4. Review your resume and prepare a concise list of your *relevant* and *specific* accomplishments.

As you can see, most of this preparation involves somehow acquiring inside information about your target employer. Does this mean hiring a spy and paying bribes? Hardly. Most "inside information" is readily available from the outside. Always check out the following sources:

- The target employer's website
- The company's annual report (available in print, but usually also posted on the company website)
- Catalogs, brochures, and other material the company publishes
- PR material and press releases
- News stories (in the popular and professional press) about the company
- The Internet (using Google or another search engine to find relevant material)
- Ads for the company's products

The idea is to invent yourself as an expert on the target company so that you can walk into the interview focused not on yourself and your needs, but on the needs of the interviewer or interviewers. Focus your preparatory research on learning something about:

- The business of the company: What does it do or make?
- The scope of the company: How large is it in terms of revenues and number of employees? Where does it do business?
- The competition: Who are the chief competitors, and what is the target company's standing among them?

Deliver Yourself

Having invented yourself by acquiring knowledge about the target employer, deliver yourself at the interview by showing that you are the answer to what this employer needs. Consult the same sources you used for finding general information about the company, but focus on specifics concerning needs, goals, and problems. Try to identify:

- Company and industry issues: What themes or issues do your sources repeatedly mention?
- Current events relevant to the company and industry: What's going on in the world, nation, community, or neighborhood that affects the company or the industry?

Create Empathy

Inventing yourself with research focused on your target employer productively reduces the element of spontaneity in the interview and gives you more control in the interview. It also increases the rapport between you and the interviewers. An argument fashioned to win you a job is, by definition, an argument that must create empathy—your empathy for the needs of the target employer, and her empathy for your desire to get the job.

A highly effective way to ramp up empathy is to reverse the way most job seekers think of the interview. Instead of looking at it as a session where you are asked a lot of questions, consider it an opportunity for you to ask questions as well. When a seasoned salesman builds rapport with a prospect, he invariably does so by asking questions, knowing that this actively engages the prospect, compelling him to invest something of himself in what the salesman is selling. In an interview situation, you'll accomplish two things by asking questions: First, you'll get answers to things about the company and the job that are of interest and concern to you. Second, you'll focus the interview on what most interests the interviewers: themselves.

Questions to ask include:

• *Have you had an opportunity to review my resume?* Don't assume that the interviewer has carefully studied your resume beforehand, especially if you are speaking to more than one interviewer in a company. It is not likely that you will get a simple "No, I haven't" in response to this question, but you might hear something like, "I haven't had the chance to review it as thoroughly as I'd like to," which, in fact, means no. This is your opportunity to reveal yourself as a problem solver: "Then, perhaps you would find it helpful for me to hit the highlights of my qualifications."

• *Is there anything else I can tell you about my qualifications?* If the interviewer answers yes, she has read your resume, so invite further questions on this subject. The more time you persuade the target employer to invest in you, the more valuable you become in her estimation.

• *How would you describe the duties of this job?* Even if you've memorized the job description from the want ad, this question is important to ask. For one thing, you may discover that the interviewer's description is a far cry from the description in the ad. More likely, you will get a snapshot of which job functions really are the most important. The answer should be a springboard to more productive conversation about what you have to offer: "I'm glad to hear that you put such a high premium on client contact. For me, customer satisfaction is building a business, each and every day, one client at a time."

• *What are the principal problems facing you and your staff right now?* The answer to this question may give you an understanding of the target employer's problems, and therefore it may create an opportunity to present yourself as a solution to those problems. The question also may uncover any truly terrible situations that should make you think twice about taking the job.

• *What results do you most want me to produce?* This question declares your intention of *doing* a job rather than *taking* one. Respond point by point to whatever answer this question elicits.

• *Based on what I've told you, don't you think I could give you all that you need in this position?* You want to ask this question straight out because it calls for action. It invites a positive response and nudges the interviewer toward agreement. At the very least, it gives you an opportunity to prompt the interviewer to tell you more about what she wants or expects.

Create Desire

Having created rapport and empathy with the interviewer or interviewers, the next step is to raise this interest to the level of desire. You want the job. Fine. To get the job, you need to make the target employer desire you.

If you have identified key themes—the employer's pressing needs, concerns, and wants—wrap up the interview by focusing on these issues, discussing how you will provide for them. Bolster your promises with actual achievements. Be as concrete and specific as you possibly can be. If you have a professional portfolio or scrapbook with you, now is the time to trot it out.

This portfolio or scrapbook should include three to six copies of your resume, an "executive briefing" summarizing your resume in a single narrative paragraph, letters of commendation (but *not* recommendation, which should always be sent by the recommender directly to the prospect and not pass through your hands), awards, copies of (nonproprietary and nonclassified) business presentations you have made, photos of equipment you have worked with, and so on—whatever physical evidence of your achievements and qualifications that is sufficiently portable for you to take to the interview.

Remain in control of the scrapbook. You may give the interviewer a copy of your resume and the executive briefing, but the scrapbook itself stays in your hands. Do not hand it over to the interviewer. Share it with her. Let her look. Of course, if she asks to look through it for herself, allow her to. But the idea is to convey to her that the work it contains is yours and is of value. Like the portfolio itself, you are not simply up for grabs.

Refute Resistance

Classic rhetoricians believed that an important part of any persuasive argument was the *refutatio*, the refutation of opposing points of view. In an argument crafted to get you a job, your object is not to win the argument but to get the job. If you put the interviewer in the position of "losing" an argument with you, you may win the argument, but you probably won't get the job. In an interview, refuting resistance means finding out more about how you can satisfy the interviewer. Do not look upon objections raised in the interview as roadblocks to employment but as opportunities for you to clarify your qualifications and make them more appealing.

In countering resistance, always begin by emphasizing the positive, the areas of agreement or satisfaction. Then proceed to address the core of the objection. For example:

Interviewer: You really don't have a great deal of experience in customer service.

Applicant: I agree. Two years is not a great amount of experience. The experience I do have, however, is quite varied and of very high quality. At XYZ Corporation, I'd say that my two years of experience is the equivalent of three or four years almost anywhere else.

Talk Salary

Unless either the interviewer or you decided early in the interview that you are not the person for the job in question, the salary discussion is an inevitable part of the interview. Prepare for it carefully by doing the following:

1. Review your needs and wants, and work out your own cash requirements before the interview.

2. Determine the going price of your qualifications and skills on the current market. Your industry research may have provided this information. You can also go to the website of the U.S. Department of Labor to download a copy of the latest report of the Bureau of Labor Statistics (www.bls.gov). It offers a wealth of salary information, broken down by industry.

3. Consult the latest edition of Les Krantz's *Jobs Rated Almanac* (Fort Lee, N.J.: Barricade Books, 2002).

4. Consult professional and trade journals in your field or industry, since these sources often publish annual salary surveys.

You should walk into the interview with three figures in mind: Start with the minimum salary you need and a midpoint salary associated with your target position. Using these two figures, formulate a third—your blue-sky salary, the amount you would really love to earn.

In most arguments, forthrightness is a very strong quality. In salary negotiation, however, you should move heaven and earth to avoid being the first to mention a figure. Try to ensure that the salary discussion does not come until the end of the interview; however, if you are asked what kind of salary you are looking for, turn the tables on the interviewer:

"I expect a salary appropriate to my qualifications and demonstrated abilities. What range did you have in mind?"

Or:

"What salary range has been authorized for the position?"

If the interviewer insists on getting a figure from you, do not start a fight. Respond with a broad salary range.

If you have determined that you need a minimum of $38,000 and your research suggests that the salary range for the target position is $34,000 to

$42,000, bracket the range you give to the interviewer so that it interlocks with the upper range of what you might expect as an industry standard and exceeds your own minimum requirement. Here, for example, a good range would be $40,000 to $45,000.

Once a salary range is finally on the table, you can respond in one of four ways:

1. You can accept the figure or the range offered. (If necessary, adding the remark that "the upper end of this range is what I had in mind and would be acceptable to me.")
2. You can continue the negotiation by responding with your own range, which overlaps the top end of the offer.
3. You can thank the interviewer for the information and ask for additional time to consider the figure.
4. You can tell the interviewer that the figure (or range) is unacceptable.

If you are truly satisfied with the figure offered, you may respond with the first option; however, most employers leave some negotiating room beyond the top end of whatever figure or range they state. Why not, therefore, respond with the second option in order to define a new, somewhat higher figure or range? Use this discussion as an opportunity to reemphasize your key qualifications. Appeal to reason by giving the employer a logical reason to pay you top dollar.

The third option risks losing the offer altogether, but it is useful if you strongly feel that this employer wants *you*. It is a gamble—and one that is best taken if you have a backup offer from another prospect or if you are not desperate for the job.

The fourth option, telling the interviewer that her offer is not even in the ball-park, is playing genuine hardball. It is a great risk and will probably end the negotiation. A better alternative, if the employer's figure is substantially below your range, is option 3. Ask for time to think the offer over. Set a specific time when you will call with your answer—usually within twenty-four to forty-eight hours. This will give you time to think things through and, more important, give the employer an opportunity to rethink her "absolute" salary cap.

Objections to your salary requirements are almost always variations on one of four themes:

1. Your figure exceeds the range authorized for the position.
2. Your figure is outside of our budget. We can't afford you.
3. Others similarly qualified within the company don't make that kind of money.
4. Your salary history does not merit what you are asking for.

The first objection may be a statement of fact. If so, you may not be able to refute it. The other objections, however, are significantly less absolute. None of them has anything to do with your value or performance. This means that, as part of your refutation, you can communicate to the target employer that she will get exceptional value and a very high return from your performance. Note that the objections all focus on cost. You must persuade the employer to refocus on *value*—that is, on *cost* versus *benefit*:

> "I understand that you budgeted less than $37,000 for this position, but I believe that we're both agreed that I bring to the table special qualifications and skills, as well as a deep commitment to performance. These things justify the $40,000 figure I'm asking for."

If you're told that others presently employed at the firm don't make the salary you are asking for, redirect the discussion to your own performance:

> "I see. But, based on our conversation thus far, I understood that my salary would be based on my performance and my qualifications, not on what others in the company earn."

Just as you need to divorce the issue of compensation for your performance and qualifications from the salaries others are earning, so too must you separate the record of what you earned in the past from what you are asking for now:

> "It is not clear to me what bearing my past salary has on the work I will do for you. What I see as relevant to salary is performance and qualifications. We have discussed these topics, and I think that we're both agreed that I offer great value to the company."

If you discover that, at the end of the negotiation, you are still far apart, you might conclude the interview with thanks and continue your job search elsewhere, or you might accept the employer's best offer now, with the explicit understanding that your salary will be reviewed in six months in light of your performance.

Know When to Close

It is possible that you may get an immediate offer; more typically, though, the interviewers will indicate to you when the interview is at an end. They may tell you that you will hear from them in a certain number of days. In this case, try to pin down the date. You do not want to give the impression that you are willing to wait indefinitely.

If neither an offer nor a "next step" is discussed, try to prompt closure—to push the employer to action:

> "Ms. Jones, I've enjoyed talking with you, and I believe I have a great deal to give this firm. Is there anything I haven't addressed to your satisfaction? What might I tell you that would prompt you to make an offer?"

Alternatively, you might ask this closing question:

> "Based on what we've discussed, don't you think I could deliver everything you need in this position?"

Arguing yourself into a job ends with action. Say what you can to elicit positive action—either an offer or a specific next step—rather than leaving without a conclusion.

C H A P T E R   1 0

Move Your Boss

Make your case and get your way with
bosses and supervisors.

All business, we know, is people business. In business, it is important to respect everyone and to try to create satisfaction in all those with whom we come in contact. In this sense, all people are equal. But, to paraphrase George Orwell, writing in *Animal Farm*, some are more equal than others.

If all business is people business, the most effective way to do business is to identify the people who have the greatest power and authority to propel your projects and promote your career. Bosses, of course, fall into this category. While it is certainly important to persuade your subordinates, colleagues, and customers, nothing is more important than to persuade your boss—every day.

WORDS TO USE

Any persuasive argument starts with the right words. The following list suggests some words to use when you speak with the boss.

able	correct	future	opportunity	reschedule
achieved	create	generous	overcome	resolve
advise	dedicated	goals	perform	resource
agree	discuss	gratitude	perspective	responsibility
alternatives	do	happy	plan	reward
appropriate	dollars	help	possible	serve
approve	duty	ideas	potential	service
asset	effective	imagination	prepare	solve
aware	efficient	improve	pride	source
balance	encourage	innovate	priorities	strategy
can	enthusiasm	judgment	productivity	strength
capable	evaluate	loyalty	profit	support
care	excitement	manage	propose	thanks
committed	expedite	motivate	prudent	time
confident	experience	negotiate	qualifications	value

consider	expertise	new	question	willing
contribute	fair	objectives	reasonable	

WORDS TO AVOID

As important as it is to use the right words with your boss, it is at least equally important to avoid the wrong ones—the words that work against your argument. The following is a list of some all-too-common nonstarters to avoid.

afraid	demand	fear	incapable	panic
bad	disaster	final	late	ridiculous
blame	doubt	forgot	luck	tired
bored	dull	frightened	mess	unappreciated
can't	dumb	hopeless	no	underpaid
crisis	fail	impossible	nonnegotiable	unfair
delay	fault	inadequate	overloaded	waste

AT STAKE

Recall that the part of persuasive communication the classical rhetoricians called "discovery" is nothing more or less than deciding what, precisely, is at stake in the situation at hand. These days, *team, teamwork,* and *decentralized decision making* are buzzwords—and for good reason. Most organizations are less monolithic, less absolutely hierarchical than they were two or three decades ago. But make no mistake: The boss still abideth.

No matter how "flat" the structure of the modern business organization has become, some people are still in charge—or, at least, they are more in charge than others. Fail to persuade these individuals and you and your projects (along with your career) will get nowhere. People in charge are the enablers, and they are also the gatekeepers. In communicating with them, just about everything is at stake. Whoever else you may *want* to persuade, it is the boss you *must* persuade.

YOUR GOAL

The goal of any persuasive discourse is to get your way. That simple definition is not much help in dealing with the boss, however. Before you plan your argument, let alone make your argument, rethink your goal. Getting *your* way is not what your boss is all about. What your boss wants is *her* way, which, if she's a good leader, is what she perceives will benefit the entire organization. Your goal, therefore, is wholly to identify what *you* want with what *she* wants and, by implication, with what will be good for the enterprise as a whole.

Having this as your goal doesn't require as much altruism and self-sacrifice as seems to be the case at first glance. Visualize the big picture. If you are a member of the enterprise, if you are committed to the enterprise, if you want to rise within the enterprise, then what is good for the organization—and your boss—is necessarily good for you. Persuading your boss that what *you* want is really what *she* wants doesn't require a cynical trick of persuasive rhetoric. It requires setting out the situation as it really is and making clear the common cause that exists between you, your boss, and the good of the enterprise. Your goal, then, is to convey a *vision* of the organization, its needs, its potential, its present, and its future.

YOUR APPEAL

Recall again that the classical rhetoricians identified three basic approaches to persuasion: 1) the appeal to reason, 2) the appeal to emotion, and 3) the ethical appeal. All are important in persuading bosses, but the first and the third are especially critical. We begin with a few words on the ethical appeal.

Nothing you say to your boss will mean much—or, at any rate, much that is good for you—if she lacks admiration for, and confidence in, your ethical character. In working with your boss, deeds speak more powerfully of character than words. Behave ethically over the months and years and you will be able to enter into any argument with an ethical appeal ready-made. If necessary, you may highlight the features of this foundation verbally:

> "You know that I am fully committed to this company and that I have always made my evaluations and decisions based on the growth of the organization."

If possible, cite a fact or a piece of personal history—the more specific the better:

> "You know, last year I could have left customer service for sales—and probably made significantly more money for myself—but my greatest strength is in service. I'm committed to it. It's where I can do the most for our company. So, with that in mind, I want to lay out an idea for introducing an upselling program into our service organization."

PREPARE FOR SPONTANEITY

The classical rhetoricians believed in the power of eloquence, but they saw nothing supernatural or magical about it. For them, persuasive eloquence was the application of hard work. Indeed, they believed that the proper preparation for an orator was not merely studying the various formulas of rhetoric, but engaging in a lifetime of learning.

General Douglas MacArthur often proclaimed that "there is no substitute for victory." In persuasion, while a command of language, a familiarity with the patterns of argument, and (often) a flair for figures of speech are all very important, there is no substitute for knowledge. Before you approach your boss to sell an idea or a project or a point of view, be certain that you know what you are talking about. This does not mean that you have to write out a formal presentation every time you want to talk to your boss about something important. It does mean that you should diligently prepare for spontaneity. Avoid shooting from the hip. Do the necessary research. Learn something about your subject *before* you bring it up.

For example, suppose you want to persuade your boss to give you a raise. You could try spontaneity by blurting out, "My adjustable-rate mortgage has gone up, my daughter needs a load of orthodontic work, my old car is ready to bite the dust; please, please, please, *I need more money!*"

Honest? Heartfelt?

Yes and yes.

But this approach won't do you a bit of good. Count on it: Your boss just doesn't sufficiently care about what you need. The far more effective approach is to avoid spontaneity and, instead, prepare a case so that you can present a persuasive argument demonstrating that it is in your *boss's* self-interest to raise *your* salary. Here's how:

1. *Do some self-research.* Compile a list of ways that you not only meet but exceed the demands of your job. Do not rely on your boss's having kept score for you.

Showing is always better than telling. Nouns and verbs are more persuasive than adjectives and adverbs. Mentally review the facts concerning people, events, and achievements that demonstrate your great value to the organization and, therefore, to your boss. Instead of using abstract adjectives like *great, efficient, imaginative*, create a presentation about your accomplishments that speaks the language of business—in other words, that talks in dollars: Two years ago, when you started in the department, sales volume was $XX. Today, it is $XXX. The promotional program you designed was responsible for $XX in revenue last year. The new program slated for next year is projected to bring in $XXX.

2. *Research what others—in similar positions, with similar duties, and in similar companies—get paid.* If you discover that the average is significantly higher than what you currently receive, congratulations! You have found a point for your argument in favor of getting a raise.

If you discover that your compensation is about average, hold this information in reserve. Should your boss point out that your compensation is about standard for the industry, you should be prepared to show the ways in which you outperform the industry standard.

Of course, it is possible that you may discover that you are getting paid substantially more than the going rate. In this case, start researching the possibilities of a promotion rather than a raise.

3. *Study the results of your research.* Be ready to reel off your most important accomplishments—"spontaneously."

4. *Focus your research, but don't ignore key peripheral facts.* For instance, you should be fully aware of how well (or how poorly) your company and depart-

ment performed during the past year. Be sure that you know *your* job as well as its place in and impact on the company as a whole.

5. *Before you meet with your boss, use your research to formulate a target salary level.* Don't just spin the wheel of fortune. Prepare yourself with a firm idea of what you can reasonably expect.

The subject of salary negotiation is just one example. Whatever idea, project, or course of action you want to persuade your boss to buy into, build your eloquence on a foundation of fact. Speak from knowledge.

MAKE A SPECIAL DELIVERY

Your attitude toward your boss, how you stand in relation to her, is silently telegraphed by your body language.

Constructive Body-Language Vocabulary

- Cast yourself in the role of an equal; however, always approach your boss politely.
- Knock on the door or, if your boss occupies a cubicle, knock on its outside wall. When you're invited in, walk in all the way. Don't just poke your head in at the door or the opening, and do not linger on the threshold.
- Maintain eye contact, but never stare. It is okay to look away occasionally in order to gather your thoughts (see the next item), but when you speak, look into the boss's eyes.
- Periodically shift your glance to your boss's forehead, focusing just above her eyes. This is a subtle way of asserting your strong presence.
- Don't rush to sit. Linger just a moment, standing in front of the boss's desk. This will compel her to look up to you, thereby putting you in a position of power.
- Once you are seated, keep your hands fully visible. Don't hesitate to use hand gestures that underscore important points.
- Gesture with open, slightly upturned palms.
- Smile.
- Lean forward. This posture strongly conveys your interest in what is being said.

LISTEN UP

Your ears are valuable tools of persuasion. They give you remarkable inside information. After all, if you listen to what your boss tells you, you will know a good deal about what to say to her. Only when you listen will you be able to shape your messages to the boss's needs. The following steps will help you to concentrate—and help you to be a persuasive listener:

1. *Reflect what your boss says.* Paraphrase her statements to let her know that you are listening and that she is being heard. This practice also helps you stay focused.

Boss: I told him that we should go with ABC because it could deliver faster, even if we had to pay a bit more.

You: Speed is an important feature.

Boss: That's right.

2. *Ask questions.* Relevant questions keep the conversation moving and keep it productive.

3. *Don't respond in ways that take the conversation in tangents.* Your remarks should be relevant to comments being made by the boss.

WORK THE PROBLEM, RESOLVE THE CONFLICT

Nobody welcomes problems, but they cannot be denied or ignored. They need to be worked and resolved. On the positive side, a problem, whatever else it may be, is an opportunity for you to communicate. If you communicate persuasively, you will enhance relations between you and your boss.

The key principle to bear in mind is that few problems, even those caused by outright mistakes and misjudgments, are fatal or beyond repair. Typically, the most dangerous feature of a problem is not the direct consequences of the problem itself, but the negative emotions it creates. Communicate persuasively and you can minimize destructive feelings and perhaps even create the positive emotions that accompany satisfactorily solving a problem.

There are three steps to approaching any problem created through error or misjudgment:

1. Acknowledge the error.
2. Realistically assess the nature and scope of the problem.
3. Work the problem. Make positive suggestions to your boss for resolving the issue.

Let's look more closely at a number of problem scenarios.

When the Problem Is Your Fault

Begin by reporting the error right away. Better your boss should hear it from you than discover it on her own or hear it from someone else. Take ownership of the problem. This doesn't mean simply accepting blame, but it does require you to make yourself responsible for mitigating or resolving the problem.

- Don't panic, and, even more important, don't behave in a manner that suggests panic. For example, avoid running breathlessly into the boss's office.

- Although you should report the problem right away, do take a short time at this stage to assess the nature and scope of the problem.
- If possible, go to your boss with a report of the problem and a suggested solution.

It is not always possible or desirable to make a quick assessment of a problem. Use your judgment. If time is of the essence, move quickly. If, however, you can secure time to resolve the problem in the best way possible, buy time by not going into great detail in your initial report. There is a distinct strategic advantage in letting your boss feel that she is assessing the error for herself rather than listening to your possibly biased version of it. Once you have assessed the problem, proceed to create potential remedies.

In this situation, it is most important to communicate a positive message about your intention, willingness, and competence to correct the problem. Second, you want to acknowledge fault and offer an apology. Do not dwell on these things, and do not let them overshadow your commitment to move forward with a positive solution.

When the Problem Is Not Your Fault

It takes real integrity to admit to having made a mistake that has created a problem. It also demands a serious ethical commitment to take ownership of a problem that is not yours. The objective in this case is both to resolve the problem and to convey your commitment to the organization by your willingness to assume responsibility for the resolution of the problem.

- Try to identify and locate the person who is responsible for the problem. Discuss the matter with him as constructively as possible. Be sure to focus on constructive solutions rather than on blame. Work the problem. Don't try to fix the person who created it.
- If the responsible person cannot be identified, and if it is a problem you cannot resolve on your own, report it to your boss.
- If possible, go to your boss with a suggested resolution to the problem or, at least, some positive plan of action.

In reporting the problem, your objective is to persuade your boss that you are a problem solver—which makes you the most valuable member of the organization.

When the Problem Is Not Your Fault, but Is Your Problem

Subordinates and others may cause a problem for which you are not directly responsible. Even if you didn't personally press the wrong button, it is, nevertheless, your problem. Accept ownership of such problems as part and parcel of your job description. You are by no means required to assume blame or fault for the problem. However, it is up to you to take responsibility for the fix.

- If you can resolve the problem correctly without resorting to higher authority, do so.
- If you must make a report to the boss, do so in a positive way. If your subordinate failed, explain the failure, but embody in your report President Harry Truman's great motto: *The buck stops here.* Take unambiguous ownership of the problem and the responsibility for finding and implementing a solution.
- As always, convert the problem into an opportunity to reveal yourself as a problem solver.

When the Problem's Got You Stumped

Some problems are simply baffling. If you can't immediately get a handle on a problem, it is difficult to present yourself as a problem solver. In a case like this, don't make excuses. Ask for help. Ask your boss for help. Make her your ally against a common enemy, namely the problem at hand.

Begin by admitting the problem calmly. For instance:

> "I need your help. We are missing four key customer files. I don't know why they are gone, but instead of wasting more time looking for them, I think it is best to call the clients. Now: How do you suggest I do this without embarrassing us?"

The fine art here is to avoid simply passing the buck to your boss, even as you solicit her aid. Suggest as much of a course of action as you can, then, in asking for help, create common cause with your boss. Put yourself in the position of working the problem together.

When a Project Fails

Most problems are solvable and most errors fixable. But note the operative word: *most*. Sometimes ideas, endeavors, efforts, and projects fail and cannot be saved. Out of even the worst failures, however, some things are salvageable, including, most important of all, information. From failure it is often possible to salvage the future—your future.

The future should be the subject of any discussion you have with your boss following a failure. The future is always valuable, and it is your task to persuade your boss that you have a role in realizing that value. Take this approach:

- To the degree that you are responsible for the failure, accept responsibility.
- Having taken responsibility for the present, refocus the discussion on the future, on potential and opportunity.

- Avoid such phrases as "should have," "wish I had," "if I had only," and the like.

  Use phrases such as "next time," "in the future," "we learned a lesson for the future," and "we won't do it this way next time." (Use *we* in preference to *I* and *you*.)

An Example

"I just discovered that I made a serious error in the sales report I submitted to our client. The numbers for X, Y, and Z are wrong, and the documents have already gone out. I have a corrected report ready, along with a cover memo, and I'll send both as e-mail attachments. I'll also phone the client to advise them of the error and the correction.

"This was a serious, but simple, error. In the future, we are going to have to build into the report process at least six hours of proofreading and fact-checking time. That's my recommendation."

There is no panic here, no excuse, and no abject apology. Your boss doesn't want to hear any such. All she wants is to know what happened, what you are doing about it, and how you will keep it from ever happening again. What's done is done. The future, however, is still available for positive action.

STYLE IT POSITIVE

Negative messages do not produce positive results. Persuasive discourse with your boss should be styled as positively as possible. This does not mean distorting the truth or hiding bad news. It does mean identifying the positive components of any situation. Understand, however, that *positive* is not a synonym for *good*. A *positive* approach simply means identifying the components of a situation that can be acted upon.

The accident investigator who gazes on a heap of twisted metal that was once an airliner does not call what he sees "good." But he does focus on the positive component of the wreckage: its value as a teacher of lessons that may prevent a future catastrophe. He does not dwell on the money and lives lost. About these things, he can do nothing. They are, truly, negative components of the situation. What the debris may say about the future is positive.

Positive styling is not about calling the bad good. It is about making productive use of everything, good and bad.

HOW TO READ YOUR BOSS

Classical rhetoricians as well as the most modern PR gurus agree: Persuasive communicators know their audience.

If you think of a speech as a one-way broadcast—you speak, others listen—you will never become a persuasive communicator. Even a prepared lecture, read verbatim from a script, is actually a dialogue—provided it is spoken to some audience. Even if that audience does not talk back, it responds mentally and emotionally. There is give-and-take between the speaker and the spoken to. The most effective speeches are written with an awareness of this dialogue. They anticipate the give-and-take. They attempt to satisfy the needs of the audience.

Similarly, when you communicate with your boss, anticipate her needs and attempt to satisfy them. Your boss is your audience. Know your audience before you open your mouth.

There is one thing all bosses want: All bosses want their problems solved. Present yourself as the solution to a problem and you will be a very persuasive communicator, indeed.

Beyond this, do everything you can to determine the specifics of what your boss needs and wants.

What Does a Boss Value?

reliability	independent thinking	caution	flattery
innovation	punctuality	small talk	pat on the back
self-reliance	execution of orders and directives	no nonsense	constructive criticism
teamwork	boldness	blunt speech	competence

What Does a Boss Deplore?

slavish execution of orders and directives	incessant small talk	flattery
too much boldness	cold, no-nonsense approach	criticism of any kind
overabundance of caution	blunt speech	incompetence

Despite some common requirements, one size does not fit all. Watch your boss. Listen to her. *Read* her. Determine what she values. Strive to communicate those values to her. And, when in doubt, *ask:* "Of these three items, which is your first, second, and third priority?"

APPROACHES FOR MANY SITUATIONS

Communication is, of course, essential to every aspect of business. But communication doesn't have to become a mundane matter just because it is a daily activity. Regard every instance of communication as an opportunity to persuade your boss of your great value to her and to the enterprise.

Delivering a Progress Report

Even the most ordinary progress report is an argument for (or against) your competence. If the progress of a project is going well, the evidence is persuasive in your favor. If there are problems, well, *you* have problems.

The persuasive progress report is one that is as clear and simple as possible. The report should unambiguously identify the project, set out key milestones along a timeline, and show what has been done and what has yet to be done. Take every opportunity to highlight achievements, whenever possible quantifying them in dollars or in units of time.

> "Phase 3 was completed four days ahead of schedule, which will get us to market at least one week early."

> "By doing the final packaging and shipping out of the same plant, we have saved $XXX and are below budget by that amount."

To paraphrase a cliché, outcomes speak louder than words. This is great when the outcomes are good, but when progress slows or proves disappointing, the progress report must become a negotiation for a new deadline.

Bosses hate missed deadlines, and no boss wants to hear an excuse. While you might succeed in persuading your boss to buy your excuse, you will never make her happy about doing so. Therefore, don't waste your rhetorical skill on the effort. Instead, approach a slipped deadline as an occasion for you to persuade your boss to "sell" you more time. Like anything else you might "buy," the purchase of time is a negotiation.

• *Focus on the value your boss will receive in exchange for "selling" you additional time.* Here is one approach: "To do this project the right way, I need three more days. This will give us the result we all want."

• *Negotiate for an alteration in "schedule," not the abandonment of a "deadline."* Manage, don't panic.

• *Propose alternatives.* Don't just ask for a blanket grant of more time. For instance: "We can finish X by Friday, Y by Tuesday, and Z by the end of next week." Or: "If I reprioritize, putting the completion of X back to Monday, I can deliver both Y and Z by the original due date." Negotiation is all about providing choices. Provide them.

As in any negotiation, you may receive more than a little resistance. Just as classical rhetoricians prepared a *refutatio*, a refutation of anticipated opposing arguments, so you should come into the time negotiation prepared to meet objections.

1

Boss: This is a critical deadline. Are you aware of that?

You: I understand, and that's why I'm talking to you about it now. I can deliver three out of the four project elements by the current target. We can start processing them immediately on delivery. What I need is four more days to get the final phase to completion. The net result will be a minimum loss of time—and a project outcome we can all be confident about.

2

Boss: What are the people in your department doing with their time?

You: We invested some time in thinking through the needs of the project so that we don't take shortcuts that will cost us quality. The result of this process is why I'm talking to you now about modifying the delivery.

3

Boss: Is this really the best you can do?

You: It is possible that we could shave off a day or two, but I'm not sure I'd be comfortable with the outcome.

Negotiating a Raise or Promotion

We have already discussed the preparation necessary for entering into a negotiation for a raise. Prepare yourself with the appropriate research. Having researched the case for your raise, call on your boss and take the following approach:

1. *Decide not to* ask *for a raise, but to* negotiate *for one.* Asking sets up a one-way transaction. The boss gives, you take. From the boss's point of view, it is not a very good bargain. As for you, it puts you in the position of a child or a beggar. In contrast, negotiation is an exchange, between equals, of value for value.

2. *Make a specific appointment.* Ensure that time is set aside. With luck, this precaution will avoid interruptions. The meeting should not appear spontaneous or spur of the moment. You don't want to "surprise" your boss with a request for more money.

3. *Think body language.* Walk into the negotiation briskly and confidently. Make strong and frequent eye contact. If your boss is behind her desk, pull your chair to the side of her desk (if possible) to avoid having the desktop serve as a barrier between the two of you. If you can't sit to the side, get as close to the desk as you can. If feasible, sit higher than your boss or, at least, at the same level.

4. *Begin by thanking your boss for the meeting.* This serves two purposes. First, it is common courtesy. Second, the thanks should serve to remind your boss that, by agreeing to the meeting, she has decided you are sufficiently important to invest time in. Your thanks affirms the wisdom of her investment decision.

5. *Make your case.* Review your record, focusing on facts. Describe your achievements using nouns and verbs, instead of making mere assertions consisting of adverbs and adjectives. Make your pitch. Here's how it might go:

> "Thanks for making time, Mary [if you customarily call your boss by her first name]. As you know, I've been with our firm for four years—two in sales, and two in marketing. This last year, I headed up the XYZ account, which I've transformed into a major profit center, generating $XX this last quarter. I have every reason to believe that the ABC account, which I've just taken on,

will show similar results. I really appreciate the creative room you've given me, and I've used it to build our business.

"Now, while I have moved up steadily here, I've amassed a great many responsibilities, and I think it is appropriate at this time to bring my salary up to the level of my responsibilities and my achievements. What do you think?"

Here, you have presented your case in brief. Without mentioning a number, you have nevertheless outlined your expectations: a salary "up to the level of" your responsibilities and achievements. You have, that is, proposed an exchange of fair value for fair value. In addition, you have given your boss the feeling that she is both fair and astute. After all, she hired you, and you are producing excellent results. You are reminding her that she has already invested in you, and that the investment has paid off. This opening makes a positive response possible, and the question at the end of the appeal actively engages the boss's thought. No demand is made. Instead, this argument shifts the focus from you to your boss, subtly translating your self-interest into terms of her self-interest and the interests of the organization.

Expect resistance, the commonest form of which is a bid to delay consideration. Your boss may reply that she can't consider the request now or that it will have to wait until later. Respond by negotiating for a specific appointment date for the salary review:

"I see. Let's set a date for the discussion, then."

Or:

"Can we set up a meeting now for a week from Monday?"

Don't leave with nothing more than a vague plan to meet again "later." Make an appointment.

Other resistance responses include:

1

Boss: If it were up to me, you'd get the raise right now. All I can do, however, is make a recommendation. The final decision is not mine.

You: Would it be better for me to talk with [name of boss's supervisor]? And can I count on your recommendation to him?

2

Boss: I've got to tell you that I have a lot of people in my department doing great jobs, but none of them has asked for the kind of raise you want.

You: Well, I'm only talking about what is appropriate in my case.

You may not encounter outright resistance; rather, you may suddenly find yourself engaged in an all-out bargaining session:

Boss: A 10 percent hike is out of the question. I just can't do it. Maybe 3 percent.

You: [Don't haggle. Remain silent, but don't leave. Don't glare. Let the silence linger.]

Boss: Would 5 percent work, if I can swing it?

You: I appreciate your consideration. I can work at that salary, provided that we have a firm understanding that in six months we'll tote up the score again and revisit the matter of salary.

The hardest form of resistance is the outright *no*. The answer may be final, as far as this particular discussion session is concerned, but don't let it be the last word.

Boss: I just can't accommodate you at this time.

You: What can I do to make it possible, say, in another three months?

Remain engaged. Use the negative response to gain insight into your place in the organization and to learn what your boss really needs and how you can be successful next time.

Selling a Project

Selling a new idea or project requires a skillful reading of your boss. If your sense is that your boss encourages innovation, the task of persuasion is easier. If, however, you have reason to believe that she is conservative and tends naturally to resist new ideas, your work is cut out for you.

Let's assume your reading of your boss suggests that she is generally receptive to new ideas. It is up to you to persuade her to act on her creative, innovative instincts:

- Take time to research and prepare your case—even if you are having an *apparently* spontaneous conversation with the boss. As always, nothing is more persuasive to a boss than a demonstration of your knowledge and command of the situation in question.

- In a formal presentation to the boss that involves written research material, be sure to provide guiding remarks, such as: "The highlight feature of the proposal is . . . ." or "As you study the proposal, take special note of . . . ."

- Arm yourself with any necessary research notes, in case you are asked for details.

    Secure at least some buy-in beforehand. Build a coalition of colleagues and subordinates. Get others involved in and committed to the project, even before you present it to the boss.

If you are facing a boss you believe does not tend to welcome innovation, your strategy for persuasion should include steps that give *her* a tangible stake in *your* project. Structure the argument this way:

*   Make it your goal to let your boss see herself as your partner in the project. This can be done with a few well-placed remarks, such as: "As you study the proposal, you'll notice how thoroughly I incorporated your thoughts in X, Y, and Z."
*   Recruit your boss before you try to persuade her. Ask for help: "I'd really appreciate your opinion and guidance on . . . ."

Come to the party well prepared to refute resistance and negative responses. For instance:

1

Boss: This is a tough one. I'm not convinced.

You: Any project in this area will involve a real commitment. What I ask is that you study the proposal. The figures are all up-front. Then let's take the discussion from there. I am confident it will make sense to you.

2

Boss: I'm swamped. I just don't know when I'll be able to consider this idea.

You: I appreciate how busy you are, but I'm confident that you'll be very excited by the proposal. It really is worth making some time for.

Accepting an Assignment

How you accept an assignment is an opportunity to persuade your boss of your competence and commitment, as well as your value to the organization. The best case, naturally, is when the assignment genuinely interests and excites you. As you accept it, speak from your feelings. Express your pleasure and your enthusiasm. Nothing will make your boss happier.

The job of persuasive communication is more complex, but perhaps even more critically important, when you are *not* exactly thrilled about the assignment. Assuming you are not in a position to decline the assignment—or feel that declining it is not the best option for both you and the organization—you are not obliged to pretend you are happy about it. Nevertheless, you owe your boss and the organization a message that conveys your intention to work cheerfully and professionally to carry out the assigned task. You need not convey more than this, but you cannot convey less.

The worst case is when you are compelled to take on an assignment you have grave reservations about. If declining the assignment is feasible, that may be your best course. If not, you need to persuade your boss that you will successfully manage the situation. Don't fake enthusiastic confidence, but avoid responding with black negativity or panic. Instead, fashion a positive response, but buy time for study by mentioning that you will be back with some questions: "Okay, I'll begin studying this immediately, then get back to you with some questions." Use this time to coolly assess the benefits and pitfalls of the project before committing to a definitive response. It is not only appropriate to buy time, it is a benefit to your boss and your organization:

> **Boss:** You seem to have some doubts. . . .

> **You:** Well, what I have are some questions. Let me get started studying the project immediately, formulate my questions, then come back to you with them.

Declining an Assignment

Depending on a great many factors—including the nature of your job, the level at which you are working, and your relationship with your boss—you may or may not possess the viable option of declining an assignment. Remember, in everything you say to your boss, your objective is to make a persuasive argument concerning your competence and commitment. This being the case, the first rule of thumb in declining an assignment is to regard this option truly as a last resort. It is almost always best to avoid an immediate negative response. Instead, begin by asking for time to review the assignment and return with questions. Only after you have studied the assignment should you decline it—and that's assuming that you are in a position to make the choice.

The argument to make is that you are declining the assignment for one of three reasons:

1. The assignment itself is unfeasible or unnecessary.
2. The assignment is feasible, but you are not the best choice for it, either because of lack of qualifications or lack of experience or because you are a resource better used elsewhere.
3. You prefer not to take on the project.

In making an argument that is likely to meet with resistance, it is almost always most desirable to address issues rather than people. Therefore, the first approach, demonstrating that a project is unworkable, is the soundest basis on which to decline an assignment. Make your case. Avoid criticizing anyone responsible for the proposed project, especially your boss. Focus on the project itself.

> "I told you I'd probably come back to you with some questions. I have carefully reviewed the project, and I have identified a number of problems we need to consider very carefully before we proceed."

Make the persuasive transition from *I* to *we*. Avoid setting up the opposition of *I* versus *you*. Be aware of the following:

- It is one thing to criticize a project if you have been specifically tasked to evaluate it. However, if your primary task was not evaluation but execution, assume your boss thinks the assignment is valid and desirable. She will be protective of it.

- You should present criticism as positively as possible. Avoid rejecting the project out of hand, but use instead such words as *questions, problems, sticking points*, and so on. These matters, you say, must be "resolved before proceeding." This approach warns the boss of difficulties even as it communicates your engagement with the project. Most important, it positions the boss such that she will see an opportunity to acknowledge the difficulties for herself—much more persuasive than your forcing the recognition on her.

The argument becomes more difficult if there is nothing inherently wrong with the assigned project, but you simply believe that it is not right for you. In this event:

- Your goal is to persuade your boss to see things your way in this *one* instance. That is, you don't want to provoke her to question your overall competence.

- The most positive—and therefore most desirable—argument to make is that you are a valuable resource far better used on a different project.

- If this argument is inappropriate in this case, suggest alternatives: "I have studied the assignment, and I have concluded that someone in customer service would be in a better position to take this one on. More than half the project involves service issues."

Never concentrate on your unsuitability. Instead, focus on the alternatives. Your boss is probably a lot less interested in who does the job than she is in getting the job done. Help her get it done. Nominate someone else for the assignment.

When you encounter resistance to your bid to decline the assignment, it is time to move with extreme caution. Your best course may well be to bite the bullet and take the work on. However, if you are truly convinced that you must decline the assignment, be prepared to meet resistance without creating animosity or doubts about your competence and commitment.

> **Boss:** I'm surprised. I just don't see how you can pass this up.
>
> **You:** I greatly appreciate the vote of confidence you've given me, but until we have reviewed the project one more time and resolved the issues I've outlined, I cannot be comfortable or confident that we will get what we need out of this assignment.

Embracing Criticism

Nobody likes being criticized, especially by their boss. Unwelcome or not, criticism should not be fended off or, even worse, ignored. The best strategy is to accept it as meaningful communication and as evidence of the investment your boss is making in you. She cares enough to want improvement. There are numerous ways to react to criticism:

• *Regard criticism as an opportunity.* Even undeserved criticism is useful, and valid criticism is downright invaluable. It is an education. The most persuasive response to criticism is to accept it with interest and gratitude.

• *Resist the impulse to feel hurt and/or to put up your defensive shields.* Listen and learn instead.

• *Remember that criticism is not absolute.* It is someone's perception. Objective measurements, including sales figures, schedules met, production quotas reached, and so on, may suggest top performance. Nevertheless, your boss may find something to criticize. Do the objective data invalidate the criticism? Not necessarily. In any case, your job is not just to perform; it is also to satisfy your boss. Explore, with yourself and with your boss, the reasons behind the criticism and the routes through which you can create greater satisfaction.

• *Do not fold.* Do not meekly agree with unjust or unfounded criticism. Do, however, learn from it. What can you do to create a positive perception?

• *Respond to the criticism in a way that strengthens your relationship with your boss.* Build on what you have.

Some criticism will come to you in regularly scheduled review sessions, but most times criticism will be provoked by some specific event. These are high-pressure situations in which your job is not to refute the criticism (unless it is indeed wholly unfounded) but to persuade your boss that you hear her, understand her, and will act accordingly. For example:

1

Boss: Three days to process these orders? Your problem is that you don't delegate responsibility effectively enough.

You: I agree. These orders should have gone out in forty-eight hours. I have some ideas for streamlining the process, which I'd like to discuss with you. And I am wide open to your suggestions.

2

Boss: I get the impression that you're spinning your wheels on the ABC account. This is very bad. Where's the progress?

You: I assure you that I am not "spinning my wheels," but we do have some problems. Let's talk just as soon as you can see me. I want to give you an interim progress report and get your input on some solutions I have in mind.

SELL THE FUTURE

The most persuasive argument you can make with any supervisor or boss always looks toward the future. While past performance can provide good evidence to build a persuasive argument, the past should never be the thrust of your communication. The future is promise, and promise is the very meat of persuasive discourse. If things are good now, argue that you will make them even better tomorrow. If they are not so good at the moment, persuade your boss that they will improve—tomorrow—because of you.

Inspire Your Staff

*Practical lessons in the rhetoric of
leadership and management.*

Your job title may say "manager," "supervisor," "chief," or even "CEO," but if you are depending on that official designation to give you all the power you need to get your staff to do what you want them to do, then you, they, and your entire organization are headed for trouble.

Leadership is not bestowed by a job description or a title. It is conferred, every day, by those you lead. Leadership requires a committed followership, and you must win that commitment every day through persuasive communication. As always, persuasive communication starts with the words you choose to use (and others you should avoid):

WORDS TO USE

advise	discuss	future	manage
analyze	encourage	help	mentor
assist	evaluate	inspire	navigate
consider	excite	invest	plan
counsel	expedite	lead	teach
determine	formulate	learn	

WORDS TO AVOID

blame	crisis	disaster	hopeless	mess
catastrophe	demand	fault	impossible	or else
command	destroyed	force	incompetent	stupid

AT STAKE

Shortly before midnight on April 14, 1912, a lookout aboard the White Star luxury liner *RMS Titanic*, at the time the biggest and safest ship in the world, warned of an iceberg ahead. The captain responded by ordering the sharpest possible turn. But the hard fact is that you cannot stop or turn a 66,000-ton ocean liner on a dime. And we all know what happened next. Within little more than two hours, *RMS Titanic* had sunk with the loss of some 1,500 lives.

Leading any enterprise is much like trying to steer a big ship. Holler as loudly as you want, threaten as menacingly as you will, issue your orders with the most crystalline of clarity, but the organization will not turn on a dime. The coordination, cooperation, judgment, and initiative of several or many are required to effect a change in course, and these things take time to activate and manage. The surest way to save valuable time, to create a flexible, agile, responsive organization, is to communicate with your staff in ways that motivate and inspire them.

YOUR GOAL

Effective leadership communication achieves three goals: being absolutely clear, absolutely truthful, and absolutely persuasive—which means that the communication is inspirational. In everything he says, the effective leader's purpose is to move subordinates to discover the best within themselves as they implement policies, decisions, and programs for the benefit of the organization. Everything that is communicated is intended to engender personal dedication, not simply by convincing the staff that they work for a beneficent manager and a great company, but by persuading them that their personal goals are necessarily in sync with those of the company, that their personal success depends on the success of the entire enterprise.

In the long run, truly effective members of an enterprise must identify their personal goals—their futures—with the objectives and purposes of the company. In the short term, however, on a daily basis, this identification is most effectively fostered by creating in your staff a sense of personal loyalty to you. To win this loyalty, you must argue for it—and argue persuasively. In all that you say and do, you should convey:

- Your accessibility
- Your willingness to hear as well as respond meaningfully to requests, wants, needs, grievances, and complaints
- Absolute clarity about what you want and expect
- Generous positive feedback and helpful constructive criticism
- Excitement and pleasure in your directives

YOUR APPEAL

An effective leader makes full use of all three classical modes of rhetorical appeal: the ethical appeal, the appeal to reason, and the appeal to emotion. To achieve *effective* inspiration—inspiration that will motivate a useful, correct, and efficient response from subordinates—no single mode can be allowed to overshadow another.

The ethical appeal is indispensable to a leader or manager. Those who report to you must trust and admire you as a person of high character, a person who deserves not just compliance but top-level, maximum-effort performance.

Good managers also appeal to reason. They make their directives clear. They provide a vivid picture of the reasoning behind the directives, the objectives of each, their desired effect, the level of performance expected, and so on. Good managers do not treat their staff members as passive receptors of orders, but as thinking human beings, competent, skilled, and talented, who deserve to understand why they are being asked to do what they are being asked to do. Clarity is essential in an appeal to reason, but it is not sufficient. Orders and directives should be presented in a way that shows how each instruction fits into the larger picture. People work more effectively and creatively when they understand the work in all of its dimensions.

Finally: the appeal to emotion, which is the mode all too many modern managers neglect. The idea of expressing and eliciting enthusiasm, of genuinely inspiring top performance, seems corny or embarrassing to many managers. But as the proverb says, "Where there is no vision, the people perish." The leader must make the objectives and goals of the enterprise clear, not just as intellectual realities but in their emotional dimensions as well.

LEADERSHIP LANGUAGE

The vocabulary of leadership is both verbal and nonverbal. Study the short list of words at the beginning of this chapter and you'll notice that the effective words are positive rather than negative. They relate to what is possible, not what is impossible. They relate, for the most part, to the present and the future, not the past. Notice, too, that they are enabling rather than coercive. They are words of collaboration and teamwork rather than coercion and strict instruction. Finally, take note that many of the words are about *management*—not *commanding* and not *obeying*. The verbal vocabulary of leadership is literally constructive. It builds.

How do you know that you are getting through? Simple. Ask the person to tell you:

"Did I answer your question?"

Or:

"Am I responding to your needs?"

These simple questions are a good start. Just be aware that subordinates do not always say to supervisors and managers what they really mean. It is therefore critical to effective leadership that you become attuned to the body language of others. Be on the lookout for signals of resistance. These body signals include:

- *Avoidance of eye contact*, which suggests that either you are not getting through or the other person has something he'd rather not tell you about
- *Hands to face or mouth*, which often suggests that the subordinate is not being fully honest with you
- *Arms folded across the chest or hands on hips*, both of which are classic signs of resistance, even defiance
- *Rubbing the back of the neck*, which signals bewilderment, frustration, and/or anxiety
- *Nervous leg movement*, which telegraphs an urge to run

If you detect any of these cues, bring the issue of communication out into the open. Do *not* allude to the body language in question: "You're covering your mouth. Is there something you're not telling me?" This will serve only to make the other person self-conscious, embarrassed, and almost certainly defensive. Instead, verbalize the content of the body-language cue you are receiving:

> "Tom, I get the feeling that I'm not being as clear as I should be. What would you like me to go over again?"

Accusation is rarely an effective strategy for leadership communication, so never accuse someone of failing to listen or failing to understand. If you sense noncomprehension, assume the burden rather than putting it on the subordinate. The question to ask is, "Am *I* making *myself* clear?"

DEFINE GOALS

One of the most persuasive classical means of argument is definition. No wonder. Just define the word *definition*: It is telling people what some thing or some idea is. It is delivering reality, furnishing truth. What could be more powerfully persuasive?

An effective leader defines reality for the organization, and no reality is more important than the future. A major leadership task is to define the future through the clear, consistent, and inspirational communication of objectives and goals.

Begin by understanding the difference between objectives and goals:

- *Goals* are long-term achievement targets.
- *Objectives* are the short-term steps necessary to attain the long-term targets.

The future of the enterprise becomes a lot less vague once you separate objectives from goals and define which objectives are necessary to achieve the goals you have also defined. In presenting goals and objectives to others, communicate the differences between them clearly, as follows:

1. Define the goal.
2. Provide a context for the goal. "Sell" its benefits to the organization and, therefore, to you and your staff. Sometimes information must be guarded, distrib-

uted on a need-to-know basis only. Yet it is also true that too many leaders reflexively hoard information, meting it out in an unnecessarily stingy or secretive fashion. It is almost always far more effective to share sufficient information to show how the goal you have set fits into the big picture and how the objectives you have defined move toward that goal.

3. Having defined the goal and its context, lay out the objectives necessary to achieve the goal.

4. Delegate the tasks necessary to achieve each objective.

5. Communicate *what* is to be done.

6. Communicate *when* each task is to be done—the deadline for each.

7. Communicate all relevant specifications, limits, budget constraints, and other requirements.

8. Try to attach some form of evaluation to each objective so you are able to measure the degree of success with which it has been attained. Nothing is more persuasive than quantifiable evaluation; for example, a particular objective may be defined as achieving a certain sales figure by a certain date.

DEFINE PROBLEMS

The definition of goals and objectives is nothing less than an argument for the future course of the enterprise. Most effective arguments include what the classical rhetoricians called the *refutatio*, the refutation of opposing points of view. In the leadership argument that defines goals and objectives, it is often necessary to "refute" problems that loom as obstacles to the achievement of those goals and objectives.

- Define the actual and potential problems associated with each goal and objective.

- Never minimize problems, but look for legitimate ways to persuade others that each problem also presents an opportunity.

- Formulate a response to each potential problem in advance.

If you discover that you cannot prevent the potential problems from overshadowing the proposed goals and objectives, or if you discover problems to which an effective response is unavailable, it is time to reevaluate the goals and objectives you propose to present. It is folly to argue for an untenable or unpromising future.

SHARE FACTS AND SHAPE REALITY

In any organization, "reality" is not nearly as objective as common sense might suggest. It is largely compounded of perception—often many, many individual perceptions. Leaders frequently find themselves in the position of presenting an argument to persuade others to buy into *their* version of reality. This, in fact, is a key leadership task: to share facts and shape reality. Fail to do this and the organization will tend to splinter into a collection of self-centered, perhaps idiosyncratic points of view. Equally bad, in the absence of a clear picture from leadership, the organization will become ripe for rumor. In this way, a randomly generated, typically inaccurate, and often highly destructive perception of reality may emerge as dominant throughout the organization.

The most effective way to counter fragmented, distorted, and inaccurate perceptions within an organization is to have a strong leader paint a persuasive picture of reality. It doesn't require magic or even extraordinary charisma. It does call for the following:

- Clear goals and objectives that are set out clearly within an unambiguous context.
- Clear instructions and directives, with verbal directions reinforced with brief memos or e-mails.
- The use of plain English.
- Quantification of instructions. Wherever possible, directives should be accompanied by specifications as to when, where, how much time, and so on.
- An explicit invitation to ask questions. Never assume that your subordinates understand that they may seek clarification. Invite them to ask questions.

Next to clarity comes enthusiasm as another indispensable component when presenting a persuasive picture of reality. Enthusiasm is not a robust commodity. It is fragile, easily stifled by insensitive supervision, and readily dissipated by cynicism. To infuse people with enthusiasm, do the following:

- Talk frequently with your staff.
- Suggest fresh approaches to stubborn problems.
- Express understanding and empathy in difficult situations.
- Continually consult and coach those who report to you.

Some of the most persuasive arguments are based on the recognition of cause and effect, or action and consequence; therefore, make liberal use of positive reinforcement. Our world is full of rewards, awards, and ceremonies of public recognition. Regularly convene "reinforcement" meetings. These get-togethers should be positive and upbeat. Their objective is to reward, refresh, and, if necessary, refocus people. Make these meetings enjoyable events by serving refreshments or promoting conversation and small talk. But when it comes to the reward and reinforcement, be specific.

Of course, you should not wait for a reinforcement meeting to praise achievement. Motivate your staff with continual feedback designed to demonstrate your confidence in their skills and abilities. Be as specific as possible, and deliver your remarks with enthusiasm, sincerity, and gratitude.

ENABLE ACTION

All effective arguments conclude not merely by directing, prompting, or encouraging a desired action, but by actually enabling action. The most familiar example is the successful sales pitch. This argument begins by commanding the prospect's attention, then develops interest, builds desire, and ends by enabling the prospect to act, to make the purchase:

"We take all major credit cards."

Or:

"We can handle the financing. It's easy."

Similarly, an argument to promote a set of goals and objectives must end by enabling the actions the leader calls for. If you have a choice about the person to whom you delegate a particular assignment, the first step in this enablement may be matching the right person to the appropriate task.

While choosing the right person for the right job saves you worry and time, it does not set you free from the responsibility of monitoring the progress of a project, and although continual communication may be required, you should not micromanage. The most effective way to monitor action is to set a schedule of regular meetings, spaced as far apart as possible while still offering the ability to address any problems that come up. Scheduling such meetings in advance is a persuasive argument for confidence in success, and it suggests that you are taking a well-planned, proactive approach. It is not a good idea to call ad hoc or emergency meetings. Any unscheduled meetings imply that you are worried about, or dissatisfied with, progress.

Once you have chosen your person or team for a particular task, empower them by demonstrating your confidence. General George S. Patton remarked: "Once, in Sicily, I told a general, who was somewhat reluctant to attack, that I had perfect confidence in him, and that, to show it, I was going home." The most persuasive argument proving Patton's confidence was made not with his voice, but with his feet. He went home.

For many managers, the most challenging aspect of leadership is delegating, and the most challenging aspect of delegating is doing so in a way that empowers the subordinate. Here are some steps to enable empowerment:

• *Don't use the sink-or-swim approach.* Ease your staff members into progressively greater levels of responsibility.

• *Give subordinates leeway to do at least some aspects of their assigned task their way.* Encourage (but monitor) creativity.

• *Mentor your subordinates.* Begin by delegating repetitive and routine tasks, if possible, then move on to more challenging jobs.

- *Hold yourself available to help—just don't offer help too quickly.* It is easy to tell people what to do. If they ask you to dictate a specific course of action, don't be in too great a hurry to respond with *the* answer. Instead, review with them the various possibilities but leave as much of the actual decision making to those you delegated the job to. This form of empowerment will help to train people who'll make your professional life easier and will benefit the enterprise.

- *Don't rush to bail out someone who is floundering.* If feasible, consider adding another member to the team. Assign that person to help.

- *Resist pressure to do your subordinates' work for them.* Point out that you have other high-priority work to handle. Do not scold. Instead, assure staff members that you have full confidence in them.

APPROACHES FOR MANY SITUATIONS

The following sections have suggestions for effectively communicating with subordinates across a wide range of common workday situations. While the situations differ, the core of communication is always the same. Everything you say to those you lead or manage is an argument, an effort to persuade them not merely to comply, but to perform at a high level for the benefit of the enterprise.

COMMUNICATING STANDARDS AND EXPECTATIONS

Rule number one: Before you make an argument promoting standards and expectations, make certain that you *have* standards and expectations and that they are capable of being expressed clearly and unambiguously. Make this discussion an argument from authority. That "authority" should be a set of written guidelines, standards, and expectations that you have for your enterprise or department. Everyone who reports to you should have a copy of this document. New hires should be handed it, asked to read it, then invited to discuss it.

Using the document as your authority, talk to your staff about the importance of adhering to standards and meeting expectations. For instance:

- Your thesis is that the stated standards and expectations benefit customers, the company, and each member of the company.

- To support this thesis, do a point-by-point review of each standard and expectation. The review should clearly demonstrate how each standard and expectation enhances the organization's performance.

This approach to presenting standards and expectations is, in effect, self-correcting. If you find it difficult or impossible to provide the support for every standard and expectation listed, you need to reevaluate the standards or expectations that are giving you trouble. If you cannot justify them in the context of the enterprise as a whole, if it is not clear to *you* how a given standard or expectation benefits the organization, then it is time to rethink your document and revise your authority. Perhaps that particular standard or expectation is no longer useful. Perhaps it needs to be modified or rejected entirely.

In presenting standards and expectations, never allow any point to appear arbitrary. Consider this situation:

> **Staffer:** I think that having to confirm customers' phone numbers and address information by repeating the numbers over the phone is really time-consuming. I don't ever get this information wrong. I could be a lot more productive—make more calls each day—if I weren't required to go over *every* number *every* time. It's just a waste of time.
>
> **Manager:** It's company policy.

That phrase—*It's company policy*—is the knee-jerk response to almost any employee question concerning stated standards and expectations. In terms of classical rhetoric, it is the worst kind of tautology or begging the question.

> **Q:** Why is X true?
>
> **A:** Because X is true.

Such an argument is both invalid and false. It proves nothing, it explains nothing, it justifies nothing, and it answers nothing. In short, it creates frustration. And no good can come from creating frustration in the people who report to you. A better way to handle the same situation is as follows:

> **Manager:** You raise an interesting question. It is true that confirming this information is both tedious and time-consuming. However, it accomplishes three things. First: It *does* reduce the frequency of errors. I'm sure *you* make very few mistakes. I'm not nearly so sure that your *customer* doesn't make mistakes. After all, I know you. I do not know him. Reviewing the information with the customer gives him an opportunity to correct his errors. Avoiding a mistake requires an investment of time and attention, but this investment is much less than what is required to correct a mistake—and mistakes are never fully corrected. They leave a negative impression with the customer.
>
> But there is also a second reason for reviewing the information with the customer: It demonstrates your interest in serving him. It demonstrates your willingness to spend a little extra time with him—rather than just taking his order and running on to the next call. Finally, this procedure also requires the customer to invest a little extra time in *us*, and that suggests to him that the business he does with us is valuable—to *him*.
>
> Does this policy make more sense to you now?

Standards and expectations allow your organization to run efficiently and to achieve excellence. They also become a shared set of values, a source of authority that helps to forge a creative sense of community within the enterprise.

CORRECTING ERRORS AND IMPROVING PERFORMANCE

Since childhood, each of us has heard a lot of talk about "constructive criticism." Few of us, however, give the phrase much thought beyond a definition that goes something like this: "Constructive criticism is criticism that doesn't hurt too badly." Not very illuminating.

Truly constructive criticism is an argument with three theses:

1. Task X is not being done satisfactorily.
2. There is a way to improve task X.
3. *I* am confident that *you* (the object of the constructive criticism) are capable of achieving the necessary improvement.

Contrast this definition with the theses implicit in what we might call "destructive criticism":

1. You (the object of the destructive criticism) are doing task X poorly.
2. You had better do it better. (Or else.)
3. *I* have little or no confidence in your ability to achieve the necessary improvement.

The argument in constructive criticism addresses the realm of possibility. In destructive criticism, the argument deals with the impossible or, at the very least, the improbable: Task X is bad. You must fix it. You are (probably) incapable of fixing it. The action that the first argument can prompt is positive. There is no guarantee of improvement, but there is the potential for it. The second argument leads only to panic, disgust, despair, and frustration. If it prompts an action, it may be for the person being criticized to lash out (express frustration), give up, or quit. Here are steps for structuring your critical argument to ward off (refute) anxiety and defensiveness:

• *Communicate in the manner of a mentor or a coach, not a taskmaster.* Your employees are valuable assets, whom you can make more valuable the more you invest in their training, mentoring, and coaching.

• *Communicate your commitment to developing employees as members of the enterprise.* Let them know that *their* success is key to the success of the entire organization.

• *Don't rush to criticize.* Are you sure that you are not using criticism merely to vent your frustration, anger, or irritation? Also, limit criticism to what can realistically be improved. Making an argument about the impossible may, in some academic and philosophical contexts, provoke interesting conversation, but it is pointless in any business endeavor. It accomplishes no good—and may do significant harm—to criticize a subordinate for something over which she has little or no control. Think first. If your remarks are not likely to improve the situation, don't make them.

• *Ask permission to criticize.* You might simply say, "We have a problem with so-and-so, which I would like to discuss with you. Is now a good time?" Asking permission in this way enhances the effectiveness of your remarks because it engages the other person as an equal, as someone of value and deserving of respect.

• *Never deliver criticism, no matter how constructive, in front of others.* Have this discussion in private.

• *Time this argument to leverage its persuasive potential.* That means avoiding criticism first thing in the morning or last thing before quitting time.

• *Be specific.* Blanket criticism, or criticism that's generalized, is confusing and usually makes a less-than-satisfactory situation worse. Do your homework so that you can cite specific issues and incidents—things that *can* be fixed or improved. It is best, as far as possible, to quantify your criticism objectively: "Turnaround time has been running long. I'd like to shoot for a 10 percent improvement. Let's talk."

• *Keep your eye on the prize.* Maintain your perspective. You are both on the same team. You have common goals. Be friendly.

• *Address issues, not people.* Issues can be fixed. People cannot.

• *Stir in as much praise as possible with the criticism.* For instance: "Hal, I love the way you handle customers, but I'd like to share some observations about how you tend to close your sales. May I talk to you about this for a few minutes?"

• *Address one issue at a time.* Do not bombard your staffers with a cluster of faults and problems.

Here is an example of constructive criticism:

You: John, I was listening to the way you handled that customer's complaint. You worked with him quickly, efficiently, and politely. But, if you'll let me, I'd like to share a few observations that might help you deal with such complaints even more effectively.

John: Well . . . yes. . . . What did I do wrong?

You: No, it's not a question of doing anything wrong. It's a matter of improving what is already good. Look, you came up with a course of action very quickly. It's good to be decisive. But in this case there were several possible options available, so it would be even more effective to ask the customer what he wants. Empowering the customer makes it possible to convert his complaint into satisfaction. Do you see what I mean?

John: I'm not absolutely sure. . . . I'm not sure what I did wrong.

You: You did nothing wrong. I just want you to be aware of an even more effective approach in this case. Whenever you have choices to offer—and that's not always the case—let the customer have more power. Don't be too quick to propose a single solution.

John: I didn't want to waste too much time.

You: That's a valid point. And the approach I suggest *will* take more time. But it isn't "wasted" time. It's time invested in a customer who has a complaint. It's time invested in converting that complaint into a positive impression, into satisfaction.

This is constructive criticism. It is delivered in a positive, approving context. It is clear and detailed. It deals with what is possible, what can profitably be improved. It is mentoring. The subordinate and the enterprise emerge from it all the better.

Reprimands

Sometimes criticism must be stronger. This more urgent kind of criticism is the reprimand. *Reprimand* is not a synonym for *punishment*. Rather:

- A reprimand is a vehicle for constructive criticism intended to correct or improve a particular situation that urgently requires correction or improvement.
- A reprimand should not scold or isolate the person. It should aid in the development of the subordinate.
- Generally, if an action or behavior is serious enough to merit a reprimand, the reprimand should be delivered verbally, but also memorialized for the record in written form. Verbal reprimands are more immediately effective than written reprimands, but the written follow-up is necessary to note any action that is to be taken, including corrective action promised by the employee. The memo should also record any consequences of failure to remedy the situation. The written reprimand becomes the "authority" from which you may make future "arguments," if the subordinate demonstrates inadequate improvement.

The tone of a reprimand should be as positive and constructive as the situation permits. Under no circumstances should you yield to the temptation to make an ad hominem argument. It serves no constructive purpose to attack personality. Address issues, not people. Make no threats, but do advise the subordinate of potential consequences if the problem is repeated or isn't remedied. Here is a recommended process for delivering a reprimand:

1. Begin the reprimand by acknowledging the generally positive nature of the employee's performance—if this is at all possible.
2. Clearly define and describe the nature of the problem or infraction.
3. Do not scold, but clearly and calmly explain the effect of the error, bad behavior, or inadequate performance on the organization.
4. Suggest remedies and appropriate steps to resolve the situation.
5. Always solicit comments and suggestions.
6. Clearly explain the potential consequences if the infraction is repeated or the situation goes unresolved. Do not minimize the consequences, but never make idle threats.

7. Enthusiastically and sincerely assure the subordinate of your willingness and desire to work with him to correct the problem or improve the situation.

Reprimands are urgent arguments for urgent improvement. They must be delivered sensitively but forcefully. Here are four situations—lateness, absenteeism, bad behavior, and uncooperativeness—that call for improvement through persuasive argument.

1. *Late to Arrive and Early to Leave.* Adhering to prescribed business hours is part of the covenant each member of an organization makes with the enterprise. Because time is a quantity, business hours can be stated with complete objectivity; therefore, it is an easy matter to establish a basis of authority for any argument about timely arrival and departure.

- Be certain that everyone understands the prescribed arrival and departure times. They should be clearly and unambiguously established.
- Have a written policy concerning legitimate reasons for arriving late or leaving early.
- Have a written policy requiring that late arrival or early departure be cleared with a designated supervisor.
- Provide a reason for your on-time policies. It can be a simple statement: "It is essential to productive operation that people be where they are expected to be when they are expected to be there. We depend on each other."

2. *Frequent Absenteeism.* Again, establish the basis for an argument from authority:

- Have in place a written policy on sick days and personal days.
- Make the argument that everyone is essential to the team. This means that attendance is critical.

Let's say you have a situation where Sarah is often absent. It is time to talk with her:

You: Sarah, you have been out X days out of the last thirty. We've missed you. I mean it. We've missed you, and we needed you. You are essential to this team.

Sarah: I was sick a lot.

You: If you are having a problem with a chronic illness, we need to discuss it. I need to be able to depend on you. What's this next month going to be like?

Conclude the argument by focusing on the future. The point of a reprimand is not to "avenge" the past, but to create improvement for the future.

3. *Bad Behavior.* The great danger in reprimanding a subordinate for bad behavior is engaging in such behavior yourself—without, of course, intending to. This is an occasion to avoid ad hominem argument. Focus the talk on a particular incident. Address facts, not personalities. For example, Joe is often rude to customers:

You: Joe, I had a disturbing phone call yesterday from one of your customers, who was angry enough to take her business elsewhere. She described an exchange with you that I can only characterize as rude, including borderline abusive language.

After detailing the customer's story, ask for Joe's version: "Joe, is this accurate? Is this true?" Listen carefully. Assuming the customer's complaint is accurate, make your argument for a better future:

You: Joe, you understand that we are a service organization. A part of what we sell is the feeling that each customer is special to us. *That* is customer service, and that gives us our competitive edge. If we lose that edge, all of us are in trouble. Service—this feeling—is as important as anything else we sell.

Now, I believe we have lost a customer. We cannot afford to lose another. Can you deliver service?

Joe: Yes. I promise.

You: I'm relieved to hear that. I would like you to call the customer to apologize. I do not expect you to win her back, but I do not want bad feelings about us circulating in the marketplace. Can you do this?

Joe: Yes, I can.

You: Great. I am leaving the content of the message entirely to you. Let me know how she responds.

There is no punishment here, no scolding. The argument is for corrective action in the realm of what is possible. No miracles are expected or called for; however, the subordinate is both empowered and held accountable. He is given the choice of creating his own message, but is asked to report on the results.

4. *Lack of Cooperation.* Lack of cooperation or outright insubordination may be the product of many things, including emotional instability, personal crisis, dissatisfaction with the job, or a failure to understand the nature of a job or assignment. Whatever the cause, the problem signals a disconnect between the individual and the enterprise, and it calls for an immediate discussion. The thesis of your argument is this: *The employee has broken his contract with you and the organization.* Which leads to the question: Can the break be fixed?

You: Brian, when you started working here, you agreed to take direction from me. Yesterday, I assigned you X. This morning, I received your e-mail saying that X is not part of your job description.

Actually, Brian, X *is* part of your job description. But that is not as important to me as the fact that we need to be able to rely on each other.

Brian: It's just that, look, I'm overqualified to do X. You can get the new guy to do it. I'd rather be doing Y.

You: Brian, I am willing to talk to you about expanding your responsibilities. But, in my judgment, you are the most qualified person to do X, and I cannot afford to accept your sudden decision not to do it. I rely on you. The department relies on you. Now, where do you want to take it from here?

Habitual Mistakes, Substandard Performance

Everyone makes a mistake now and then. But what do you say when error becomes a pattern and substandard performance the norm? As in building the case for any important argument, you do the following:

1. Begin by gathering the facts. Resist the emotional temptation to look for a person to blame. Instead, look for sources of the error.
2. Analyze the facts.
3. Review procedures and processes as necessary.
4. Do not criticize those involved in the pattern of errors without also furnishing direction and alternatives.
5. Create a solution, the more collaborative the better.

A meeting addressing repeated errors can all too readily degenerate into a blame-fest. Keep the focus on problems, not people. For example:

You: Ann, have you finished studying the error reports generated by customer service for your accounts?

Ann: Yes.

Put the facts front and center. Argue from the facts (in this case, the error reports generated by customer service). Avoid subjective assessments.

You: I am not terribly concerned with this or that mistake. It is the *pattern* of errors that is the problem. Why are we making so many mistakes so consistently? What is going wrong with our system? Ann, since the errors fall into your area, you are going to have to be most responsible for creating improvement.

Be careful not to isolate or alienate the subordinate from the group. Be as inclusive in your analysis as possible. Argue for individual responsibility, but in a way that will be most likely to have a positive effect on the future.

You: I want to give you my directions, and then I'll ask for your comments and suggestions.
Review your processing procedures to ensure that your routine meets the requirements of company policy. Once you complete this review, report to me no later than the twelfth. Your report needs to describe what has been going wrong and why it has been going wrong. Finally, I want your suggestions for reducing the rate of error.
I truly believe that once you identify the errors, you will be able to improve overall performance.
Now, do you have any questions and comments?

Ann: Well, in my defense, I just don't believe the situation is as bad as you think it is.

You: What I think is not at issue. The error reports reveal a pattern. But, it is true, we will have a much more accurate idea of the scope of the problem after you have prepared your report.

Don't be led astray by the red herring that the subordinate offers. There is nothing subjective in the foundation of your argument. Keep the reality of the situation centered on the facts.

RESPONDING TO COMPLAINTS AND CRITICISM

How you respond to complaints and criticism from subordinates makes a powerful argument about your leadership style. Beyond this, complaints and criticism are a valuable means of monitoring the state of your organization and the level of its performance.

Nothing is more persuasive than your willingness to listen to what others tell you. When you listen to complaints and criticism, be certain that you really do listen (watch your body language!) and that you withhold all judgmental or defensive responses. It is very destructive to invite criticism, to express your openness to criticism, then bite the critic's head off. If you ask for frank feedback, make certain that you are prepared to hear it—and to profit by it. Never invite criticism or complaint if you have no intention of making any changes. Naturally, you are not obligated to act on every item of criticism or complaint. Each circumstance needs to be assessed. But you do have to be willing to change what should be changed, provided that change is possible.

People complain about a lot of things. When they work together in groups, they complain about even more.

Excessive Workload

Work overload is a common employee complaint, but just because it is common doesn't mean that you should not take it seriously. Before responding, consider two possibilities:

1. Your expectations of the subordinate are excessive or unrealistic.
2. The workload in question would be hard for anyone. Maybe additional personnel are required. Move beyond subjective feelings about the situation and get the facts, then assess the facts.

You need to appear receptive and nonthreatening in hearing out the employee, and you should always express appreciation for the comments.

Subordinate: The volume of work in this department is getting beyond us. People are starting to burn out.

You: I agree—the workload is heavy, and I now have some idea of how you feel about it. Thanks. What we need to do next is get some hard data. Let me gather production and time figures for the past two quarters. Let's sit down with the figures and assess what we need. Maybe the answer is more personnel. Maybe something else.

Working Environment

Many managers automatically react to complaints about working conditions by taking the attitude that the workforce is spoiled. It is more productive to respond to complaints rather than simply react to them. Of course, it may or may not be possible to remedy the issues, but it is probably of less immediate importance to solve the problems than it is to listen to and respond to the complaints. This is an opportunity to argue for productive community, for teamwork. In this kind of situation, you may want to say:

> "I am glad that you and the others have taken the time and effort to report to me on the problems with the break room. I wish I could just tell you that we'll remodel the facility, but I cannot. Our funding for the physical plant will not begin to cover all of the improvements some of us would like. Nevertheless, I have a suggestion for making some significant improvements. The department staff should choose a representative to meet with me in order to home in on which items on your 'want list' are most urgent. Once we have a core of must-do improvements, let's price them out and, based on available funds, decide what changes can be made now and which ones can be put off—either for a certain amount of time or indefinitely."

Coworker Disputes

These are the situations that give the word *argument* its bad rep. Disputes between coworkers are rarely arguments in the classical sense of structured debates based on a set of facts. More typically, they are emotionally motivated eruptions about which there may be little absolute right or wrong.

There are risks to intervening in disputes among subordinates. One party may believe that you are showing favoritism to the other, or both parties to the dispute may be dissatisfied; some people may feel intruded upon; some may feel that their issues have not been resolved but simply dismissed by your arbitrary authority. In all of these cases, resentment may be turned against you. The risks are real, but leadership requires taking risks, and the consequences of failing to intervene can be far more devastating.

The most persuasive approach in situations of coworker disputes is to avoid getting entangled in emotion. Get everyone talking—in your presence:

1.   Meet with the parties and acknowledge the existence of a problem.

2.   Listen to both sides without comment, while also watching for nonverbal body-language cues. If you need facts clarified, interrupt as necessary. Do not, however, interrupt with opinions or judgments.

3.   After hearing all or both sides, offer no argument or proposal. Instead, ask those involved what *they* would like to see happen. The object is to formulate a resolution that will satisfy the disputants—not a third-party solution that may fail to satisfy any of them.

4.   Ask for time. Withhold any judgment or proposed solution. Say that you need time to evaluate the problem. Set another meeting time. However, before ending the present meeting, state the necessity of working cooperatively together—for the good of everyone. Do not request cooperation. Make cooperation an expectation: "In the meantime, I expect you to cooperate with one another and work together."

5.   Take the time to study the problem.

6.   Call another meeting and announce your decision, which may be in the form of suggestions or directives, as appropriate.

SOME POSITIVE WAYS TO SAY NO

Managers say yes, and managers say no. That is their responsibility as well as their prerogative. No argument is absolutely required—but, as always, a persuasive argument can be valuable. The object is not to persuade others that the decision to say no is correct, but to persuade those to whom you say no that they have not been rejected—even if their project or idea has—and that they still hold their stake in the enterprise.

The danger in saying no is that the decision will be received as an ad hominem argument. The way to avoid this danger is to ensure that your "no" is directed at a proposal, an idea, an issue—and not at the person or people associated with that proposal, idea, or issue. You must clearly separate people from issues. A manager has to say no, but saying no to people is a sure way to undermine and even dismantle an organization.

The general rules for saying no are these:

*   *Say no clearly, unmistakably, but gently.* Resist the temptation to translate emphasis into volume.

*   *Provide a reason for saying no.* You don't have to justify your decision, but you are obliged to provide a context for the negative response.

*   *If possible and appropriate, offer alternatives.* It is always best to shift the emphasis from negative to positive, from impossible to possible, from what you cannot do to what you can do.

- *In general, do not apologize for saying no.* Apologizing suggests that you've made something less than a good decision. Do not confuse providing a reason for your decision with apologizing for it.

Even if you cannot give a subordinate the answer he wants, you can give him a full and thoughtful hearing.

1. Express appreciation for the request, which comes from a valued member of the organization.
2. If there is any part of the request that you *can* satisfy to some extent, begin with that.
3. State what you cannot do.
4. Put the subordinate's request and your response in context. Develop your response in the context of department or company needs and goals, which benefit everyone.
5. If possible and appropriate, suggest alternatives.
6. If possible and appropriate, outline future conditions under which the request might be met. Be as specific as circumstances allow.
7. Thank the subordinate (again) for his request or idea: "What you have to say is always valuable."

Request for a Raise

Managers are often put in the position of responding to requests for salary increases. Saying no presents a sensitive situation, since salary is (at least in some degree) a quantitative measure of an employee's value in the organization. How do you say no yet persuade the employee that he is valuable to the organization?

As usual, it is always best to provide a context of authority for the arguments you make. In the case of salaries, the organization should have clear guidelines and policies governing compensation, including annual or semiannual performance reviews. These reviews provide an absolute context for both the salary request and the response, preventing both from becoming merely subjective. Without the capacity to appeal to authority, arguments more readily degenerate into fruitless disputes with plenty of hard feelings and little genuine resolution.

When you do have to say no, do so straightforwardly and without emotion. Avoid judgmental content or tone: "You don't deserve a raise!" Avoid judgmental rhetorical questions: "Do you really think you deserve a raise?" Avoid apology: "Oh, gosh, I really wish I could. . . ." Instead, give a straightforward reason for your response and, if possible, offer rational, realistic, and clearly defined hope for the future: "I am certainly willing to revisit this issue at your next review in six months." If the person seeking a raise has a presentation to make, listen to it. If he has a rebuttal to your no, listen to it. However, do not *ask* for a discussion or justification unless there is a real chance that you will change your decision. Being

told no may be disappointing, but being made to jump through hoops for no productive purpose will (quite rightly) create resentment.

Consider this situation: After five months in your department, Ed wants a raise.
He does a good job, and you want to retain him in your department, but you cannot
raise a salary after only five months. You say:

> "Ed, I am very pleased by what you have been doing for us these past five
> months. In that short time, you've made an impact. However, I cannot even
> consider a raise before one full year of employment. That's not only policy,
> it's good policy, because it is essential to our being able to control costs. If
> we cannot control costs, we have no company—which means no money for
> anyone.
>
> "Okay. That's what I *can't* do. What I *can* do is tell you that I will be very
> receptive to this discussion in June, which is when your first salary review is
> scheduled. Let's pencil in an appointment right now."

That was relatively painless—an easy argument to make. More difficult is the
situation in which you must say no to a request for a raise from a subordinate
whose performance does not merit one. Regard this argument as an opportunity to
help the staff member improve performance and develop professionally. Propose
the performance conditions that will make a raise possible in the future:

> "I have to tell you, Jill, that your current level of performance does not merit
> a salary increase. I need to see improvement in three areas before I will con-
> sider a raise."

No punches are pulled, but no punches are directed at the person making the
request, either. The target is *performance*, not Jill. The no is unambiguous, but it
is not presented as an enduring obstacle. Rather, it is modified with the word *current*, which implies the possibility of improvement and, with it, the possibility of a
raise later. The argument must be completed with an enumeration and discussion
of the three areas that require improvement. This is an opportunity to state or
restate performance goals. Make your requirements clear. Conclude positively so
that you strengthen the mutual commitment between you and the subordinate:

> "Jill, I believe that, together, we can bring your performance to a level that
> will merit an increase and that will improve the productivity of the entire
> department."

Perks, Privileges, and Miscellaneous Ideas

Take every request seriously, even those that seem manifestly outlandish or unwarranted. Rejecting anything out of hand comes across as an attack on the person
who makes the request. For example, Ben wants to change his working hours. The
last thing you want to do is try to coordinate a major shift in the department. But

you also recognize the request as an opportunity to demonstrate your willingness to take all requests seriously and in good faith. After all, the people who report to you may be disappointed if they don't get what they ask for, but they will be downright angry if they feel that their requests are automatically dismissed by a boss who won't give them the time of day. You say:

> "Ben, the department needs you to be available as you are currently scheduled, and I'm in no position to shake up the entire department. That said, maybe *you* can do something about your situation. If you can work out a swap with anyone else in the department, come back to me, and we'll shift you guys around."

Here's another example:

Jane: If I were moved out of a cubicle and into a real office, I could be much more productive.

You: It is not possible or appropriate for me to assign you a private office at this time. First, we don't have one available, and I don't have the funding to cover major remodeling. Second, your job does not require client conferences or other private meetings. Third, other staffers with positions equivalent to yours do not have private offices.

WHAT TO SAY WHEN YOU ARE WRONG

You will make mistakes. Some mistakes do substantial damage, which may or may not be capable of repair, but you can be certain of making a bad situation worse if you refuse to own up to the mistake, admit error, and work toward a solution.

The fix for any error begins with an argument based on the proposition that you are still in control and worthy of being in control. Present an orderly response to the error that is aimed at containing and reversing the damage:

1. Do not panic or rush to confess culpability. Do not wallow in remorse.
2. Assess the error, problem, and damage.
3. Explain the problem or error.
4. Offer a brief apology.
5. Meet with those affected by the problem or error. What do they need?
6. Empathize.
7. Propose remedies.
8. Present arguments to support the proposed remedies.

Here is an example of a dumb—and quite typical—mistake:

> A member of your staff submits a documented request for travel-expense reimbursement. Three weeks later, she sends an e-mail to you asking about the

status of the reimbursement. You then discover that not only has the accounting department not received the endorsed request from you, you have lost it, documentation and all.

You: Claire, I've tracked down the reason for the delay in getting you your reimbursement.

Claire: Wonderful!

You: Not really. The reason is me. I lost your request and documentation. I cannot account for them. Please tell me that you have copies.

Claire: The report is on my computer, but I didn't photocopy the documentation.

You: Well, let me handle this for you. E-mail a copy of the report to me. I can reimburse you out of petty cash right away, and I'll send the report to accounting with an explanation that I have misplaced the documentation and have initiated a search. That at least will make it an issue between me and accounting—not between you and me. I'm sorry your money has been delayed.

The most persuasive argument you can make following a mistake is to commence with a fix that requires little or no effort from anyone except yourself. An apology is also required, but it is no substitute for a fix. Don't dwell on the apology. Move quickly to the fix. Make certain the proposed solution is acceptable to the injured party.

THE CARROTS AND THE STICKS

Motivation is largely an argument based on actions and consequences. To make a persuasive argument for a particular course of action, you often need to paint a picture of the anticipated consequence of the action. Along the way, as the individuals in your organization progress toward some goal—a desired consequence—it is helpful to offer additional arguments in order maintain a high level of performance. For this, no argument is more powerful than praise. Its presence is keenly felt, and so is its absence.

Praise costs you nothing, but you must not make it cheap. Avoid dispensing empty, meaningless praise. Always attach praise to something specific: an idea, an action, a good result. More specifically:

• *Always look for things to praise.* Although you must avoid empty praise, you should praise everything that deserves it. Make an effort to identify praiseworthy events, acts, words, and ideas. Then praise those responsible for them.

• *Praise whatever you want more of.* Praise isn't just a polite thank-you, it is positive reinforcement. If you want your staffers to be more attentive to customers, praise the very next example of good customer service you see.

• *Keep praise timely.* Behavioral psychologists, who study the effect of reinforcement techniques on learning and on shaping behavior, have long recognized the importance of associating positive reinforcement as closely as possible with a desired behavior. The time that passes between the behavior and the reinforcement reduces the effectiveness of the reinforcement. Don't put off praise.

• *If possible, praise in public.* Although it is a fine thing to take a subordinate aside and praise her privately, the value of the praise is greatly amplified when you deliver the praise in front of the person's colleagues. Hence the Academy Awards.

• *Be specific.* Tie praise to specific accomplishments, actions, or events: "You did a sensational job with X." If possible, quantify the achievement: "Revenue from X will bring our fourth-quarter figures up by 3 percent or 4 percent. Outstanding!"

• *Praise for the future.* Praise necessarily relates to the past: what *has been* accomplished. Interject a note of the future: "I can't wait to see what you'll do next year."

Praise is the carrot. But sometimes you also need a stick. We have already discussed constructive criticism for particular problems, but it is also possible to take criticism to another level, beyond correcting a particular problem. We're talking about more generally and permanently nurturing the kind of creative thinking that maximizes performance and minimizes the need for criticism.

First, do what you can to create an environment where it will not be necessary to offer criticism: Make objectives and goals clear from the beginning. Set unambiguous performance criteria. When you believe that improvement is needed, set realistic improvement objectives. Do not waste a persuasive argument on the impossible. Setting objectives you know are far beyond the reach of a particular staffer will not inspire that person to stretch and to achieve; it will create disappointment, frustration, and bad feelings all around. To persuade the people on your staff using this approach:

• *Do not make an empty argument.* If you want your criticism to create improvement, resolve not to abandon the people you criticize. Coach and mentor them. Monitor the achievement of objectives and deliver praise for each achievement. Offering criticism creates a contract between you and your staff members. Both parties are now obligated; your employees will be obligated to meet new performance objectives, and you must not turn your back on them.

• *Don't just talk. Listen.* Never censor what the employee says. Do not interrupt. Be patient.

• *Don't just make declarations. Ask questions.* The most effective questions do not call for a yes or no, but elicit open-ended responses: "What would you do to make communication with customer service more effective?"

• *Offer direction—and ask for feedback:* "Do you think this suggestion will help the situation?"

• *Provide positive emotional support.* "If you can achieve X now, Y and Z will present no problem for you later."

CHAPTER 12

Motivate Your Colleagues

Learn the language of team building and teamwork, and beware the subtle, high-stakes rhetoric of office politics.

Your enterprise can be an effective team, a disorganized rabble, or a snake pit of intrigue and backstabbing with every man for himself. You choose. All three scenarios are built in large part from words, but most business people, made aware of the choices, will want to argue for teamwork.

WORDS TO USE

As teams are built person by person, team-building language is put together word by word. The following are some positive, team-building words you should use.

adapt	contribute	merge	revise
admire	cooperate	modify	study
advise	differ	objective	suggest
agree	disagree	opinion	talk
collaborate	facts	our	team
combine	feasible	respect	together
confer	goal	results	us
consult	input	rethink	we

WORDS TO AVOID

If the right words can help to build teams, the wrong ones tend to tear them apart by wrecking the rapport that should bond collaborators together. Avoid words that define one ego against another.

absurd	insane	stubborn
bad	misguided	stupid
crazy	refuse	unworkable

impossible   ridiculous   wrong
incompetent   selfish

AT STAKE

Working effectively with colleagues is more than just getting along with people—although that helps. Persuasive communication with colleagues also requires creating a working atmosphere in which everyone feels that something has been gained. At stake in any argument for teamwork, for effective workplace collaboration, is the proposition that everyone needs to feel like a winner and, indeed, everyone needs to win. The argument for teamwork must therefore refute the notion that communicating with colleagues is a game of dirty office politics, a zero-sum game where someone must lose if someone else wins. To defeat a colleague is to defeat yourself. If the people you work with come to believe that talking to you means losing, very few of them will approach you, let alone work with and support you.

YOUR GOAL

To advance the proposition that your enterprise is one in which *every* member must win for *any* member to win, you must set up a communication environment based on four principles:

1. *Show respect all around.* This is the golden rule: Do unto your colleague as you would have him do unto you. Listen to the people you work with, then demonstrate that you have heard them and that you value what they say. Often, it is the small gestures of respect that are the most cumulatively effective. You can demonstrate how you value what your colleagues say by peppering conversations with such phrases as "That's interesting," "I never thought of that before," "I see," and the like.

2. *Agree on the ground rules.* Human beings are remarkably territorial animals. The territorial instinct is built into the genes, and much workplace hostility, including many barriers to communication that seem silly or irrational, are in fact primal turf disputes. Therefore, define responsibilities. Mark out territories. Discuss everyone's areas of responsibility, understand them, and agree on them.

3. *Sound your horn.* Don't stew and suffer in sullen silence. If something someone says or does bothers you, discuss it in a calm way that addresses the issues rather than the personalities behind the issues. Talk about *what* bothers you, not *who* bothers you. The object of your argument is to change behavior (a possible goal), not people (an impossible one).

4. *Make small talk.* A lot of managers have a knee-jerk reaction against small talk, which they define as conversation not directly related to business. They see it as unprofessional and a waste of time.

Quite the contrary, small talk in the workplace can be an important medium through which coworkers bond into an effective team by learning to appreciate and respect one another as human beings, not just job titles. Propose the thesis that you are interested in the people you work with. Prove the thesis by asking your colleagues about their families, hobbies, interests, and outside activities. Exercise sensitive good judgment and moderation in small talk. Develop a sense of when enough is enough and it's time to get down to work. Be sensitive to the signals. When you sense that your colleague needs to get back to the job, stop talking. By the same token, you can terminate the small-talk exchange by politely and specifically pointing out what you have to do. Don't say, "Tom, I've got work to do," but try something like: "Tom, you'll have to excuse me, but the Smith report has got to be ready for the ten o'clock meeting." If you don't have a pressing task, but just want to get back to work, be as specific as possible: "Tom, I'm just settling down to catching up on my e-mail. Let me drop by your desk in a few minutes."

YOUR ARGUMENT

Everyone's heard of "office politics," and we will discuss the subject at the end of this chapter. For now, take note that the phrase has a decidedly negative connotation, suggesting the machinations of ruthless individuals who are adept at manipulating others. The fact is that office politics is about manipulation, but it does not necessarily have to be bad. In essence, office politics is a set of strategies people within an organization use to further their careers. If your organization is a healthy enterprise, these strategies also benefit the organization as a whole. Remember, what is at stake in working with colleagues is the thesis that everyone must win.

Your most effective argument in dealing with colleagues supports the thesis that getting *your* way is to *everyone's* benefit. This argument is won through office politics: through manipulation—but specifically through *ethical* manipulation.

Most offices have one or more Machiavellian schemers. Recall that Niccolò Machiavelli was the sixteenth-century Italian political theorist who wrote a book (*The Prince*) arguing that a ruler could and should act with complete moral indifference because the sole object of power was to amass even more power. For many, this is a most seductive idea, and it would be foolish to deny that some people climb a corporate ladder they themselves build out of the knives protruding from the backs of their colleagues. Even if you don't find this approach morally repugnant, you need to be aware that it has a serious drawback. What goes around comes around. If you draw a long knife, you might just get cut with it.

The good news is that you don't have to be Machiavelli to practice successful office politics. Ethical manipulation is based on the assumption that the more influential you can make yourself, the more powerful you become—and are perceived to be. The more powerful you are perceived to be, the more powerful you will become. A tautology? No. A perfect circle.

The way to go about building influence is to sell your influence to others. The more ideas and initiatives of yours that you persuade others to adopt, the more influential you become. Now, just about anyone can sell a single idea. But to sell more, to win more arguments, to build influence over time, you must promote ideas that benefit the entire enterprise. With ethical manipulation, it is, in fact, impossible to be selfish, because you acquire influence in proportion to how you and your ideas benefit others.

SELLING YOUR POSITION AND GETTING YOUR WAY

The first step to selling your influence is to find the right customer. The classical rhetoricians and orators were highly conscious of the importance of audience, and you should be, too. Two strategies are useful:

1. Approach ready-made allies, people you have reason to believe will already be receptive to your idea.

2. Approach a person or people with power and influence. Such people include highly regarded coworkers or, perhaps, a boss. The idea is to emulate the ancient Greek geometrician and philosopher Archimedes, who famously proclaimed: "Give me a lever and a place to stand, and I will move the world." Find yourself the right "lever" and you, too, may be able to move the world. Win over an influential person and you multiply the appeal of your idea.

The second approach can be persuasively developed into what is often called the "bandwagon strategy." When the trendsetters, the most influential people in the organization, buy into your idea, others naturally want to hop on the bandwagon. Even if you don't begin by winning over a trendsetter, you can make the argument that other influential people, groups, or companies are using an idea like yours. Or you might make a compelling comparison between your new idea and a time-tested concept that has already proved successful.

Leveraging your audience and creating a bandwagon effect are good ways to prepare the ground for the successful reception of your idea. But they are not in themselves sufficiently persuasive. Sharpen your argument by rethinking what it is that you are selling. Don't sell your idea. Sell the *benefits* of your idea. More specifically:

• Sell the benefits of compliance with your idea or suggestion. Be certain that these benefits are compelling to the person or persons you are trying to persuade: "Starting the kind of tech support group I am talking about will give you a greater voice with upper management."

• Make a case for how your idea will benefit the company, but put your main emphasis on the *direct* benefit to the person(s) to whom you are speaking right now.

Make it your business to create a receptive audience for your ideas. Be friendly. Cultivate warm personal relationships with colleagues, coworkers, and the people who hold the power and influence in your firm. It is easier for everyone, from coworkers to boss, to trust the professional judgment of someone they know socially. It is more difficult for coworkers to shoot down their own friends or a friend of the boss.

OVERCOMING RESISTANCE

The classical rhetoricians included the *refutatio*, the refutation, as an important part of most arguments. In selling an idea, it may be necessary to directly refute opponents, objections, and opposing points of view. But there is an alternative strategy to consider as well. Sometimes, the most effective way to counter an opponent or potential opponent is not to refute but to embrace her.

> You want to start a special customer support group, but you suspect that Jane Doe in sales will see your idea as trespassing on her turf, which will cause her to oppose the idea. You could present an argument that you are not invading her area of expertise. The more effective strategy, though, is to recruit rather than refute: "Jane, I really need your input on developing the special customer support group. Do you think you could find time to work with me on this project?"

Recruiting a potential opponent can be a highly effective way of gaining support. Moreover, making an ally of a potential opponent may convert other potential foes into friends. A good ally leverages others.

CONFERRING OWNERSHIP

It is one thing to sell an idea, but another to confer ownership. That is, persuasion is always easier if the person or people you are trying to persuade are first persuaded that your idea is really *their* idea.

Confer ownership of your idea by giving others an ownership stake in it. Get them to discuss the idea with you. Get them to contribute to it. Get them to invest time in it. Start referring to it with the plural possessive: not "my project," but "our project."

DISAGREEING WITHOUT BEING DISAGREEABLE

Whenever you advance an idea or project, you can count on at least some opposition. Working productively with colleagues is not about avoiding disputes, but neither is it about defeating those who disagree with you. Ruthless debaters talk about "demolishing" their opponents. Can you truly afford to demolish today someone you will need to work with tomorrow, the next day, and perhaps for years to come?

The key to strategy in refuting opposition is neither to deny its existence nor to beat it down. The more effective approach is to disagree with your opponent without, however, being disagreeable. Here's how:

1. Start by identifying issues on which you and your colleague differ.
2. In your mind and in your speech, clearly separate these issues from the personalities associated with them.
3. Pit issue against issue, not personality against personality or ego against ego. Argue issues, not people.
4. As you argue the merits of your proposal and refute objections, continually work toward shifting the focus from the disagreement to areas where agreement can be reached. Bring about a shift from a negative to a positive.

You cannot depend on your colleagues' ability to separate issues from personalities, so you must take the lead in this process:

Colleague: You're deluded if you think the customer will pay a premium price for a widget. Were you absent from class the day they taught marketing?

The bait has been dangled. Will you bite? Or will you take the lead in shifting the dispute from personalities to issues?

You: So you think the market won't accept a premium price point for a premium widget?

The question is emotionally neutral. There are no personal words here, just conventional business terms such as *market, premium,* and *price point.* Note especially the absence of the possessive pronoun. It is not "my price point" but "a premium price point." No personal claim is staked on the proposal.

Move on from here. Having shifted the focus from egos to issues, identify areas of agreement rather than dispute. Build up and out from there. No law says that agreement has to be 100 percent. Move from 100 percent disagreement to 25 percent agreement and you have made a positive step. Develop it.

SECRETS OF SUCCESSFUL MEETINGS

Dispute is inevitable, but if you are looking for a "safe" thesis, propose the theory that "all business meetings are useless." It is unlikely that anyone will dispute this assertion.

Business meetings should be natural forums for productive discussion, presentation of ideas, and argument. However, all too commonly they consume so much time and effort that participants go into them expecting to waste both. Any forum that offers the opportunity to promote your ideas and projects is much too valuable to be wasted. It is important to rescue the business meeting and to make productive use of it. Meetings fail for many reasons. Here are some of the individual attitudes that sabotage meetings even before they begin:

• *The self-fulfilling prophecy.* If participants expect a useless meeting, they will almost certainly create a useless meeting.

• *"I will tell all."* Some people see a meeting as an opportunity to impart knowledge to others. They are prepared to talk (and talk some more), but not to listen or to genuinely exchange ideas.

• *The "rant and whine" mind-set.* Some people see meetings as gripe sessions, nothing more and nothing less. A business meeting may well be the appropriate place to air a grievance, but it should be much more, too. Avoid any approach that creates a negative context for the meeting.

• *Field of dreams.* Purposely or helplessly, many meeting attendees zone out and drift off in the course of discussion. The result is a convocation of empty suits.

• *"Be afraid, be very afraid."* At meetings, a good many attendees say nothing. They fear speaking in public, perhaps, or, more to the point, they fear the pain of being shot down for what they say. Fearful attendees create two problems. First, by failing to offer their insight, they do not pull their weight. Second, the emotion of fear typically descends like a fog, obscuring all that goes on. It's hard to pay attention if you are thinking about how scared you are.

• *Left out.* Many junior-level staffers don't feel entitled to participate in meetings, even those they are required to attend. Encourage all to participate.

To refashion the business meeting as an appropriate forum for persuasive argument, avoid holding routine or arbitrary meetings. Pare the meeting schedule down to those that truly serve a productive purpose. Before *you* call a meeting, ask yourself whether the purpose of the meeting could be more effectively accomplished with a simple conversation, a telephone call, an e-mail, or a memo. Whenever possible, use these less formal, less time-consuming procedures in preference to a meeting.

When you do convene a meeting, approach the event as you would approach a persuasive argument. Define a subject—an objective or a manageable set of objectives. Using these objectives, draw up an agenda. An agenda need be nothing more elaborate than a list of issues that must be addressed to attain the stated objective(s).

Even if you are not the person who called the meeting, you can still promote the creation of an agenda by speaking with the person who has called the meeting and asking agenda-related questions:

"Please send me a copy of the agenda."

"What issues will we address?"

"What do I need to prepare for the meeting?"

"What would you like from me at this meeting?"

If these questions don't produce satisfactory results—that is, an agenda—you have a good argument for opting out of the meeting.

A Reason to Meet

The classical rhetoricians had good reasons for attempting to classify, categorize, and rationalize the nature of argumentation. We can emulate them with regard to meetings. Virtually all meetings fall into four categories:

1. They may be occasions of presentation or information sharing.
2. They may be occasions for identifying problems and generating ideas.
3. They may address and attempt to solve a particular problem that has already been identified.
4. They may be occasions for motivation.

The inability to place a proposed meeting into at least one of these categories suggests that the meeting has no clear purpose, and that's a strong argument for choosing not to have the meeting.

Once the meeting has been categorized, it is easier to define its objectives. That accomplished, plan the agenda:

1. Begin by listing the topics to be addressed.
2. Consider polling prospective participants for topics. (Ask them how much time they need to present or discuss their topics of concern.)
3. Assign an approximate length of time to each topic. Be certain that any one meeting addresses a manageable number of topics.
4. Based on the time allotted to each topic, set a time limit for the meeting as a whole. Do not call open-ended meetings.

As the classical rhetoricians devoted considerable attention to the nature and concerns of their audience, so you should give careful thought to who should attend a given meeting. Remember, the more people, the more complex the meeting, and the more complex the meeting, the longer the meeting.

If you take care to define the subject areas of the meeting clearly, you should find it relatively easy to decide what people from what departments need to attend. Try to invite only people who absolutely should be heard. Do not assume the more the merrier, and do not yield to the temptation to gauge the importance of your meeting by the number of attendees present. Generally speaking, presentation or informational meetings work best among fewer than thirty attendees. Meetings devoted to problem identification or review and evaluation are best conducted with ten or fewer participants. Outright problem solving requires intimacy: five or fewer active participants. Only motivational meetings tend to work on the principle of the more the merrier.

Preparing for Spontaneity

Meetings, even primarily presentational meetings, are not lectures. The essence of a meeting is an exchange, a pooling of mental resources. However, you should not rely on the spontaneity of the participants to drive the meeting. Much as the persuasive orator prepares a presentation by doing the research necessary to define the issues and theses of the argument (what the classical rhetoricians called "discovery"), so a productive meeting may begin with "discovery" of the most relevant issues. People experienced in conducting meetings often start a session by conducting a problem poll. This process works as follows:

1. Bring the participants into a room with a whiteboard or the equivalent. Ask those present to call out the problems and issues of greatest concern to them. Have someone write them on the board. Do not pause to discuss the problems or issues. Nothing should interrupt the flow of ideas until the flow stops.

2. When the flow does stop, look at the whiteboard and go through one point after the other, restating each concern in *positive* terms. For example, "I'm worried about quality control" becomes "Our objective is to improve quality control." (Positive statements invite action, whereas negative statements often make action impossible.)

3. Develop this positive point as specifically as possible: "Our objective is to improve quality control in order to reduce returns by 15 percent." Now you have a manageable topic that is clearly of concern to the participants in the meeting.

4. Having defined an issue, generate some approaches to addressing it. Brainstorming is a time-tested method for generating ideas. It works best in small peer groups, usually of five participants or fewer. Encourage brainstorming participants to hurl the ideas out as quickly as possible. Write them down on a whiteboard or computer screen that everyone can easily see and read. Aim for *quantity* of ideas. Don't concern yourself about quality. Don't judge. Don't evaluate. Don't criticize. Don't discuss. Just keep moving.

5. After the stream of ideas peters out, ask the group to select those ideas they wish to discuss further. Focus on how to establish criteria for judging the value of each idea. At the end of the brainstorming process, you should have a few viable ideas relating to the issues under discussion.

6. Since ideas don't readily emerge from very large meetings, break up into small discussion groups of four or five participants each. Assign each group a particular problem or issue. Also assign someone in each group to record the proceedings, then, after a set period, reconvene the smaller groups into a larger group and ask all of the recorders to share their results.

7. If you are leading a meeting, resist the temptation to use it strictly as a forum for your own views. The purpose of the meeting is to pool intellectual resources, not to exhibit your own. As leader, you should ensure that everyone is agreed on the objectives. You should also present an argument explaining why each agreed-on objective is important. As the meeting proceeds, put an end to any discussions that tend to drift from the agreed-on objectives.

The leader of a meeting is, among other things, a timekeeper and time manager. Set time limits for various phases of the discussion, and enforce those limits. People tend to work more effectively when they are aware of a deadline.

The leader should both *reflect* and *facilitate* the discussion. Reflection is an ongoing summary and paraphrasing of major points. Facilitation helps the group make logical, productive transitions from one point to the next. For example:

> "X, not Y, is the major obstacle to effective quality control" reflects the course of the discussion, but "Let's now focus on X. How can we solve this problem?" is the facilitation that logically follows the reflection.

Support Conflict

The most productive meetings are not necessarily the most harmonious. The more important the issue under discussion, the more likely it is that conflict will arise. Do not try to eliminate conflict. Instead, support it productively:

- Focus disputes on issues, not people.
- Argue for your point of view, but don't let this blind you to the points of view of others.
- Consider the possibility that the sum may be greater than the parts. From differing points of view, try to synthesize a third point of view that is better than either of the original two. Conflict can be a powerfully creative force.

Argue for Action

Why do so many people so often complain about business meetings? It is because they waste time. In other words, it is because they call for an investment of time that yields no productive action. Every meeting should conclude with a clear call to action.

The call to action may be a set of specific actions:

> "We have decided, then, that we will implement A, B, and C."

Or it may be a decision that another meeting is necessary:

> "We have defined A and B, but we still need to define C. This should be the subject of a meeting Friday."

If you are the leader of the meeting, review and restate all action items. Poll the group to ensure that nothing has been misunderstood or left out:

> "Are we all agreed, then?"

Each action item should be specific and should be assigned to someone at the meeting so that participants leave the meeting with action assignments in hand.

APPROACHES FOR MANY SITUATIONS

All communication with colleagues is an argument for attention. Your thesis must be that what you have to say is of concern to your colleagues and offers a benefit to them. What follows are some common situations calling for persuasive communication.

Getting Colleagues Up to Speed

Much of what we say to one another in a business context is informational. You know something your colleague doesn't know. You want to convey that information, generally for the benefit of the organization you both work for. Sounds simple enough. Does merely conveying information really require an argument?

Yes, it does. Here's why: You need to command attention. Your thesis is that what you have to convey is of more than routine importance. How you present the information, therefore, must be a persuasive argument in support of that thesis. You and the people you work with are awash in words. To make what you say stand out and get noticed, you must sell the notion that what you have to say is valuable—*to those around you.*

1. Begin your presentation by getting the other person's attention. The surest way to do this is to appeal to the person's self-interest. Instead of saying, "I want to talk to you," consider opening with "This will interest you" or "You've got to hear this," or even "I have important news for you."

2. Now that you have the other person's ear, make use of this opportunity to communicate. Convey your information, and ask questions that focus on the person's needs and concerns. Listen to the response. Make certain that the information you are sharing is understood and accepted.

3. Structure the information you present in a way that will be most useful to the person you are speaking with. If the subject matter lends itself to a chronological narrative, present events in chronological order. If the subject matter involves prioritizing information, be certain to make the priorities clear.

Asking for and Offering Help

The concept of "asking for help" is in need of revision. Nobody likes to ask for help, especially in a business or professional context. After all, we feel that we occupy a more powerful and more persuasive position when we can *offer* something rather than *ask for* something. Therefore, begin by revising the notion of asking for help so that it becomes *offering someone an opportunity to help.* The fact is that most people enjoy being offered the opportunity to help.

Never introduce your offer with an apology. Remember, you are not *taking* something; you are *offering* something. Offering an opportunity to be helpful is offering an opportunity to feel good, and that's powerful.

If time is of the essence, be straightforward: "Ben, I need your help." If the situation is not urgent, give the other person more options:

"Ben, I need your help. When can we talk for a few minutes?"

Offering the opportunity to help is a positive proposal, provided that you don't simply dump a problem in someone else's lap. Own your problems. Seek help with them, but take responsibility for them, and do not try to palm off responsibility to someone else.

If offering the opportunity to help creates rapport between you and the helper, offering help to someone else is even more powerful. The golden rule is: *If you are asked for help, give it.*

If you are unable to furnish the help that has been asked for, you can still be helpful by assisting the person to find someone who *can* help:

"Ed, I don't know a thing about database programs, but Sally Jones does. Let me introduce you to her."

If you are not directly asked for help, but you see a colleague in obvious difficulty, make an offer:

"Jane, may I help you with that?"

Do not say anything even remotely judgmental, such as "You look like you can really use some help!" Just make a neutral inquiry: "May I help?"

Apologizing for Errors and Misunderstandings

No one likes to be in a position that calls for an apology. Mistakes, after all, can be costly and painful. However, the apology itself need not be an occasion for agony. Of course, it is true that there is never anything to cherish about the reason for making an apology, but there is a very good reason to value the apology itself. It is an opportunity to build and strengthen a collegial relationship.

An apology to a coworker or colleague should be an argument in support of the thesis that you are worthy of forgiveness, that you are a competent, valuable, and reliable colleague who happened to make a mistake.

An apology should say much more than *I'm sorry*. The apology should be helpful. It should contain an offer of whatever assistance you can render to set things right. Such an apology goes a long way toward repairing the damage an error has done, and it certainly helps to repair (or to build) collegial relations.

- Begin the apology with an *apology*—the "I'm sorry" part.
- Express understanding of the other person's feelings. In other words, empathize.

- Offer help. Collaborate on a remedy. Unless you can simply fix things yourself, structure this conversation so that the words *you* and *I* become *we*, as in "We'll fix this."

An apology is not an excuse. Know the difference between the two. What you owe is an explanation—a rough outline of the facts and circumstances associated with the error—but nobody wants to hear you explain why the problem was not really your fault. If the explanation, an outline of the facts, serves to excuse or exonerate you, fine. If not, you should offer no additional excuse.

THE RHETORIC OF OFFICE POLITICS

Earlier, we discussed "ethical manipulation" as the heart of office politics at its most positive. Ethical manipulation is an argument in support of your influence in the workplace. We close the chapter with a discussion of office politics in its more commonly understood incarnation: *unethical* manipulation—at *your* expense.

Rumors

At the root of most office politics is rumor. No workplace that employs more than two people is free of rumor. The impulse to gossip is natural and virtually inescapable. In some ways, gossip can be a positive thing, a sign that people like each other sufficiently to share information freely—perhaps too freely. The office grapevine is a feature of the culture of the workplace. Gossip actually builds relationships among coworkers. It socializes the office, and it may even create personal bonds that facilitate professional working relationships.

It is also true that gossip can be destructive. You need to be on top of destructive gossip, especially when a rumor concerns you. The best defense against gossip is to:

- Behave and speak in ways that provide very little material for the gossipers.
- Practice discretion. Don't air your dirty linen in the workplace.
- Not gossip about others. Gossip is an invitation to further gossip.

When you are approached with gossip concerning someone, respond clearly that you are not interested in hearing it:

Gossiper: Did you hear about Ed and Jane?

You: John, I have a report due today, and I cannot take the time to discuss Ed and Jane.

You need say nothing more. Don't moralize. Through your response you want to stop the spread of gossip—at least through yourself. This response is sufficient to achieve that objective.

Few office events are more chilling than discovering that you have become the subject of malicious gossip. When you make this discovery, your urgent rhetorical task is to persuasively refute the gossip. The worst thing you can do is ignore it in the hope that it will pass; it almost certainly will not. To allow gossip to flow unchecked is to deliver up your identity to others, to allow yourself to be defined by what others say. This, clearly, is unacceptable.

The first step in an effective refutation is to identify the source of the gossip, if possible. Seek out the individual. Instead of lodging a complaint or making an accusation, ask for help:

> **You:** Bob, have you heard this rumor going around about Mary and me?
>
> **Bob:** Uh, well . . . I might have heard something. . . .
>
> **You:** Maybe you can help me, then. This kind of talk can be hurtful. There is absolutely no truth to the rumor. Now, you are very influential in this office. People listen to you. So I would be grateful if you could spread the word: There is nothing to this rumor. The sooner people understand that, the less potentially damaging embarrassment Mary and I will suffer. Can you help?

Some rumors are pure fiction, others are distortions of an underlying truth. In the latter case, provide information that sets the record straight. If gossipers can use the office grapevine to spread destructive rumors and untruths, you can use it to circulate more accurate information. Commandeering the grapevine in this way requires pitching your argument at the level of the grapevine. To do this, find the person you believe to be the source of the gossip and, in a confidential tone, talk to her:

> "Jane, those rumors about what I'm doing with the XYZ account project are fantastic! Have you heard what's being said?" As if in confidence, tell Jane the story you *want* people to hear. Jane will spread that version, too—especially if you presented it as privileged information.

In the case of a distortion you believe requires immediate correction, consider sending an e-mail to everyone in the office. Be straightforward; you have something of great value to offer: the truth.

> "It has come to my attention that a rumor is circulating to the effect that I intend to [summarize the rumor you are concerned about]. Misinformation like this can be very destructive. Here is the truth." Then narrate the correct version of the story. Do not lecture. Do not accuse. Do not blame. Provide clear and unadorned facts.

Plots and Plotters

Gossip may start out innocently enough, without malicious intent, but there are some people who are sufficiently selfish, ambitious, or just plain nasty to try to do real damage to you through office politics.

Sometimes the knife in your back is pretty obvious. You know you've been stabbed. Often, however, the working of a scheme is subtle. This is dangerous; for the longer a schemer works, the more destructive he can be. Conversely, the sooner you detect the knife in your back, the sooner you can remove it, control the damage, and even reverse the damage.

If you find yourself excluded from certain meetings, if you begin to feel that you are being cut out of the loop, if you fail to get a realistically anticipated promotion, you should suspect the work of a schemer. In this situation:

- Refute the schemer preemptively. Prevention is always better than cure.
- Persuade others of your decency and value by cultivating good workplace rapport. Be considerate of others. Earn the respect and affection of your colleagues.
- Engage in small talk. Ask your colleagues about their lives outside of the workplace. Ask about family, friends, and outside interests. Get to know them as fully rounded human beings, not just as accountants and copywriters.
- Make dependable friends and strike firm alliances.
- Do not generate or listen to gossip.
- Do your job so well that you become indispensable.

The most common forms of nasty office politics are credit grabbing and idea stealing. Typically, the idea thief listens to you talk casually about an idea, then simply appropriates it, presenting *your* idea as his own.

One way to prevent such theft is not to share your ideas. That, of course, is counterproductive. However, you might consider doing the following:

- Put your idea in written form before you discuss it. Distribute the written idea, dated, with a note that it is a draft, that you are seeking input, and that you intend to have the completed proposal ready by such-and-such a date.
- Choose reliable confidants on whom you can try out your ideas.
- Challenge anyone who presents your idea as his own. Stay calm. Do not express emotion. But do offer a clear challenge: "Martha, that's the idea I presented to you on Friday, isn't it?" If Martha denies it, persist: "No? How is the idea you're discussing different from the one I discussed with you Friday?"

Sneaks and Snakes

Some people try to create bad blood that undermines relationships. A colleague who has never been particularly friendly suddenly becomes *very* friendly. He says, "I don't like to talk behind anyone's back, but Jack has been saying some pretty unpleasant things about you. I think you should know about them." Then he goes into the details.

In a situation like this, you need to suspect that your new pal wants—for some reason—to undermine your cordial relationship with Jack or, perhaps more generally, to undermine your self-confidence. Hearsay evidence is usually inadmissible in a court of law. There is a very good reason: Hearsay is inherently unreliable.

Hearsay is not proof. Do not act on the basis of hearsay. Instead, go to the purported source, explain the situation, and ask questions: "Jack, I was just told something quite strange about something you have been saying. . . ." Talk it out.

Another variety of office politician to watch out for is the passive-aggressive manipulator. This person may approach you with an "offer you can't refuse":

"You've got to support me on this project or I'm sunk. You *can't* say no!"

Never relinquish choice. This is the equivalent of accepting a fallacious argument that attempts to put you on the horns of a dilemma: *Either you're for me or against me.* If a coworker tells you that you have no choice, you'd better choose right then and there whether you want the weight of this individual hanging around your neck.

People who make inappropriately emotional appeals may or may not be consciously manipulative. Perhaps they just can't help themselves. But that hardly matters. Whether their actions are deliberate or not, they can be dangerous. Anyone who cannot resist crossing the line between professional conduct and plain old whining might just as readily cross the line between persuasion and extortion: "If you don't back me, I'll tell Smith about . . . ." What can you do?

- Choose not to allow emotional manipulators to attach themselves to you.
- If you can avoid working with a manipulative individual, do so.
- If you feel you are being coerced, threatened, or blackmailed, go to the boss. Act preemptively. Explain the situation. Once an issue is out in the open, it no longer poses a threat.

There is yet another course to take in dealing with unethical office politicians. Avoid dealing with *them* and instead address the *issues* they have raised or the mess they have made. If, for instance, you are accused of something you did not do, fight back with the facts:

"I hear that you have some problems with the way I've been handling the X account, Bob. I am not aware of anything wrong with the account. Help me out here. What do you see going wrong?"

Avoid letting the manipulator know that you have been hurt or offended by what he says. Why let him win? Instead, after getting at the facts, conclude on a positive note—despite your negative feelings: "Bob, I'm glad we cleared the air. I hope that, from now on, we can keep the lines of communication open between us." Offer a handshake. You've won.

Win Your Customers

Truly "classic" approaches to prospecting
customers and winning new business.

Persuasion is selling, and selling is persuasion. The rhetoric of the Greeks and Romans was designed as a vehicle for the sale of ideas, propositions, and points of view. It was—and remains—a set of approaches for demonstrating that what you advocate creates a benefit for the person to whom you are making your appeal. This chapter applies some approaches that have stood the test of a *very* long time.

WORDS TO USE

Persuasion is a matter of logical argument, but it also depends on giving people the "right" feelings and preventing them from getting the "wrong" feelings. The right words are invaluable in producing the right feelings. Choose carefully.

accommodate	create	listen	satisfy
act	decision	need	save
advise	demonstrate	new	serve
agree	direct	offer	service
alternative	discuss	opportunity	smart
answer	enjoy	option	solution
appreciate	establish	order	solve
appropriate	expedite	our	special
approve	experience	partners	style
ask	extra	personal	successful
assure	free	please	sure
authorize	fresh	pleasure	talk
available	generous	possible	time
benefits	guarantee	promise	trust
choice	hear	quality	truth
choose	help	question	understand
comfortable	immediate	relationship	unique

commitment	information	reliable	value
confidence	invest	requirement	we
consider	investment	satisfaction	yes
convenient			

WORDS TO AVOID

If the right words can spawn the right feelings, the wrong ones can produce the wrong feelings. Here are some words to avoid. Think of them as poison pills.

bargain	cheapest	expensive	no
cannot	costly	final	rock-bottom
cheap	cut-rate	impossible	sacrifice

AT STAKE

The stakes involved in any argument supporting the proposition that customer A should buy item B from you would seem to be self-evident. What is at stake? The sale of item B to customer A.

And this is true—as far as it goes. But it does not go far enough. A sales argument aimed at making a single sale to a single customer is insufficiently ambitious in scope. A good salesman makes a sale. A *great* salesman creates customers. It follows, then, that a good sales argument makes the sale, but a great one creates a customer and, indeed, creates many customers. A great pitch produces present business and also the likelihood of future business, including repeat business from this particular customer as well as word-of-mouth business inspired by the confidence and satisfaction that have been created in the current customer.

YOUR GOAL

The goal of sales rhetoric is to claim the highest possible stakes inherent in the sales scenario, which means not just making the sale, but creating a customer who will generate multiple sales. To reach this goal, you must create a value relationship with the customer by persuading her that what you have to offer is of benefit to her and is a fair value delivered on reasonable and honorable terms.

The hardest thing to do when you are intent on making a sale is focusing your pitch where it should be focused: on the prospective customer. But this hard thing is also the most important thing. Persuading the prospect of the value of what you are selling means persuading her that the merchandise is of value *to her*. It is difficult to maintain this perspective when your principal objective is to persuade the prospect to part with her money. Really, however, the problem of the sales pitch is the problem inherent in any argument. We tend to think of the purpose of an argument as convincing someone to accept *our* point of view. This mind-set automatically puts the focus on ourselves instead of where it belongs: on the person we are trying to persuade. Any argument is persuasive to the degree that the other person recognizes a benefit in allowing herself to be persuaded. Your first goal in crafting the sales pitch, therefore, is to adjust your own focus. Sell the benefit—the benefit to the prospect, not to yourself.

YOUR APPEAL

As consumers, we like to think that we are susceptible to only one mode of appeal: the appeal to reason. We purchase an item because we've done our research and have determined that item A is a better value than item B and offers more benefits than item C. Moreover, we have carefully reviewed our bank balance and determined that we can safely afford the purchase. So, all in all, it simply makes sense (that is, it's "reasonable") that we buy item A.

Doubtless, some people really do base their buying decisions heavily on reason. Doubtless, too, many of the items we purchase lend themselves to a buying decision based strictly on need and a sober, objective evaluation of product features and benefits. Yet, if we honestly examine our buying habits, most of us have to admit that the appeal to reason is only one of the factors on which we finally base a buying decision. Depending on the item and the circumstances, the appeal to emotion may play a significant role. In the case of big-ticket items, which represent a one-time major investment, or commodities, which we purchase on a regular basis, the ethical appeal is also very important. Whether we're making a one-time big purchase or establishing a relationship with a supplier of some commodity, we want to feel good about the seller and enjoy confidence in his integrity and reliability.

In short, all three modes of appeal—to reason, to emotion, and the ethical appeal—can be legitimately used in the sales argument. Generally speaking, the greater the value of the merchandise involved, the more important it is to draw on all three modes. Also, the nature of the merchandise often determines which of the three modes should be dominant.

> *Example 1.* In selling a lawn mower, you will probably use the appeal to reason first and foremost, enumerating in a factual manner the features and benefits of the product. You'll also present an ethical appeal ("We stand behind what we sell. . . .") while using the emotional appeal only to a limited degree ("This model gives your lawn a manicured look that will make your neighbors drool with envy").

> *Example 2.* In selling a diamond ring, however, you might put the greatest emphasis on the emotional appeal, since the purchase of high-cost jewelry is inherently tied to emotion—as a token of love, a symbol of status, and so on: "What woman wouldn't be thrilled to own such a diamond? She will think of you every time she wears it."

> *Example 3.* Next in order of emphasis is the ethical appeal. The great fear in purchasing jewelry is that the dealer is dishonest, offering inferior goods at

inflated prices. A persuasive ethical appeal goes a long way toward enabling the customer to act on the decision to purchase: "Each of our diamonds is certified by an independent gemologist, and we furnish a full, notarized appraisal with each gem. This has been our policy for the thirty-five years we've done business in this town."

The appeal to reason emphasizes the facts or attributes related to the merchandise in question. These facts include features, functions, materials, quantities, availability, and price. Do not underestimate the power of the appeal to reason in a sales situation. Buying and selling is, in the end, actually a very rational transaction based on quantity: An item is exchanged for a specific quantity of money. For that reason alone, much of the decision to purchase item A versus item B—or to make no purchase at all—is a decision concerning quantity. How many features do I get for how much money?

Emotion plays a persuasive role in many purchase decisions, especially when the merchandise in question tends to create strong feelings. This is the case with jewelry, clothing, automobiles, many consumer electronic products, and even with housing. Reading the prospective customer's emotions requires sensitivity, a sympathetic imagination, and a willingness to listen.

Finally, the ethical appeal is always present in sales. No customer wants to believe that she is dealing with a crook. Fail in the ethical appeal and you may lose a sale; make a successful ethical appeal and you are likely not only to make this particular sale, but also to create a steady customer who will do more business with you in the future and encourage others to do business with you as well.

THE NONVERBAL RHETORIC OF SELLING

Recall the emphasis the classical rhetoricians and orators placed on persuasive delivery. The physical presence of the salesperson, including nonverbal communication—body language—is important, especially as an adjunct to the ethical appeal. Of course, the classical orators were always physically present when they spoke. They never phoned in their arguments. In contrast, much prospecting for customers is done by telephone these days. No role for body language on the phone, right?

As a matter of fact, wrong.

Persuasive delivery is as important on the telephone as it is when you are presenting an argument face-to-face. There are two key nonverbal techniques you can add to your telephone sales calls:

1. Try standing up rather than sitting down when you make the call. If you stand while you speak, your voice tends to acquire more resonance, power, and authority. When is the last time you heard an operatic diva deliver her big aria from the comfort of an armchair?

2. Smile when you speak. Of course, the person on the other end of the line can't see your smile, but she *can* hear it. Smiling imparts a cordial, open, and inviting quality to your voice.

Clarity of speech is always important, but it is especially critical when speaking on the telephone. Speak slowly and distinctly—more slowly and more distinctly than in ordinary conversation. Some authorities on selling advise the salesperson to speak somewhat more rapidly than in normal conversation. This is a mistake. Not only will slowing down a bit make what you have to say clearer, it will ensure that you are not identified with the negative image many people have of the "fast-talking salesman."

When you are meeting someone face-to-face, bear in mind that the most persuasive nonverbal strategies convey openness, trustworthiness, and honesty. Eye contact is the single most important nonverbal element of persuasive presentation, especially in a sales situation. Establish and maintain eye contact. In addition:

*   Adopt a posture of giving rather than taking. Keep your hand gestures open, the hands slightly spread, palms turned upward, as if you are offering something.
*   Stand with your feet slightly apart and firmly planted.
*   Smile.
*   Be responsive. Don't interrupt the other person verbally, but do provide frequent nonverbal feedback. Nod gently to show that you hear, understand, and appreciate what the prospective customer tells you.

ASK QUESTIONS

No part of the classical persuasive argument is more important than the "discovery" process, which is the first phase of composition. If you are creating a formal discourse, discovery may require hours, days, or even months of investigation and research. If you making a sales pitch, however, discovery requires at the very least that you listen to your prospective customer. And the best way to ensure that you have something useful to listen to is to ask questions.

The rhetoric of effective selling is interactive. It is not a one-way pitch, as in a television commercial, but a dialogue where you discover the prospect's needs, desires, concerns, and doubts, then address them directly. People sometimes say of a persuasive political candidate: "I feel that he's talking to *me*." That is precisely the effect that persuasive salespeople strive to create. It doesn't require special talent, let alone clairvoyance. It does require that you ask the prospective customer what he wants, then address those issues.

You: Is feature A important to you in product X?

Prospect: It's important, but even more important is feature B.

You: You're right. Feature B is a great add-on option to product X. Let me tell you all about it.

Although asking questions is especially important as part of the discovery phase of your argument, you should not stop asking them until the sale has been closed. Keep thinking interactively. For instance, instead of declaring, "Product X completely solves problem Y," put this statement into the form of a question:

"Would you invest in a product that completely solved problem Y?"

Asking questions engages the prospective customer. It invites her to think, to imagine, to consider. It requires her to invest time and attention in you and your argument. Having invested this time, it is more likely that the prospect will go on to invest money—to make the purchase.

Asking questions is also a highly effective tactic for overcoming resistance or doubt. Never argue with a prospect, but do keep working until you understand and can address the sources of resistance. For instance:

You: Is price the problem here? Or is there something else?

Prospect: Yes. Five hundred dollars is more than I want to spend.

You: What would you consider investing to own this product?

Prospect: At most, $300.

You: I can offer you our model X, which has all the features of model Y, except for feature A. It is priced closer to your figure—at $375.

Maybe you will make the sale, maybe not, but the longer the dialogue continues, the better the chances for closing. It's not a question of "wearing down" the prospect, but of addressing her needs and wants so that she feels you are speaking directly to *her*, about her concerns.

HOW TO SELL BENEFIT

There is another step in the all-important discovery phase of the sales argument that is often overlooked or misunderstood. It is this: Before you begin to make a sale, ask yourself just what it is you are selling. The answer is not as self-evident as it may seem to be on first consideration:

"I'm selling a new digital tire-pressure gauge."

This statement says very little and certainly will not help you to build an argument sufficiently persuasive to sell the customer on your product. Go deeper:

"I'm selling a new digital tire-pressure gauge that features a digital readout of tire pressure. It is more accurate than old-fashioned mechanical gauges."

This statement is better, because it allows you to build an argument based on enhanced accuracy. Whereas the first response simply describes the product you are selling, the second begins to enumerate the features of the product. But the fact is that your customer is not really interested in buying a product, even one with certain features. She is interested in buying the *benefits* ownership of that product will create for her.

What are you selling? *A digital tire-pressure gauge capable of greater accuracy than an old-fashioned mechanical gauge.* That is a start. Now, translate this start statement into a benefit:

> "Because the digital readout is more accurate than the old-fashioned mechanical gauge, you can be confident that your tires are inflated precisely to the recommended pressure, and as any expert will tell you, nothing is more important to your safety on the road than four tires inflated to precisely the pressure that the tire and the vehicle are designed for. This gauge will help ensure your safety, and your family's safety, on the road."

Features are inert physical or mechanical properties of the product. Benefits are the good things the features will do for anyone fortunate and wise enough to own the product. They are the real *human* reasons to invest in the product. Always sell benefits rather than features.

USING TESTIMONY, AUTHORITY, STATISTICS, AND PRECEDENT

Recall from Chapter 2 that testimony is one of the classical "topics" of argument and that it is divided into four major subtopics: authority, statistics, precedent, and law. For purposes of creating a persuasive sales argument, only the first three subtopics are relevant.

Authority

Authority relies on testimony from a specially qualified source to persuade others of the validity of your thesis. We seek the advice of authorities before we make many of our decisions. If your neighbor George is an auto mechanic, we may consult him before purchasing car X as opposed to car Y.

If you choose to support your sales argument with the testimony of an authority, be certain to choose an authority relevant to the product:

> "The ViewEx television is personally recommended by three award-winning film directors because of the amazing cinematic realism of its picture."

Depending on the product and the situation, you may want to present the testimony of more than one authority, and you may also need to present—briefly—the expert qualifications of each authority. Authoritative testimonials are most powerful if you can quote the authority verbatim:

"I have been a professional chef at the four-star Le Food restaurant for ten years, and SuperSharp cutlery are now the only knives I use in my kitchen. Nothing cuts cleaner and faster."

With some products, it is most persuasive to furnish the authoritative testimonial in detail, as an expert's report on the product.

When you choose an authority to support your sales pitch, make sure the authority's opinion is internally consistent and neither self-contradictory nor illogical. Be certain that the authority you cite is genuinely and obviously qualified and expresses an opinion that is demonstrably unbiased. The vitamin supplement you are selling will benefit from the authoritative testimony of Dr. X, provided that Dr. X is not the inventor of the vitamin supplement in question.

The authority's opinion must also be based on current data and generally accepted by other authorities in the field. If the authoritative testimony is cited at length, there should be nothing obviously amiss concerning the basic assumptions behind the authority's opinion.

Finally, ask yourself: *Is the authority really an authority?* Advertisers love to use celebrity endorsements—but what does a 1960s TV sitcom star really know about bargain healthcare insurance plans?

Statistics

Some sales professionals avoid quoting statistics because they believe people are bored by numbers. True, numbers can be dull—unless they are immediately and directly connected to something of immediate and direct interest to the person you are trying to appeal to. Used skillfully, statistics are highly persuasive in a sales argument because, as numbers, they come across as perfectly objective evidence of performance and value.

Indeed, statistics are so powerful that we often grant them more power than they actually merit. While good statistical data may confirm a certain set of facts, the numbers presented do not necessarily support all inferences made from them. Telling your customer that your product commands 70 percent of the market does not necessarily mean that it is the best product on the market. Perhaps it is merely the most effectively distributed and most widely advertised. Make certain that the statistics you call upon really do support the conclusions you want them to support.

Precedent

Precedent is another highly persuasive subtopic on which to build a sales argument. People feel confident purchasing products that have stood the test of time. Of course, you don't want to put yourself in the position of appearing to sell old-fashioned or outdated technology, so be certain that the precedent you offer is genuinely valuable:

"The XYZ Widget is a new and innovative design that is nevertheless based on an exhaustively proven technology that has been used successfully in over one million installations over the past ten years."

ARISTOTLE MEETS AIDA

Recall that the classical structure of argument consists of certain discrete parts. The Roman rhetoricians followed the example of Aristotle and divided persuasive discourse into five parts:

1. The *exordium* was designed to capture the attention of the audience.
2. The *narratio* was a statement of the facts relevant to the argument.
3. The *confirmatio* (sometimes called *probatio*) was the part of the argument in which the speaker presented his proof, marshaling support for the thesis.
4. The *refutatio* was the section in which opposing points of view were introduced and persuasively refuted.
5. The *peroratio* was the closing section, in which, typically, the audience was called to act on the argument presented.

This organizational scheme was proposed thousands of years ago. As a formula for effective selling, however, it continues to work very well today. But instead of breaking down the sales pitch into five sections with Latin labels, the modern sales professional often divides the pitch into four phases, which may be expressed in a somewhat operatic-sounding acronym: AIDA. It stands for:

> *A*ttention
>
> *I*nterest
>
> *D*esire
>
> *A*ction

Commanding Attention

The "A" part of the AIDA acronym corresponds to the classical exordium. It is the part of the sales argument designed to capture the prospect's attention. Not surprisingly, the most effective means of commanding attention is to persuade the prospect, from the very beginning, that what you have to say is not simply important, but very important to the prospect. Here is one way to go about it with a telephone call:

"Hello, Ms. Jones. This is John Doe at ABC Company. I'm calling to follow up on a conversation we had a short time ago about high-performance widgets. I wanted to let you know that we now stock the brands you and I spoke about . . . ."

Command attention by recalling the past. Demonstrate that you are not a total stranger offering random information, and point out to the prospect that she wanted something in the past, and you are now prepared to offer it to her. By reminding the prospect of this *past* interest, you stand a good chance of capturing attention *now*.

Even if you don't have a past history on which to base your call for attention, you can still command attention by identifying a need your prospect has—even if the prospect is not (yet) herself aware of the need. For example:

> "As a widget user, you know that conventional widgets are limited in speed as well as endurance. We now have a technology that overcomes the conventional barriers so that you can get your widget work done faster and, over the lifetime of the widget, at a significantly lower cost. Would this be of interest to you?"

Note the question on which this attention-getter ends. Any sales argument benefits from questions that engage the prospect and make the presentation interactive.

Creating Interest

Having commanded the attention of his audience with the exordium, the Roman orator proceeded to the narratio, in which he presented the facts of the case. The narratio equates to the "I" in the AIDA formula, or the phase when the salesperson develops the prospect's *interest* in the merchandise. Here you may present the relevant facts that demonstrate the benefits of the merchandise—that is, the facts that show how the merchandise will satisfy the need(s) of the prospect, which you identified in the opening of the presentation:

> "The New-Era Widget includes XYZ technology, which works four times faster than the conventional technology, and because it has 40 percent fewer moving parts, it lasts up to six times longer. Moreover, the New-Era requires refilling every 100 hours, whereas the best conventional widgets have to be refilled every 60 hours. We are able to offer the New-Era Widgets at a special introductory price."

Generating Desire

Just as the purpose of the *confirmatio* in a classical argument is to make the facts presented in the narratio more than interesting—indeed, absolutely compelling—so the purpose of the "D" in the AIDA formula of a modern sales presentation is to raise interest to the level of a positive *desire* to own the merchandise. The more you know about your prospect's taste, wants, and needs, the easier it is to crank interest up to the level of desire. That is why it is important to ask questions and listen to the response.

"For just $500 per unit, the New-Era Widget will give you all of the perform-ance benefits I just mentioned. Typically, this widget will save you 25 percent in costs over a one-year period, and you and your clients will enjoy the satis-faction and confidence that comes with possessing the latest and best tech-nology."

There is no separate phase of the AIDA formula that corresponds to the *refu-tatio* of the classical argument. That is because the sales presentation may be inter-rupted at any stage by resistance and objections from the prospect. Typically, however, the strongest resistance will be met in the "D" phase.

To refute objections and overcome resistance, argument is not the most effec-tive strategy. Instead, ask more questions. Understand the source of the objection or resistance, then address this source as directly and effectively as you can. For example:

Prospect: The $500 price is pretty steep. We currently spend $400 per unit.

You: Well, let's think in terms of value, not just cost. If you work out the savings in terms of time saved and the increased durability of the New-Era Widget, it becomes clear that our product is a significantly greater value. That one-year savings of 25 percent I mentioned fully takes into account the higher initial cost of each unit.

And the news gets even better. We offer quantity discounts. Would you like to hear about these?

Prompting Action

Listen for the prospect's "buy signals"—indications that she is on the brink of making the commitment. In this case, a buy signal would be an affirmative response to the question, "We offer quantity discounts. Would you like to hear about these?"

Describe the discounts, then move to close the sale. Make the call to action—in other words, begin the *peroratio*.

You: For thirty units, the per-unit cost comes down to $460. We have thirty units available for shipment right now, and I can lock in that price. We can make payment with a credit card, a wire transfer, or I can set up an instant account for you over the phone. We can have an installer at your site next week.

Make the call to action brief and clear. Tell the prospect what she needs to do to complete the sale, and help her to do it.

APPROACHES FOR MANY SITUATIONS

When you speak or write, you do so for an audience. You don't need to read Aris-totle to understand the importance of knowing that audience so that you can shape your communication to its needs, wants, and desires. Here are some ideas for persuading typical audiences.

Open Doors

The first step in reaching any audience is, quite literally, to *reach* the audience. Traditional approaches include writing letters (or e-mails) and making phone calls. Whichever of these avenues you use, your first task is to get your prospect's attention. This is most effectively done by identifying a need the prospect has. Having done this, show how you can satisfy the need, then make an argument that persuades the prospect to allow you to satisfy that need. Conclude by inducing the prospect to act—now.

There two ways of getting to know your prospective customers (your audience):

1. By simply meeting them (that is, being introduced to them by current customers, then talking to and, even more important, listening to them)
2. By imagining that you know them

The second of these two methods requires some further discussion. Before you communicate with a prospective customer you do not know, summon up all that you *do* know about what you know best: the product or service you sell. Really think about the customer who typically buys your merchandise. For example, if you are selling custom accounting software, don't make a sales presentation to the owner of the deli down the street, but do identify accounting firms and other organizations likely to have complex accounting needs. Having made a list of likely firms, understand that nobody speaks to a company. People talk to people. So take the time and the steps necessary to identify just whom in the company you should address your letter, e-mail, or phone call to. Is it the head of accounting? Or the CFO? Or someone else?

Having identified likely prospects, try to learn something about their company—what it does and the nature of the opportunities and obstacles it most likely faces. Imagine how your product will address that company's needs and solve its problems. Craft your sales argument accordingly, so that you are speaking persuasively and directly to the prospect, as if you already know him.

Be aware that a ready-made pool of needy prospects are the businesses and individuals new to your area. All of these people have an urgent need to establish local contacts, including reliable vendors. Along the same lines, keep your ear to the ground so that you will hear about new hires and promotions at established companies. Make contact with the new people. They need your help.

The more focused your argument is on the needs of the prospect, the more persuasive it will be. Whether you do so through knowledge of your territory, through research, or through plain old common sense, begin your sales argument by establishing a community of interest. The message you wish to convey is not

"Gimme," but "I have something you want." Focus on the prospect's needs and you will be certain to command attention.

Having commanded attention, do not instantly reveal what you have to offer. Instead, *tell* the prospect what *he* needs:

> "I know that your business makes some very special and specific demands on accounting software. You need a solution that's right for what you do every day—not some hope-for-the-best, one-size-fits-all approach."

Next, build on both the community of interest and the identification of need by persuading your prospect that you are supremely capable of satisfying the need you have identified. At this stage, you do not have to be clairvoyant or in possession of extensive knowledge of what the prospective customer requires. Just remember that the one thing everyone needs is simply to be heard:

> "I am familiar with your business, and I am also a champion listener. The only thing I do better than listening to problems is working with my customers to solve them."

Inertia is both a physical and psychological fact. It can be hard to get things going, and once something is going, it can be difficult to speed it up, slow it down, or change its direction. Conclude your communication with a call to action, then make it easy for the prospect to take action:

> "I have set aside the week of May 4 to meet with accounting managers for the major firms in our area. I will call shortly to set up an appointment with you. I hope that we can get together."

Sales letters or phone calls that are intended to open the door are often called "cold letters" or "cold calls." They are much less about selling merchandise than they are about persuading the prospect to invest a little time in *you,* so that you can solve a problem or answer a need. If a cold letter or cold call sells something, great! But that's not the main purpose of these communications. The goal of a letter setting up a sales call is to persuade a busy person to see you. Therefore, consider adding an argument from authority. It can take the form of a brief listing of past or current satisfied customers—perhaps even a few testimonial remarks. You might want to close by mentioning any special offers you are prepared to make: discounts, coupons, free estimates, free appraisals, and so on.

Appeal to CEOs and Owners

The advantage of addressing a cold call or letter to the top person in a company is that you are dealing with someone you know has the authority to make decisions and act on them. The disadvantage is that CEOs or owners may be too busy to concern themselves with a vendor.

If you decide to aim high, be certain that you do your homework and address issues appropriate to the top level. Also be aware that the smaller the firm, the more likely it is that aiming for the CEO or owner will produce results. Here is an example of what you can say during a cold call:

> "Ms. Jones, thanks for taking a minute to speak with me. I just read in *The Commercial Concierge* that you are expanding your concierge service into our state. I am marketing director of the largest importer of fine stationery and specialty papers in this state, and I would like to be a part of your success. I've put in the mail to you our latest catalog, and I hope this call will encourage you to look through it. I know that you will be impressed by our extensive inventory of very special papers, which will enhance the service you give to your clients.
>
> "Please give me a call at 555-555-5555, or send me an e-mail at xyz@xyz .com, if you would like to see any samples. The catalog will arrive with a discount schedule that applies even to relatively small quantities. I would love to serve your specialty-paper needs."

When you are dealing with CEOs or owners, whose great advantage to you is that they have authority to act and make decisions, make it easy for them to act. Ask for a decision.

Appeal to Managers

Managers are problem solvers. Boiled down, that is the essence of each and every manager's job description. If you want to persuade managers to open their door to you, present yourself as the very person who will solve at least some of their problems for them. Consider this letter:

> Dear Mr. Smith:
>
> As operations manager for XYZ Company, one of your biggest responsibilities is managing costs, and one of your biggest cost-management problems is liability insurance.
>
> I don't know if you have the best liability insurance for your needs, and I don't know if you are paying too much for it. What I do know is that if you give me a half-hour of your time, I can give you a definitive answer to both of these questions, and I can offer you the right insurance at the best cost.
>
> The ABC Agency is an independent full-service liability agent. We work with a wide variety of insurance suppliers, and our only job is to find you the best insurance—the policy the best suits your needs—at the lowest possible cost. We have been doing this in our community for three decades, and our clients include . . . .
>
> Call me or send an e-mail; my contact information is on the enclosed business card. I would like to set up an appointment with you so that you can solve at least one of your most important cost-control problems—now.

Appeal to Entrepreneurs

Three assumptions are usually appropriate in communicating persuasively with entrepreneurs:

1. They are typically small-business people with limited discretionary funds.
2. They are looking to invest rather than spend.
3. They tend to be trendsetters, often willing to be the "first kid on the block" to obtain the latest technology.

Craft your sales argument accordingly. Be a problem solver. If it is possible to offer good financing terms, emphasize this benefit. Also emphasize the financial (and other quantifiable) benefits of owning the product or using the service you offer. Be prepared to sell cutting-edge technology. Here is a sample e-mail:

> **Dear Mr. Johnson:**
>
> The one asset you cannot accumulate, recover, or build is time. As a successful entrepreneur, you know that better than anyone else. You also know that what *you* can do with time is avoid wasting it. That means leveraging every workday minute to the maximum.
>
> I would like to offer you a way to do just that.
>
> XYZ Car Service offers a wide variety of limousines and other automobiles for your every business need, from the understated elegance of Mercedes, to the full-out display of our stretch fleet, to the high-passenger capacity of our minivans.
>
> When we do the driving, you save time, and because our vehicles are equipped with the latest in mobile communications technology, including high-speed Internet access, you not only save time, you leverage it, so that you can hit the ground running when you arrive at your destination.
>
> Our advanced scheduling system ensures that when you want a car, you are never put on hold, and we will get to your location exactly when you want us there.
>
> What is the price of such high-end service? We have a wide variety of plans available, and we can custom-design one for you. Our terms are not only affordable, but represent an investment that will build your bottom line.
>
> Let's talk. Reply to this e-mail with your phone number and the best time for me to call back—or dial me direct at 555-555-5555.

SELLING SERVICE

Selling a service is selling a relationship. As with selling any other kind of merchandise, the emphasis must be unmistakably placed on the benefits to the customer. It is also important to include a strong ethical appeal that persuasively illustrates your integrity. For example:

Dear Ms. Reynolds:

Savvy and prudent managers like you routinely protect their firm's investment in office equipment—copiers, fax machines, and computers—with on-site service contracts. But *busy* managers like you rarely have the time available to get the very best deal on such contracts. And that's a shame. Because, *as with any other insurance product,* guaranteed on-site service comes in a bewildering variety of levels and prices, and it's not always easy to get the best deal.

Until now.

Minuteperson Specialists offers you:

- The best factory-trained, factory-authorized service for virtually all your office equipment including copiers by [brands], fax machines by [brands], and computers by [brands].
- The greatest flexibility of coverage programs, including guaranteed three-hour response, guaranteed next-day response, and guaranteed 48-hour service, and programs that range from emergency repair to installation to regularly scheduled maintenance.
- Proven integrity. (We've been providing service nationwide for XX years and have over XXXXX clients. We will always be there when you need us.)
- And, of course, the lowest prices, period.

Now, let's talk about that last item just a bit. We know from experience that the overwhelming majority of service suppliers charge the equivalent of X percent to Y percent of the original purchase price of your equipment for each annual contract. That's a sweet deal—for them. But it is a stiff price for you.

You can do much better with us.

Figured as a percentage of the original purchase price of your equipment, our fees typically range from X percent to XX percent.

Look, you're right to protect your investment. But why throw money away to do it? Let one of our service representatives put together a service plan custom-made for you and designed to grow with you. Send us an e-mail at name@&&&.com or call us at 555-555-0000 today.

Sincerely yours,

FOLLOW-UP COMMUNICATION

After you have successfully set up and made a sales call, there are four possible strategies for the rest of the sales process:

1. You make the sale as a result of the call. No additional communication is immediately necessary, but see Chapter 14 for strategies on ongoing communication with current customers.

2. You must supply additional information as a result of the sales call. Do so quickly and accurately. Until you supply the information and answer any outstanding questions, the sale will not be closed.

3. You need to confirm details, requirements, specifications, and preferences relating to the transaction.

4. The sales call results in the customer telling you that he has no interest in purchasing your product or service. You write a letter to accomplish some or all of the following:

- Thank the prospect for her time, courtesy, and attention.
- Attempt to determine why the prospect declined to buy.
- Attempt to determine what would make it possible for her to say yes *next time*.

Follow-up letters or conversations after the initial contact can nurture a budding relationship, develop a sale, collect and/or furnish information, rescue a sale, and retain a customer for the future, even if the current sales attempt has been unsuccessful.

Satisfy Your Customers

*A chapter on ''the rhetoric of relationships'' and
using persuasive communication to transform
making the sale into creating a customer.*

The title of this book is *Getting Your Way Every Day*. The last two words are meant to be as significant as the first three. Like life itself, business is more than a snapshot. It resembles a movie in that it develops and changes over time. Make a sale and that's great, but what comes next? You have to think of the next day and the one after that. You have to think about every day. In business or anything else that really matters, persuasion cannot be a one-shot proposition. It needs to be an aspect of a relationship over time that creates sustainability and growth.

WORDS TO USE

Whenever we make a purchase or transact any business, we all listen for certain words that predict whether or not we will be satisfied. Try to include some of the following in what you say or write to customers and others with whom you do business.

able	detailed	invite	response
advance	develop	latest	responsive
advice	direct	new	review
advise	discount	nominal	safe
answer	discuss	opportunity	save
answers	easier	options	secure
anticipate	enterprise	outstanding	security
approach	exceptional	personal	send
attention	excited	please	service
choice	expect	pleasure	shrewd
choose	expedite	pledge	special
client	experience	prefer	specifications
collaborate	expertise	pride	specify
colleagues	extensive	project	standard

competitive	extra	promise	style
complete	facilitate	prompt	support
confidence	facts	protection	thanks
conversation	features	purpose	time
counsel	free	quality	update
create	improvements	questions	upgrade
creative	include	reaction	upgradable
custom	innovative	ready	warranty
customize	interest	realize	willing
cutting-edge	invest	requirements	winner
deliver	investment		

WORDS TO AVOID

The following words tend to create anxiety over the business at hand. Avoid them.

bargain	cheapest	expensive	sacrifice
buy	costly	impossible	sidetrack
cannot	cut-rate	lost	unload
cheap	delay	obsolete	wait

AT STAKE

Too many sales professionals are taught that *the* sale is the one and only objective of the persuasive sales argument. This would be adequate if you intended to stay in business for a day or two at most; but, of course, your intention is to stay in business for a long time—and not only to stay in business, but to grow in business. Thus, each sales argument you make must persuade your customer to do business with you and then to do even more business with you.

YOUR GOAL

The goal of communication with customers is to create business by contributing to the creation of satisfaction. Satisfied customers give you business today as well as tomorrow, and they tend to provide positive word-of-mouth that brings additional business.

Satisfaction depends in large part on how well a product or service performs, but it is also critically linked to the communication that takes place prior to the sale, in the process of the sale, and in the follow-up to the sale. Satisfaction is heightened and sustained on an ongoing basis through persuasive communication; therefore, increasing and sustaining customer satisfaction is a reasonable goal in communicating with your current customers. Note, however, that the customer is not always right. The customer's performance expectations may be unrealistic or mistaken, or the customer may be suffering from a common affliction known as "buyer's remorse." We will discuss these issues in just a moment.

YOUR APPEAL

When it comes to sustaining and enhancing a relationship with a customer, nothing is more important than the ethical appeal. People do not do business with companies. They do business with people, who happen to work for companies. An appeal that emphasizes your character, integrity, honesty, good judgment, and reliability is highly persuasive in building a sustained relationship.

The ethical appeal must be built on a record of ethical dealing; however, it is up to you to bring this record to the customer's attention:

> "We have served this area since 1975. Total customer satisfaction is the core of our success."

> "We are a member of all of the major industry associations, and we hold a Certificate of Excellence from the XYZ Association."

> "I have worked for WXYZ, Inc. for fifteen years. You can always reach me directly at 555-555-5555. I am personally responsible for your account—and for your satisfaction."

As important as the ethical appeal is in building and sustaining a strong customer-company relationship, the first and final language of business is money. For this reason, good value is always a prime motive for doing business with a firm on an ongoing basis, and it is most persuasively conveyed through an appeal to reason. Use hard numbers to quantify the good value you deliver:

> "We value our relationship and therefore will give you the best possible value. Your standing order receives a $X discount per unit."

> "As a customer since [month and year], your low price is locked in as of the date of your very first order with us. That puts you X percent below the average market price right now."

For building and sustaining a long-term business relationship, the emotional appeal is less important than either the ethical appeal or the appeal to reason. Of course, the ethical appeal can produce strong feelings of loyalty, but loyalty is always linked more directly to the ethical than to the emotional appeal. All of this said, you should not abandon the emotional appeal. It remains important to help your customers feel good about their purchase decisions. Even your most established customers can suffer from occasional attacks of buyer's remorse.

BUYER'S REMORSE AND OTHER PROBLEMS

Experienced sales professionals are not surprised when they are called on to make a particular sale not once, but twice. Many customers make the decision to buy, only to be assailed a short time afterward by what is universally known as "buyer's remorse." This is not an unusual, exceptional, or abnormal phenomenon. Many, perhaps most, people have some doubts after making a purchase, especially when it's a big-ticket item or an item that requires complex performance or price/performance decisions. Did I make the right choice? Did I make the best choice? Did I get the best price? Did I get the best value? Did I choose the best technology? The questions are practically endless, and because buyer's remorse is so common an experience, the best course for a persuasive sales professional is to anticipate the phenomenon and think of it as just one more phase in the sales process.

As with so many other things, the old adage about an ounce of prevention being worth a pound of cure applies here. Preempt buyer's remorse by assuring your customer immediately after the sale that she has made a wise decision. Do not wait for the customer to raise the issue of doubt. Emphasize value and benefit, which, after all, are the sound motivating reasons for making the purchase decision in the first place.

> "I'm so glad that you invested in the Model X. I know that you will appreciate the enhanced throughput. That ought to get you out of the office a little faster in the evening!"

Use your knowledge of the customer's specific needs and concerns to make your preemptive argument even more persuasive. The object is to reassure the customer that the merchandise is, in fact, exactly what she needed and wanted, so remind the customer of how it fills the need. You might highlight a feature the customer especially liked or thought especially important during the buying process:

> "Model X will certainly address your throughput issues. The new converter is just what you need, given your demand for extra capacity. And, as you yourself pointed out, this system is much more upgradable than the conventional system. It's fully modular."

If the initial sales process involved significant decision making, in which you and the customer worked together, speak in terms that portray you as a team:

> "We spent a good deal of time determining your needs and choosing the model that will give you just what you need. I am very pleased with the decision we made."

Remember that buyer's remorse is a feeling. Although the customer may raise doubts about particular features and issues related to the product purchased, her motivation is more emotional than rational. Parting with a significant amount of money can be stressful. Direct your comments toward giving the customer the best possible feelings about her purchase and about her decision. Emphasize value and benefit.

THE RHETORIC OF RELATIONSHIPS

Classical rhetoric is based in large part on the assumption of an adversarial relationship between the speaker/writer and the audience or between one speaker/writer and another. That is, the classical rhetoricians and orators assumed that the speaker's or writer's task was to persuade others, to win them over, to get them to *change* their minds, or else the task was to win a debate with someone who espoused a competing proposal or point of view. For many purposes, these assumptions are accurate and useful, even when dealing with prospective as well as current customers. After all, your job as a salesperson is often to overcome resistance—that is, to refute an opposing point of view. Often, too, you are engaged in a debate (even if it is not live and face-to-face) with competing proposals and rival products. However, it is a mistake to approach customers, whether prospective or current, as opponents. The rhetoric of the vendor-customer relationship should never be adversarial, but collegial and collaborative; it's rhetoric that establishes and maintains a partner relationship between you and your customer. Your objective is not to triumph over your customers, but to win *with* them.

The rhetoric of the vendor-customer relationship should establish a basis of value exchange. You should never feel that you are taking something from the customer or that he is taking something for you. The customer should never feel that he is giving away his money or that he is taking advantage of you. Instead, the relationship should be one dominated by a mutual sense of fair value being exchanged for fair value. This symbiotic relationship—in which both parties to each transaction enjoy valuable benefits—should be the foundation of all communication with the customer.

Symbiotic communication can be enhanced by the following actions:

• *Keep your customer informed of the latest products that offer genuinely useful benefits.* Help your customer to stay current with the latest technology and services. This action may result in a sale for you, but providing such information should never take on the feel of a sales pitch. It is an informational service—something one business partner would naturally provide to another.

• *Furnish useful facts.* Share information concerning your products and services, including new information about the product or service your current customer has already purchased from you. For instance, you may tell a customer about a new use for the widget he purchased six months ago. You may also share important industry news that you believe your customer will find useful.

• *Solve problems and facilitate doing business with you.* Keep your customer advised of new and improved ways of doing business with you, especially in the areas of credit and financing. Everyone appreciates information, advice, and help from a problem solver.

• *Follow up on product performance.* When a customer makes a significant investment in a product or service, follow up with a phone call some time after the purchase to check on the customer's level of satisfaction with the product. If he's satisfied, great! If not, find out why not. Maybe you can make things better.

The Special Value of Small Talk

The rhetoric of relationships is not solely about making sales and following up on sales. The reason? Good business is never solely about business. It's about people.

Always bear in mind that no one does business with a business. People do business with people, and that means it is about getting to know people not just as customers (that is, as sources of revenue), but as human beings. You need not force your friendship on everyone you meet or pry into the lives of each and every one of your customers. Rather, you can learn more about your customers simply by making it your business to talk about more than business. The most natural and unobtrusive way to do this is by making what is commonly called small talk. Now, the very idea of "small talk" alarms many old-school business professionals who see "shooting the breeze" as nothing more or less than a waste of time and an enemy of productivity. And so it can be—but, then, the same is true of just about any business activity. You may, for example, invest hours of work in a sale that does not pan out. Just as investing time with some prospects pays off while with others it amounts to nothing, so some small talk is productive and some is not. But just as a failed sale doesn't make you stop trying to sell, you should not give up on small talk.

Effective small talk:

- Heightens your presence in the mind of the customer
- Creates a positive impression of your ethical character, thereby building a foundation for an ethical appeal
- Builds mutual confidence
- Educates you about the customer's needs and desires
- Makes the vendor-customer relationship more pleasant, thereby facilitating business

By giving you deeper insight into your customers as people, small talk can also help you to understand the basis for resistance to certain sales. Some sales professionals believe that, in the majority of instances of failed sales, the customer will not readily volunteer the real reason for not buying. Many people give a reason they believe will sound good to the salesperson while keeping to themselves their deeper feelings. Small talk creates a climate of trust so that you'll be free to probe gently when you suspect that you are not getting the whole story: "Is there any other reason you've decided not to buy at this time?" Or, "Is something else bothering you about the product?" If you can get accurate feedback from your customers, then the more you'll know about them and the more effectively you can communicate with them. The more readily and fully you can identify your customer's needs, desires, and concerns, the more effectively you can craft your sales appeal to the particular customer.

Effective business small talk doesn't mean talking about yourself; it's about getting the customer to talk about herself. You want a dialogue, not a monologue. Most of all, you want the customer to open up. To do that, you have to eliminate all of the "conversation killers" that commonly discourage small talk.

The primary conversation killer is your failure to listen. In a crowded business day, this failure is quite common. You are understandably preoccupied, with a lot on your mind. You are also understandably so focused on your own immediate problems and projects that you find it difficult to concentrate on what someone else is saying. To counter these obstacles to small talk, put yourself in a position to listen:

• *Choose the right time for small talk.* If you are engaged in something urgently important, don't interrupt yourself to start a conversation.

• *Make and maintain eye contact.* Don't let your eyes wander. Eye contact will help you focus your attention on what the person is saying, and it will also send the message that you are paying attention.

• *Ask questions.* This does not mean peppering your customer with queries, but it is helpful to insert a question if the conversation flags. When the other person trails off, say, "And then what happened?" Or, "What did you do next?" Or, "How did you feel about that?"

Another conversation killer is the urge to interrupt the speaker. This habit often brings a conversation to an abrupt end, and it may also give the impression that you are rude. All conversation, including small talk, is a process of give-and-take. Wait your turn.

Negativity of any kind stifles small talk, which should be generally light and breezy. This is not an appropriate occasion for criticism, complaint, sarcasm, ridicule, or gossip. Nor should you ever use casual conversation with a customer as an occasion to demonstrate that you're smarter than she is. Give the other person a chance to tell you what she knows.

Now that we know what discourages small talk, let's review the ingredients necessary for effective relationship-building conversation. By its nature, small talk is spontaneous, catch as catch can. Nevertheless, you can prepare for small talk in these ways:

• *Keep well informed on current events.* Be especially alert to news that you know will interest your customers—for instance, news items related a particular customer's business or outside interests. Consider keeping a diary or informal scrapbook in which you jot down or paste in interesting news, commentary, statistics, and other significant items you may run across.

• *Make it your business to look for small-talk opportunities and seize them.* These include encounters in passing (on the street, at professional meetings, and in hallways, elevators, and commuter trains). A good time for small talk is after a sale has been made or discussed, or during business-related social occasions.

As always, be sensitive to what your customer needs. Never force small talk on anyone. If your customer is obviously in a hurry, help him save time. If your prospective conversation partner does not follow through with a conversation, stop. If your customer indicates in any way that he is busy, don't intrude.

As in almost everything else, getting started is the hardest part. Overcome the inertia that discourages small talk by asking an open-ended question. An open-ended question is one that cannot be answered with a terse yes or no, but requires something more conversational. For instance, "Have you used the new freeway extension to get to the North Side?" is a question that's best avoided, since it may push the conversation no further along than yes or no. Instead, ask: "What do you think of the new freeway extension to get to the North Side?" This question requires a more elaborate—conversational—response.

Another weapon against inertia is self-revelation:

"This is my first time attending this convention."

Some topics are generally appropriate for small talk, and some are not. Appropriate topics include:

• *The weather.* Always safe, but almost always dull—unless the current weather happens to be exceptionally pretty or exceptionally bad.

• *Commuting conditions.* Rush-hour experiences are of genuine interest, especially if you have some useful information or tips to share.

• *Current events.* A good choice, but you should generally avoid the controversial topics, such as issues involving political affiliation, liberal versus conservative position on an issue, and so on.

• *Travel tales.* Another good choice, if you ask your customers where *they* went on vacation.

• *Interests or hobbies.* Ask about them.

• *Positive comments about a place or an event, such as a recent business meeting.* Share these kinds of stories.

• *Recent books, movies, shows, or other cultural events you've really enjoyed.* Share these, too.

• *Sports.* Just be certain that the customer is interested in a particular sport. It is a mistake to use sports topics as an icebreaker with persons you know little about. Trying to start a sports-related conversation with someone who has no interest in sports makes the other person feel uncomfortable.

In general, avoid weighty or controversial topics. Also beware of broaching the following subjects:

- *Certain financial matters.* Unless you are a qualified professional, don't give tax and investment tips.
- *Cost of personal items.* Never ask a customer how much he paid for a piece of jewelry or an article of clothing. If you admire something the customer is wearing—a watch, perhaps—offer a compliment. If you are truly interested in the item, there is nothing wrong with saying something like, "That is a beautiful watch. Do you mind if I ask where you bought it?"
- *Income.* This topic is not appropriate for casual conversation.
- *Misfortune and personal problems.* Don't unload your personal problems on your customer. If, however, the customer opens up to you, listen with sensitivity. Just remember, you are not a psychiatrist, priest, or rabbi. Express condolences and sympathy for a customer who has experienced a loss.
- *Gossip.* Gossip is never appropriate in conversation with a customer.
- *Off-color stories.* Sexual jokes, questionable language, racially or ethnically based humor, and the like have no place in conversation with a customer.
- *Religion.* This topic is inappropriate for small talk.
- *Politics.* Political discussions, especially in support of or in opposition to particular candidates, can undermine any business relationship.
- *Controversial or highly charged issues.* Best to avoid these subjects as well.

APPROACHES FOR MANY SITUATIONS

Whenever you communicate with an established customer, keep in mind the goal of nurturing a collaborative relationship. The relationship should never seem adversarial. Ideally, your customer should perceive you as a trusted partner. The strongest basis for this relationship is the mutual conviction that a fair exchange of values is taking place.

From Precedent to Future Tense: Making the Second Sale

Many sales professionals approach the second sale to a new customer with a degree of trepidation. They do not want the customer to feel that, having purchased one item, he is being hounded to buy more. The cure for the uncomfortable feeling that you are being pushed is simple: Don't be pushy. Approach your customer as a partner to whom you want to offer something that will provide a genuine benefit.

Recall from Chapter 2 that, according to the classical rhetoricians, precedent is one of the most powerful "subtopics" on which to build a persuasive argument. One thing the ancients thought long and hard about was human nature, and a strong faith in precedent, they believed, was a cornerstone of human decision making and human behavior. It just seems natural that what was true in the past and worked well in the past is likely to be true and work well today, too. Therefore, build your second sale on the first.

It is most logical to approach a customer who has purchased product A with new merchandise related to product A: "I am sure you want to get maximum value from your widget. We now have available three different widget extenders, which I know you will find useful."

Precedent works very well in conjunction with an ethical appeal:

"You know how we do business, Ted. When we say it will be delivered in three days, that's what we mean."

Use your knowledge of your customers to suggest new goods and services that will be of genuine value to them. To uncover these opportunities, ask questions rather than make statements. Engage customers in a dialogue rather than subject them to a monologue or a sales pitch:

"Your having bought X from us last month suggests to me that you are doing the A process. Would you like to hear about our specialized line of products for the A process?"

Furnishing Facts

Most of the time you spend communicating with customers is devoted to receiving and conveying information. How well you accomplish this common task makes a strong argument for you as a great vendor and a worthy business partner. Come across as a good listener and an acute problem solver, and you will create customer satisfaction. Here is a recommended process for handling incoming and informational calls from customers:

- *Save your customers their most valuable asset: time.* Focus incoming calls with the question "How may I help you?" Be sure to use the entire sentence. "May I help you?" is polite, but *"How* may I help you?" directs the customer to ask you a specific question—one that will get at what she needs that much faster.
- *Clarify the customer's inquiry.* When the caller answers the "How may I help you?" question, be ready to focus her response even more sharply. If the answer is "I need the price list for your widget line," reply with, "Do you want the *complete* price list, or the price list for the standard models only?"
- *Strive to create customer satisfaction.* The less guesswork you have to do, the more satisfaction you will create. Once you have a clear understanding of what the customer wants to know, provide the information asked for.
- *Try to transform an informational call into a sales call.* For example, you can ask, "Will you be ordering those widgets today?" If the customer doesn't want to order at this time, then ask, "Have I answered all of your questions?"
- *Lay claim to the future.* Start by asking, "May I help you with anything else today?" and then invite further calls—directly to you: "Ms. Smith, please feel free

to call anytime. Just ask for me. I'm Joe Johnson, and my direct number is 555-555-5555."

Taking an order is perhaps the most basic exchange of information in business. But that doesn't mean you can't make the activity something special.

- Take the order quickly and efficiently.
- Communicate an attitude of helpfulness, service, pride, and accountability.
- Do not use the caller's time to advertise your company, but do use some of the caller's time to review the order to ensure accuracy.
- Be a problem solver and a time-saver. Create an order-taking process that has you doing the work, not the customer. Do not force the customer to look up item numbers or memorize account numbers.

Never demand information. Request it. Obtain permission before asking more questions. Briefly explain what you are doing, and be certain to put your explanation in terms that show how what you are asking will benefit *the customer*.

Offering choices is always a persuasive rhetorical strategy. Choice empowers the customer. Take care how you ask questions concerning choice, however. Use words such as *prefer* (which emphasizes the customer's choice) rather than *want* (which suggests that you are impatient to have the customer make up her mind). For example:

> **You:** We usually ship via United Shipping Service, with a three- to five-day turnaround time. We can, however, provide expedited shipping, if you prefer. Would you be interested in that, Ms. Smith?

Credit and Financing

Extending credit is an investment in a customer. You make investments in people, companies, and things of value—whatever you believe will return to you greater value than your original investment. Because credit is not something you give, but an investment you make, approach the customer with the firm knowledge that you are offering additional value. The credit package is an additional benefit of the merchandise you sell. Promote it as such.

In presenting a credit proposal to a customer, distinguish between the *benefits* and the *features*, just as you would in selling any other product. For instance, nonbreakable material is a feature of a certain coffee mug. The *benefit* of this feature is that you can enjoy your piping-hot coffee without worrying about the cup breaking.

> To make your credit proposal persuasive, explain the *features* of your credit program, but *promote* their *benefits*.

Features might include the interest rate, the absence of a prepayment penalty, the option to pay online, and so on. Benefits might include increased purchasing power, enhanced cash-flow management, more control, and greater flexibility.

No one enjoys applying for credit, so keep the selling tone light:

> "The credit package we offer not only will give you increased purchasing power, but will help you manage your cash flow. Our terms are flexible enough to put you in charge."

If you are responsible for taking the credit application information, create and maintain rapport by doing the following:

- Request information, never demand it.
- Express your appreciation for your customer's efforts. Filling out a credit application requires a certain amount of tedious work on the part of the customer; acknowledge this.
- Persuade your customer to take the time to furnish all requested information fully, correctly, and promptly to speed the application process:

> "I need you to do me a favor. Please send me copies of your financial statements for the last three quarters so that I can expedite your application and set up a line of credit right away."

If the process of making a credit decision is time-consuming, be sure to report to your customers on the progress of their application. Keep them "in the loop."

> "John, I was calling to let you know that we're in the home stretch in setting up your line of credit. I *expect* the line to be established before the end of the week, but I'll be sure to let you know if we hit any unexpected snags."

At the end of the application and evaluation process, it's time to deliver the news. If you can extend the credit requested, you should create a tone of welcome. Do not offer wildly enthusiastic congratulations; this reaction suggests that you are surprised that your customer qualified. If you deliver the good news in person, a warm handshake is certainly in order:

> "I'm pleased to offer you the line of credit you requested, and I look forward to working together. This line of credit will give you a lot of flexibility and cash-flow control."

Sometimes, you cannot give customers all that they have requested. The most effective strategy is to emphasize the positive. Talk about what you *are* offering, not what you *cannot* offer. Although you should keep the focus on the good news, do provide reasons for giving customers less than they asked for:

"Ms. Young, we are pleased to extend to you a line of credit of $XXX at this time. I know that this is less than you asked for, so let me explain what we've done. Your financial statements indicate a healthy business with a very promising future, but we have to weigh this against the fact that you have been in operation only eighteen months. As soon as you've crossed the two-year mark, let's sit down with your updated financials and see if we can increase your line."

If you decide that you cannot extend credit to a customer, you are faced with making what may be a difficult argument. You need to persuade the customer that, in declining credit, you are not rejecting him—and you do not want him to reject you. Structure the argument this way:

1. Begin with thanks for the application. Never start with an apology.
2. Tell the customer that your company "is unable to extend the requested credit at this time."
3. If possible—and even before explaining the reasons for declining the application—offer genuine hope for reconsideration at a later time and under different circumstances. Keep it positive, but keep it real. Do not offer baseless hope.
4. Be specific about the conditions that must be met to make successful reconsideration possible.
5. Be specific about when the customer should reapply.
6. Persuade the customer that you value his business.
7. Pledge continued top-level service on a cash-with-order basis.

All financial transactions are put into writing, of course, but when you have to deliver bad news to a valued customer, move preemptively. Don't wait for the customer to call you.

"I want to thank you for applying for credit with us, but at this time, your credit report shows a history of slow payment, and given your current obligations, we must postpone acting on your request for three months in order to give you the time required to catch up on your open accounts.

"I know this isn't the news you wanted to hear, but let's make it our business to review your financials again next quarter and reevaluate the application. For now, of course, we remain eager to serve you on a payment-with-order basis."

New Lead, Old Customer

Most people dread asking for a favor. They hate to "impose on you" or "put you out." And as long as that's the way a favor is defined—as an imposition, a request for something in return for nothing—there is very good reason to hate asking for a favor. But we don't have to think of favors in this way. Instead, let's redefine what it means to request a favor. Rather than thinking of a favor as a bid to get something for nothing, think of it as your chance to provide the customer with an opportunity—an opportunity to help you. The fact is that most people enjoy helping others. Being asked to help empowers the helper. It is a vote of confidence, and as such, it is very flattering. It is an opportunity to feel good about oneself.

The favor most commonly asked of established customers is a referral of business. No advertising is more effective than word-of-mouth. Persuade your established customer to help you by building an argument on four steps:

1. Lay the foundation for the request. Usually, this is the fact of the established business relationship itself: "We've worked together for so long that I feel comfortable asking you for a favor."
2. Be explicit and clear about what you want.
3. Explain how the favor will benefit you. Tell your customer just how much he will be able to help. In making this explanation, express your high esteem of the customer: "You are so influential in our community that a good word from you would be a big boost to my business."
4. Express gratitude and thanks.

A word on the third point: *esteem.* You should hold your current customers in high esteem. Be grateful for them and grateful to them. Businesses generally devote much time and money to acquiring new customers. That's fine, as long as you remember that your *best* customers are your *current* customers. They are sources of additional sales and new customers.

If you persuade a current customer that you and he are partners in a mutually productive and profitable relationship, he will be eager and pleased to recommend and refer your products and services to others. This is a favor to you, of course, but it is also of direct benefit to the customer:

- It gives the customer an opportunity to do you a good deed, which makes him feel good as well as influential.
- It gives the customer an opportunity to build goodwill with her own colleagues by turning them on to a good thing—you and your products.

Keep the approach simple, friendly, and low-key. Being persuasive in this case requires clarity, not pleading:

You: Ed, I'm calling to ask you for a favor. I've enjoyed working with you over these years, so I feel comfortable asking. Here's what I need: a brief letter of recommendation to the XYZ Corporation to help us secure a major contract with them. Can I tell you what's going on?

Customer: Sure.

You: We've been asked to bid on XYZ's new widgets, including installation and maintenance services. This, of course, would be a big chunk of business for us, and a referral from you would be just what we need to put us over the top with XYZ. You are so influential in our industry that I just don't see how XYZ could say no.

Once the customer agrees, it is a good idea to move him to immediate action by telling him more precisely what you would like from him. This will ensure that you get the best possible recommendation—one tailored to the needs of your prospect—and it will make your current customer's task of recommendation that much easier. Help the customer to help you:

You: Ed, I will ask XYZ to call you. When they do, I'd appreciate whatever kind words you can give them. However, the points I am most eager to get across are these three: We provide high value, a high level of first-rate client support, and we deliver three-hour emergency response. I really appreciate this, Ed.

FACE-TO-FACE WITH AN ESTABLISHED CUSTOMER

Your personal presence makes the most powerful impression on your customer. A face-to-face meeting lets you combine your verbal sales argument with nonverbal signals that build and reinforce rapport.

In dealing persuasively with established customers, your familiar smile is the single strongest signal you can send that you are happy to see the other person, that you feel comfortable with him, that you anticipate nothing but positive results from the meeting, and that you are open to all conversation, discussion, and suggestion. No business succeeds by closing its doors. The smile is as welcoming as an open door.

Add to the smile the use of open body language. Face your customer. Avoid all negative gestures, such as folding your arms across your chest (indicates resistance) or putting your hands on your hips (conveys defiance). When you gesture with your hands, favor open gestures, palms upward.

In American business and professional culture, maintaining personal space is a major body-language issue. Most people are comfortable with face-to-face distances of about three feet. Respect this comfort zone, but do feel free to lean forward from time to time to make a point or to show that you are listening very attentively. There is no need to touch the other person, and you should not point, but leaning forward from time to time dramatically emphasizes your interest in what the other person is saying.

Your ability to listen—and show that you are listening—is another persuasive asset. You don't have to constantly interject comments into the conversation to show that you are listening. Instead, simply nod from time to time. Nodding sends a powerful body-language signal that communicates understanding and acceptance of what is being said. In addition, nodding signals the other person that she should continue talking. The more a customer talks to you, the more you learn about what she needs and wants. This knowledge will help you make a far more persuasive sales argument.

Of course, you should not limit your part of the conversation to smiles and nods. Employ verbal communication that helps you listen and learn. A helpful technique is to reflect what the customer says. Paraphrasing the customer's statements lets him know that you are listening. It reassures the customer that he is being heard and understood, even as it keeps you sharply focused:

Customer: We are leaning toward investing in new desktops rather than laptops. Our people don't do a lot of traveling, and most of them are on the keyboard all day. Laptops give you a lot of flexibility, but nothing is more comfortable over the course of a long day than a desktop with a decent keyboard and a good monitor.

You: The desktop is the way you want to go, then?

Customer: For us, yes. I think so.

No encounter is more interactive than a face-to-face meeting with a customer. Exploit the interactive element to its fullest. Don't make a speech or deliver a monologue. Ask questions. Learn as much about the customer as you can. Craft your responses to fit the needs you hear the customer express. No argument is more persuasive than one built on your insight into the customer's wants, needs, problems, and anxieties.

As you listen, avoid the distracting temptation to eavesdrop on any neighboring conversations. Don't let your eyes wander. Don't interrupt. Wait your turn to speak.

Always listen carefully, but avoid overly critical listening. Some people listen to others mainly to find fault with what they say. It is far more productive and persuasive to listen with the intention of profiting from what you are told. The more you know about your customer, the more persuasive your sales arguments will be.

Convince Your Customers

Educating and informing customers, and
persuading even the most difficult of them to
cooperate and collaborate.

The previous two chapters were devoted to making persuasive arguments designed to create common cause with your customers, to forge a collegial or even partner relationship with them. This chapter addresses those situations that typically put you and your customer at odds: credit and collection problems, customer complaints, and other potentially rapport-wrecking scenarios. As usual, it is important to learn the right words.

WORDS TO USE

The following words speak of cooperation and collaboration. They tend to build positive relationships.

able	cooperation	latest	replace
accommodate	create	maintain	resolve
active	current	modify	respond
advantage	custom	mutual	response
advise	delighted	necessary	responsive
agree	dependable	opportunity	satisfaction
allow	discount	optimum	satisfy
alternative	double-check	option	save
apologize	easy	patience	scheduled
appreciate	error	performance	serious
appropriate	expedite	personal	service
assist	experience	pleased	significant
assure	explain	pleasure	solve
attention	extend	possible	sorry
benefit	fair	privilege	special
budget	features	promise	specifications
choice	grateful	promised	standard

choose	guaranteed	prompt	substantial
communicate	happy	promptly	support
competitive	help	proposal	talk
confident	immediate	propose	together
confidential	important	proud	unavoidable
configuration	information	quality	understand
confirm	inquiry	reason	understanding
convenience	investment	reasonable	value
convince	invite	reliable	willing
cooperate	issue	reminder	

WORDS TO AVOID

These words speak of an adversarial relationship and evoke opposition. They do not promote a constructive relationship.

blame	fault	policy	unfair
cannot	inadequate	poor	unreasonable
can't	incompetent	refuse	won't
fail	no	tough	wrong

AT STAKE

Business professionals are accustomed to planning on the basis of the money they have and the money they are going to get. Maybe it's a good idea to factor in as well the money you do not have and that you cannot seem to get. This doesn't mean the sales you haven't yet closed or the customers you haven't yet identified. That's all about *making* money. Making money is important, of course, but business, over the past decade or more, has been moving steadily into a twilight zone between what is receivable and what is collected. Receivables consist of money you have made but not yet collected, and the growing gap between theoretical revenue and actual cash on hand can become mighty dangerous. In fact, a business can get lost in it.

At stake is cash flow, the lifeblood of your business (covered in the first part of this chapter). This issue also puts at stake your relationship with your customers (the subject of the rest of the chapter).

YOUR GOAL

The goal is to use persuasive strategies to repair breaking or broken relationships with customers—and to do so without compromising your business.

YOUR APPEAL

The two main issues in this chapter are collecting on overdue accounts and addressing customer complaints. The temptation in both areas is to make an appeal to emotion. In the case of collections, you feel justified in trying to make customers feel some guilt or shame. In the case of complaints, you want customers simply to feel satisfied in a situation they are anything but satisfied with.

The emotional appeal has a place in the persuasive arguments covered in this chapter. After all, whatever else happens, you want your customers to continue feeling good about the product or service they've bought and about doing business with you. But, in presenting persuasive arguments in difficult situations with customers, it is far more essential, first and foremost, to make a strong appeal to reason.

When making collections calls, always begin with the facts. Demonstrate what is owed and for how long it has been owed. Allude to any operative or underlying terms, contracts, and agreements. Make the connection between the price offered and the terms agreed to; if the customer has unilaterally altered the terms by failing to make on-time payments, then the price offered is no longer valid.

Collections can be fraught with emotion, on the part of the creditor as well as the debtor. Generally, these emotions are destructive; that is, they diminish rather than enhance persuasion. Therefore, avoid them. Direct your appeal to the issues, not the people (and the emotions) involved.

Underlying the appeal to reason is always an ethical appeal, based on a mutual assumption that you and your customer are honorable, ethical people who have entered into a business arrangement in good faith. In most cases, the ethical appeal does not have to be made explicit, but because it is implicit, it is important that you do nothing to undermine this productive assumption. Therefore:

- Do not state or imply that the customer is being dishonest, deceptive, or dishonorable.
- Do not make threats—although, in cases of real delinquency, you should state, as fact, the consequences of failure to pay (e.g., loss of credit privileges, referral to a collection agency or attorney, etc.).

In the case of customer complaints, the appeal to reason is equally important. True, your customer is likely to approach you with negative emotions ranging from anger (over the failure of a product to perform) to anxiety (about squandering his investment on a faulty product, or repair or replacement being inadequate or taking too long, and so on). These emotions can be persuasively dealt with by assuring the customer that you will help solve the problem so that he will be satisfied. Nothing more in the way of a strictly emotional appeal should be made. Instead, get to the facts of the complaint or problem and respond to them as factually as possible. In the case of customer complaints, the key is learning about the nature of the problem, then acting on what you learn and educating the customer. Most of the negative emotions the customer feels and conveys result from a lack of information. Supply that information and your customer will feel better—a major step toward creating or restoring satisfaction.

COLLECTING ON OVERDUE ACCOUNTS

It is up to you to construct arguments that persuade the customer that the terms of the sale are serious and real, and that delaying payment beyond those terms is not routine, but wrong. One way to present this argument is to make collection calls and write collection letters. That can be hard and unpleasant work, which always risks alienating a customer. The more effective argument persuades your customers to avoid slow payment or delinquency in the first place. This argument is based on a simple premise so obvious that it is easy to overlook: *The people who owe you money actually want to pay you.*

It is not that people enjoy parting with money. In fact, few people like to pay. But they like owing even less. Your job is not so much to persuade your customer to *pay* you as it is to persuade him to accept your offer of getting him out of the position of *owing* you.

When you approach a slow-paying or delinquent customer, you do so in the belief that you have a problem. That's true enough. You do have a problem: Your customer owes you money. But that problem also gives you something in common with your customer. He has the very same problem you have: He owes you money. You may think of the creditor-debtor relationship as naturally adversarial. In fact, these two individuals have a common cause: solving the problem of debt.

The concept of cash *flow* is a metaphor. As long as cash flows into and through a business, the business is "in business." If the flow stops, the business begins to die. Money is fuel. Think of fuel flowing through the systems of an automobile. Gasoline, the fuel, flows in and circulates. Should you fail to refill the tank in a timely manner or should the fuel line get clogged, the fuel pump break down, or the injector fail, the engine dies.

There are two kinds of car owners: those who practice regular preventive maintenance and those who scratch their heads at the side of the road, staring blankly at a dead engine beneath an upraised hood.

The most persuasive arguments you can make to keep cash flowing from your customers are the arguments you make before there is any problem. Cash flow is most readily maintained through preventive maintenance:

> Cash-flow management should not be reserved for coping with crises, but should be integrated into daily business by continually keeping in touch with customers, vendors, and lenders before, during, and after money changes hands.

Talk to your customers. *Listen* to your customers. Help them to master *their* payment problems before they become *your* cash-flow problems. Anticipate trends and needs so that you can exploit potential opportunities for profit even as you avoid or prepare for possible liabilities. If you address cash flow from the very beginning of a business transaction, it is less likely that you will have to address a cash-flow problem later on.

When a payment problem does occur, adopt a helping approach instead of the adversarial posture your emotions may be prompting you to take:

1. Assume that your customer wants to pay you—or, more precisely, that he does not want to *owe* you.
2. Understand that you want to be paid.
3. Conclude, therefore, that you and your customer share a common interest.
4. From this conclusion, draw another. As people with a common goal, you should communicate in ways that facilitate collaboration toward achieving that common goal.
5. Call the customer, with an offer to help.

The Telephone Call

In collecting receivables, the best time to make your first phone call is *before* any money is due, let alone overdue. Begin persuading your customer to pay you even before a deal is concluded:

> "Hello, Mr. Smith. This is [your name] at XYZ Widgets. I understand how important it is to get this order to you quickly, so I wanted to let you know that we'll have the bid prepared early this afternoon and fax it directly to you. Because we want your business, we are cutting the numbers as close to the bone as we possibly can. However, I also want to alert you to the opportunity of saving an additional 3 percent if you pay the invoice total within ten days of our invoice date."

The most persuasive element in any sales argument is the benefit offered to the customer. Obviously, prompt payment is a benefit for the vendor, but how can you present it as a benefit to the customer as well? Silver-tongued oratory won't do it, but a tangible incentive just might. Be certain to repeat the incentive discount for quick payment in writing with such items as statements of bids, cover letters accompanying proposals, cover letters with payment schedules, inserts accompanying shipment, and invoices or invoice flyers.

If you encounter resistance to your incentive offer, don't give up:

You: Notice that you have the option of taking an additional 3 percent off the total for making payment within ten days.

Customer: In other words, you've tacked on 3 percent for bills past ten days.

You: No, not at all. Our standard terms are thirty days net. After thirty days, we charge 1.5 percent per month, up to ninety days. Beyond ninety days, the account is referred to our collections department. The 3 percent discount for prompt payment is a genuine discount off our best net price. It is *not* based on a hidden charge. Nor is it in an act of generosity. It is simply an incentive. We are a small firm, and it is worth 3 percent to us to facilitate our cash flow.

If it is a good idea to begin the collection argument before there is a problem, it is even more urgent to intervene when there is even the slightest indication of difficulty. For instance, you have received payment from a new customer, but it is a week late on thirty-day terms. Most companies let this kind of thing pass without comment. Consider instead a friendly phone call where you say:

> "This is [your name] from XYZ Widgets. We've just received your July payment. Thanks. As you know, payments received after thirty days are subject to a $20 service charge, which you included. Your payment arrived just six days after the due date, so I wanted to alert you to the fact that if you can get us your next payment by August 15, you will avoid a service charge on that payment."

This phone call bends no rules, but it nevertheless offers the customer help by suggesting an action that will save him money—in the future. The benefit you, the vendor, want is prompt payment. The benefit you offer the customer is an opportunity to avoid additional expense.

Once a customer has slipped significantly past the thirty-day net period, you might want to offer a more compelling incentive to pay:

> "Hello, Mr. Jones. This is [your name] at XYZ Widgets. I'm calling to save you some money. Your account with us has just gone past thirty days, which means that it is now subject to a $25 service charge. It is, to tell you the truth, better for us to have that account paid in full right now than to collect an additional $25 later on. So if you can get payment to me by Wednesday, I will waive the service charge. Is that something you would be interested in?"

As relations with a customer become more established, the most effective rhetorical strategy in most transactions is to approach the customer as a business partner. This reflects the very real fact that you are in business together and have interests in common. The most persuasive arguments appeal to common interests.

One of the most frequently encountered payment problems with established customers involves missed installment payments. The best approach is the most positive one. You should demonstrate that you are calling because the missed payment is exceptional—not something you have come to expect from this customer:

> **You:** Hello, Sarah. This is [your name] from XYZ Widgets. I'm calling because your payment of $XXX, which was due on Friday, hasn't reached us. You're always so punctual with these payments, I was concerned. When did you send that out?

Express concern—for the customer—then get information. Money matters should be about facts, not feelings.

Customer: Well, I was planning on sending the payment out later in the week.

You: It was due on Friday. Can you get it into the mail today?

Focus the argument on the facts. Get a factual response. The best response to the customer's vague promise is not criticism—"Later in the week isn't good enough"—but a statement of fact that makes no direct reference to the customer: "It was due on Friday."

Customer: I'll try.

You: So, we'll look for it by the first of the week?

Customer: Yes.

You: Terrific. Thanks.

The classical rhetoricians always believed in beginning at the beginning. Before you make a collections call, be sure you know what it is you want. Do you want to vent your frustration and anxiety at the customer? Or do you want to get paid?

If the answer is the second alternative, make an argument that will help your customer pay. This is especially important as the overdue account approaches sixty days. In this case:

• *Argue from facts, not feelings.* If you have a schedule of service/finance charges in place, make a phone call to remind the customer how much is owed now and how much more will be due after a given date.

• *Build on your relationship with the customer.* Appeal to the common basis of your mutual interest by explaining that prompt, personal service at the best prices requires the cooperation of the customer in the form of timely payment, which keeps costs down.

• *Argue from authority.* Point out that the prices agreed to, by contract, are based on thirty-day net terms. They do not apply beyond thirty days.

It is unlikely that your customer will attempt to dispute or counter any of the facts you present. The resistance commonly encountered in slow payment situations is vagueness and evasiveness. How do you offer counterarguments against these tactics?

• Engage the customer by asking questions—questions that can be answered, such as those related to dates and amounts.

• If the customer tells you that now is a bad time to talk, remind her that "we" are running short of time, and ask when it would be a good time to call back. Your immediate goal is to get a definite time.

• If the customer is vague about when she can make the required payment, suggest that she think the matter over, and tell her that you will call back at a specific time to get her response.

- If the customer passes the buck to her "accounting people," ask permission to speak directly to accounting yourself.
- If the customer wants to negotiate, do so.

Once you have cut through evasion and vagueness, make a bid for definition and direction:

- Remind the customer of her obligation. This is an especially compelling ethical argument.
- Review all relevant dates and the amounts.

After you have done these things, shift the argument to consequences. Cause and effect is basic to human experience and therefore makes for a compelling topic. For instance, in the case of payment due for commodity goods or services that are delivered or performed on an ongoing basis, discuss the following:

- The fact that the commodity or service delivery will be stopped unless payment is received by a certain date
- The costs *to the customer* of interrupting and then restarting delivery or service

Here is a sample exchange:

You: Hello, Ben. This is [your name] from XYZ Widgets. Your account is approaching sixty days. I'm calling to ask when we can expect payment. As you know, the contract prices are based on thirty-day net terms. Now that we're closing in on sixty days, you're looking at a $250 carrying charge on this account. If you can get us a check by Friday, I'll waive the carrying charge. That will save you $250.

Customer: I need to talk to my bookkeeper.

You: Would it be better for me to talk directly with your bookkeeper? I can give him or her an opportunity to save you some money.

Customer: No. I'll talk to him.

You: May I call you at this time tomorrow to get a payment date from you, then?

Customer: Tomorrow is a bad time.

You: We are running very short on time. After Friday, the account is subject to the $250 carrying charge. What *would* be a good time to call?

If the customer responds with a genuine problem, it is in your interest to help him solve it:

Customer: I'm in a terrible cash-flow bind just now.

You: Maybe I can help. We need to come up with a plan that we can both live with. The balance due is $XXXX. If I can get $XXX by Monday, I would be in a position to waive the carrying charges on the entire balance due, as long as the account is settled in total by November 6. Does that sound workable to you?

Even when an unpaid account becomes more seriously delinquent—approaching ninety days open—you still have compelling arguments to make, especially because the customer is probably anxious to preserve as much of his good credit as possible and is, if anything, even more anxious to settle now than he was earlier.

Now is the time to set up an argument from authority by beginning to separate yourself from such entities as "company policy," accountants, attorneys, and the passage of time itself. That is, whereas *you* would like to grant more extensions, "company policy" (or "our accountants" or "our attorneys") will not let you. Why? Because time is running out. Your argument proposes that time is the adversary you and the customer have in common. Shouldn't "we" work together to defeat this adversary?

The persuasive strategy here is intended to strengthen the cooperative bond between two people who have to work within certain rules. Your implication is that, at present, you and the customer are in control—but soon, very soon, the architects of company policy, including the lawyers, will be in charge. This approach is not intended as a threat, but as a factual expression of cause and effect. Fail to pay now, and the consequences will be yet more costly.

It is always more persuasive to offer something positive than to complain or threaten. Engage the customer by asking questions that can be readily answered:

You: Mr. Johnson, this is [your name] at XYZ Widgets. I just put your current statement in the mail. You already have two statements from us, but I've sent this one a little early, because I wanted to offer you the opportunity to beat the ninety-day deadline so that you can avoid paying a service charge of $150. Are you interested in saving some money?

Customer: Always.

You: Well, if you put your payment into the mail today, you'll save $150. Can you do that?

Customer: Actually, I'm short on cash just now. I can't send anything for another couple of weeks.

You: Well, I would still like to save you some money. If you could pay 50 percent now and the balance by the end of the month—which *will* put you beyond ninety days—I would still be willing to waive the service charges.

It is not always possible to offer positive incentives. In such instances, negative incentives can also be effective, especially because arguments based on cause and effect—action and consequences—are naturally persuasive in that they appeal so strongly to common sense. For instance:

You: Ms. Perkins, this is [your name] at XYZ Widgets. Your account is about to pass ninety days—which is not the end of the world, but I did want to alert you to the fact that, because the account is about to slip through another month unpaid, you will be charged a $150 service fee. Might I suggest that you send out a check today to avoid that charge? The problem is that once the unpaid account goes past the twelfth of the month, I have no choice but to assess the charge.

Customer: I appreciate the call, but I can't make the payment before the twelfth. I'm a regular customer. Can you give me a grace period on that service charge?

You: When would you be making payment?

Customer: In two or three weeks. Thirty days tops.

You: In another thirty days, the account will be delinquent. Neither of us wants to see that happen. What portion of the total *could* you send by the twelfth?

The Collection Letter

Just as a friendly phone call made shortly after an order is placed can help to avert collections problems, including a letter or an insert with your first invoice or—even sooner—with the project proposal can serve as the proverbial ounce of prevention that will save you a pound of cure later.

Here is an example of a cover letter that might be included with a bid or proposal:

Dear [Customer's Name]:

Enclosed are the prices for the [merchandise] we discussed. The prices quoted include all freight and handling, and there are no additional costs— based on our thirty-day terms. All unpaid balances beyond thirty days are subject to a [percent amount] service charge. We appreciate your helping us maintain our low prices by paying promptly.

Sincerely,

You can carry the argument for prompt payment through to the invoice stage. Consider adding an insert with your invoice that reads:

"It has been our pleasure to serve you. Remember, you are entitled to a [percent amount] discount from the total due as our thanks to you for prompt payment. You may take advantage of this discount by choosing to pay the balance in full no later than [date]."

Offering useful help is always a persuasive argument. Send a letter or e-mail at least ten days before a payment is due. Keep the tone informational. This message should not come across as a collection letter, but as a service to the customer:

"Just a note to call to your attention the fact that your account with us will reach the thirty-day mark on [date]. To avoid scheduled service charges, you have the option of paying the account in full before [repeat the date]."

The goal of most collection letters is *to get the money*. This would seem self-evident. However, it is more productive to think beyond this short-term goal. Just as it is better to create a customer than to make a single sale, so it is preferable to persuade a slow-paying customer to change this behavior (once and for all) than it is merely to collect a single payment due. Consider responding to a slow payment with a thank-you—and an offer of helpful information:

Dear [Customer's Name]:

Thank you for your payment, which we received on [date]. Please note that, while your account is in good standing, your payment was received [state the number of days after the due date] and is therefore subject to a service charge of $XX, which will appear on your next bill.

By making your remaining payments on time, you will avoid additional service charges.

Sincerely yours,

A positive incentive—the offer of a direct benefit to the customer—always makes for a persuasive argument. Here is an e-mail to a new customer whose payment has just gone beyond the thirty-day net terms:

"Your account with us is past due thirty days and subject to a $XX finance charge. Because you are a new customer, with whom we look forward to years of business, we will waive the finance charge provided that we receive payment in full by [date]. Please put your check into the mail today, if you would like to take advantage of this offer."

If you cannot—or choose not to—waive a service charge, you can still base your argument for payment on a positive incentive:

Dear [Customer's Name]:

A friendly note to advise you that your account with us is past due thirty days and is now subject to a service charge of $XX. You can avoid an additional service charge by making your payment no later than [date].

An alternative to the incentive is the offer of help. The basis for this argument is the thesis that you and your customer are business partners, bound together in a mutual undertaking:

Dear [Customer's Name]:

You are a great customer, and when a great customer misses a payment due, there's always an important reason.

I am concerned, and I want to help. Now that the balance due on your account has passed the sixty-day mark, isn't it time we talked? If there is a problem, I am confident that we can solve it together.

I ask that you call me at 555-555-5555. If I am unavailable when you call, be assured that any voice mail message you leave will be treated in strictest confidence, and I will return your call as soon as possible.

Sincerely yours,

If an offer of help makes a persuasive argument, *asking* for help can be even more compelling. Empower your customer to pay by soliciting his assistance:

Dear [Customer's Name]:

I need your help. One of the reasons you do business with us is that we are a small firm geared to deliver a high level of very personal attention. That's the big advantage of being small.

The disadvantage, of course, is that we have to do business on a budget lean enough to keep us more than competitive with the bigger firms. The value we offer you depends in large part on your making all payments promptly.

It has been nearly sixty days since we invoiced you, and your account remains unpaid. Help us to continue providing great small-company service at prices you can afford. Please send us your check for $XXX today.

If you have any questions, I'm here to help. Please call 555-555-0000.

Sincerely,

It is hard to make an argument, persuasive or otherwise, if the other person isn't listening or doesn't respond. Unfortunately, this happens often with customers you are trying to reach in order to collect payment due. You want to be paid, but, in these instances, your first objective is to persuade the customer to respond to you. At some point, it may become necessary to take legal action, but before you reach that stage, try more positive persuasion. As always, begin with the facts. Mention the negative consequences of continued unresponsiveness, but make them subordinate to the positive steps the customer can take—now—to secure cooperation and help from you:

Dear [Customer's Name]:

You now have our monthly statements for [list all months past due]. We have attempted to reach you by telephone X times, on [dates]. We have also sent you correspondence on [dates].

We have received no response.

Because we value and appreciate your business, we are puzzled by your unresponsiveness. Please communicate with us concerning your seriously late account. If you have a problem with the merchandise you received or with your finances, please let us know so that we can understand the problem and work with you to resolve it before your account is turned over to a third-party collection agency.

A phone call today will help us both. My direct line is 555-555-0000. You may leave a confidential voice mail message. If you prefer, reply by e-mail to [name@xyzwidgets.com].

Your immediate attention to this matter is greatly appreciated.

Sincerely,

HANDLING CUSTOMER COMPLAINTS

Problems are opportunities in a different set of clothes. The manner in which you respond to an error or mishap—the persuasive discourse you offer and the actions you take—constitute an opportunity to give your customer exceptional service. It is possible to transform disaster into a productive episode of customer satisfaction.

Responding to customer complaints requires that you persuade your customers of the positive power of your relationship with them:

First, you care about your customers and their problems.

Second, you will work to solve the problem.

If the widget your company sold to Mr. Jones fails, he will be upset—probably in direct proportion to the cost of the widget. If Mr. Jones then calls your company and finds no help available, that "upset" will be transformed into outrage, anger, fear, frustration, and a feeling of having been cheated and/or abandoned. You will "lose" the customer in every sense of the word. Worse, this customer's negative word-of-mouth may cost you many more customers.

Obviously, you need a strategy to prevent the escalation of negative emotion. This response strategy has several objectives:

- Responding to complaints is damage control, but also much more than damage control.
- Responding to complaints is satisfying warranty and contractual obligations, but it is more than simply this.
- Responding to complaints demonstrates your company's willingness to stand behind its product or service. It must be a promise to make things right again—and a persuasive argument that you are both capable of and willing to make things right again.

Make an effective argument in response to mistakes, mishaps, and disasters and you will not only redeem your company in the customer's estimation, you will actually build or strengthen the bond between your firm and the customer. Nothing will change the fact that Mr. Jones's widget sprung a leak, but he will feel a whole lot better about your company. He may even tell his friends and colleagues about the widget problem, but the main thrust of his story will be how the company mobilized its forces to *help him out* and *make things right*.

Constructive Listening

As always, persuasion begins with your ears. Some people find it difficult to listen to negative information, especially complaints. There is an unconscious tendency to block and to censor negative comments. Be aware of this habit, and deliberately focus on hearing everything the customer says. Gather as much information as you can. You need to deal with emotion—the customer may be angry, disappointed, and/or anxious—but you need most of all to get the facts. Without the facts, you cannot help. The more the customer tells you, the better—even if part of what she says sounds like nothing more than venting. Resist the temptation to respond defensively. Encourage the customer to reveal as much as possible. Ask questions in order to get specific answers. Express empathy and mirror the customer's comments so that she knows that you understand what she is telling you:

> **Customer:** It shuts down before it's done. I spent a fortune on this thing, and I'm beginning to think I threw away my money.
>
> **You:** I understand the feeling. You work hard for your money. But, rest assured, we *will* make this right.
>
> Now, can you tell me exactly at what point in the cycle the widget stops? This information will help me diagnose the problem.

Note here the full weight given to the customer's feelings, but also note that the focus is quickly shifted from feelings to facts.

The Appeal to Reason

Dealing effectively with customer complaints means, at the very least, solving the customer's problem with the product or service, but your rhetoric should aim even higher. Your objective should be to transform the customer's problem into a positive experience with your company. To do this, you must collect all of the facts relevant to the problem.

1. Determine what product(s) are involved.
2. Find out under what circumstances the failure occurred.
3. Ask, "What happened and when?"
4. If possible, walk the customer through diagnostic steps.
5. Determine if the problem is with the product or caused by the customer's (mis)-use of the product. Is she operating the product correctly? Is the product being

used appropriately? If the customer is at fault, educate her. Be as positive as possible when giving advice. Do not criticize or blame the customer.

6. Ask more questions: How is the product failing to perform to expectations? What would the customer like the product to do that it is not doing?

7. Depending on warranty terms and available services, offer appropriate options for a fix or other remedy. Explain the options and the desired results.

8. If appropriate, offer an apology—but always put the emphasis on the remedy.

The Ethical Appeal

Effective communication in dealing with customer complaints is essentially problem solving, and problem solving is, first and foremost, a rational process. Nevertheless, always back up and support your appeal to reason with an ethical appeal. Your customer relies on your expertise (which is manifested in the appeal to reason) as well as your ethical character. She wants to know that you stand behind your product or service, and that you feel a moral obligation to make things right. As far as the customer is concerned at the present moment, the failure of the product is a problem, perhaps a very big problem. But there is something worse: If the customer is made to feel that she is being cheated or abandoned, the problem suddenly becomes a catastrophe for you as well as the customer. Do not neglect the ethical appeal:

> "We are committed to your satisfaction, and we will ensure that the widget works to its specifications. We will work the problem until it is solved."

Transforming Error into Opportunity

To make the leap from solving a problem to transforming that problem into an opportunity for building a positive relationship with your customer, approach the complaint with the understanding that your customer is anxious, frustrated, and possibly angry. These feelings will not respond well to condescending assurances that "everything will be all right." Instead, communicate your *commitment* as well as your *competence* to help.

As mentioned, listen carefully to the complaint, asking whatever questions are necessary to get the relevant details. Be certain to acknowledge the complaint. You needn't admit any fault or wrongdoing, but do acknowledge that the product or service is not satisfying the customer. *That* is a fact you cannot debate.

You may discover, in talking further with the customer, that the problem is not with the product per se, but results from a disconnect between what the product is designed to do and what the customer expects from it. That is, the product may be operating properly and *still* fail to satisfy the customer. This is an issue open to discussion. The customer's dissatisfaction, however, is a given.

Express empathy, understanding, and concern. Saying that you are "sorry that this problem has happened" or that you are "sorry that the product is not performing to your satisfaction" is important to the customer. It is not the same as accepting blame but is an acknowledgment of the customer's feelings and a sensitive response to them.

If you know that you can fix the problem, explain to the customer precisely what you propose to do. Explain as well what the customer must do, including whatever steps she needs to take to make the repair, replacement, or adjustment possible—for example, she may need to take the product to the nearest authorized dealer. Make clear how the steps you propose to take will fix the problem. Be helpful. Provide all of the information the customer needs, such as a list of authorized repair facilities in her area. If, in fact, the product or service is faulty, provide closure by apologizing, but do not dwell on the apology. End the exchange on an upbeat note by focusing on the remedy you will provide; however, also include an expression of your gratitude for the customer's patience and understanding.

Some complaints do not yield to a quick fix. In these cases, the ethical appeal becomes paramount. You need to persuade your customer that you will not abandon her. A response such as "Sorry, but there's really nothing I can do" is unacceptable. Formulate and provide a plan of further action or a set of alternatives. If possible, propose a stopgap or temporary solution.

APPROACHES FOR MANY SITUATIONS

The most persuasive argument you can make in response to any complaint is an immediate solution to the problem. Short of this, provide the credible promise of a solution. Devote time to the "discovery" portion of your argument: Be certain that you obtain all of the facts relevant to the complaint.

Product Fails to Perform to Customer's Satisfaction

After listening to the customer, you determine that the product in question is indeed defective. You say:

> "I am very sorry that your widget is not performing up to spec. I can offer two options to make things right. I can send you a replacement widget part, which comes complete with instructions for replacing the defective part. This will resolve the problem with your unit. Or, if you prefer, you may return the entire unit to us, and we will perform the part replacement, as well as thoroughly test the unit, which will be returned to you with reimbursement for your shipping costs."

After listening to the customer, the alternative scenario is that you determine that the product is not defective. The customer has purchased the wrong product for his application. Instead of blaming him, you offer help:

> "I am sorry that the widget is not performing as you expected, but based on what you have told me, the problem is not a defective widget. The problem is

that this model is unsuited to the requirements of your application. For your purposes, our Model 2 Widget will work far more satisfactorily. It is specifically designed for . . . .

"We can exchange your widget for a Model 2. The difference in cost is $XXX. Perhaps you would like to speak with George Smith, our in-house technical expert, before making your decision. I can connect you with him, if you like."

In another case, a product fails in use. After listening to the customer, however, you determine that it has been misused. This voids its warranty, but it does not give you an excuse to abandon the customer. Explain what you cannot do and why you cannot do it, but put the final emphasis on what you *can* do. Remember, whatever you mention last makes the strongest impression on the listener; therefore, end with whatever positive steps you can offer:

"I understand your concerns about the durability of the widget; however, these products are thoroughly tested and certified as durable when they are used in applications for which they are designed.

"Your widget model is designed—and priced—for light-duty and moderate-use applications. It is not intended for the kind of heavy-duty work you've described. Now, we do offer a product that is more appropriate to your needs. It is . . . .

"Unfortunately, because your widget failed as a result of inappropriate use, I cannot make an in-warranty repair or exchange. In any case, if you intend to continue using it as you have been, I would not recommend repairing it, because it will certainly break down again. Your best option is to upgrade to the product I mentioned. Although I cannot extend full exchange value for your widget, I can take it in trade—as is—and sell you the appropriate product for $XX. Would you be interested in that?"

Delays in Shipment

The most effective communication concerning a delay in fulfilling an order is preemptive rather than apologetic. If you know that a shipment is going to be delayed, notify the customer. Explain the reason for the delay, and give an accurate revised estimated time of arrival. You need not offer the option of canceling the purchase, but do invite the customer to contact you if he has any questions. It is bad enough that the shipment is being delayed. Do not compound the disappointment by removing yourself from the situation:

"Mr. Smith, I am sending this e-mail to tell you that your shipment, which was promised on November 3, will be delayed about ten days. I'm sorry, and I hope this delay does not inconvenience you. Demand for the product has far exceeded our expectations, and we've had to mobilize all our forces to get the orders out quickly and accurately. Even so, they are not moving out of here as quickly as we would all like.

"If you have any questions, please reply to this e-mail or call me at 555-555-5555."

If a shipment is late, offer an argument intended to preserve the future of your relationship with the customer:

"Mr. Jones, I have good news. Your order shipped this morning. I breathed a sigh of relief when I looked through my e-mails this morning and saw the confirmation. As I explained earlier, a combination of shortages from our suppliers and unusually heavy demand has really impacted our shipping schedules. However, our suppliers are now up to speed, so I do not anticipate any delays on future orders. As for this one, thanks for your patience and understanding."

Errors in Order Fulfillment

Many customer complaints concern errors in order fulfillment. In responding, never challenge the customer. Instead, begin with a brief apology—a simple "I'm sorry" is sufficient for a start—then proceed to "discovery." That is, get the facts:

"I'm sorry for the problem. According to my records, we shipped [state the items and quantities]. Is this what you ordered?"

If the customer answers yes, proceed this way:

"And what did you receive? (Or what was omitted from the shipment?)"

If the customer answers no, proceed this way:

"I'm sorry. There must have been a miscommunication. What did you order?"

Once the facts are obtained, it may only be necessary to ensure that the error is corrected. However, you may want to go the extra mile by explaining how the error occurred and providing assurance that it will not happen again. Usually, this is best accomplished in a follow-up letter to the customer's complaint. Do not keep the customer tied up on the phone by going through a long apology or explanation. What she wants at the moment is for the mistake to be corrected. Here are two follow-up notes that will restore you to your customer's good graces:

Dear [Customer's Name]:

I'm writing personally with my apologies for our having shipped the wrong item to you on [date]. I have no excuse to offer for the error, but I can offer my promise that we will take extra care to ensure that we do not repeat the error. Just test us with another order.

I thank you for your patience in this matter.

Cordially,

Dear [Name]:

You know the facts better than I. You ordered [quantity] of [merchandise], we shipped [wrong quantity] of [wrong merchandise product], you called us, and we rushed to you an additional [wrong quantity] of the [wrong product].

You have every right to be angry, and I find your grace under pressure remarkable. I am very grateful for your patience and understanding.

Please be assured that we will not let this mistake be repeated. Why not put us to the test with another order? The freight charges for that one will be on us.

Sincerely,

Billing Errors

Billing errors are another common source of customer complaints. Again, after a quick apology, review and assess the facts. Make certain that there really is an error before you make adjustments. This situation is, by definition, a dispute. It should not be permitted to grow into a crisis. However, just as you must not allow your opponent in any dispute to put you on the horns of a dilemma, forcing you into an instant either/or, agree/disagree posture, do not permit your customer to force you into a snap decision before you have gathered all the facts. If you need time to review the records, tell the customer. Tell him what you need to do and specify a time at which you will call him back:

> "I need to review our billing records, then get back to you, so that we can resolve this promptly. Will you be available at [time and day]? I will have everything sorted out and will call back then."

If you determine that a billing error has been made, expedite the adjustment. Information is key here. Tell the customer precisely what you are doing to remedy the situation. Follow up any phone calls with a letter:

Dear [Customer's Name]:

I am very sorry that our mistake put you to the time and trouble of checking your records and having to call us. I thank you for the effort you have made to help us correct our mistake.

As we discussed, your account has been credited in the amount of $XXX. I also assure you that we are taking steps to ensure that such an error does not recur.

Sincerely yours,

Turn the mistake into something positive by adding to your apology a thank-you to the customer:

Dear [Customer's Name]:

Many thanks for pointing out the error in our invoice of [date]. A corrected invoice is enclosed, and I hope that you will accept our sincere apology for any inconvenience our error may have caused you.

We appreciate your understanding and your business.

Cordially,

If you determine that the source of a dispute over a bill is the customer's error, respond fully and factually. Never accuse the customer of wrongdoing. Never try to diagnose the reason for the customer's error. Just present the facts. You can also transform a negative experience into something more positive by offering helpful advice. Problem solvers present the most persuasive arguments:

Dear [Customer's Name]:

I understand the issues you raise concerning the number of hours for which you have been billed, and I have reviewed my time sheets, which I will fax to you for your review. As the time sheets will make clear, I performed all of the services you requested and only those services.

Please take a few moments to review the time sheets, and if you still have questions, please call me at 555-555-5555.

In the future, you can significantly reduce the time charged to you by sorting and classifying your records before you submit them. Most of my clients find that it is more cost-effective to presort rather than to pay me for doing that task.

Cordially,

Do not criticize the customer, but if the source of his error is apparent, point it out—strictly as a matter of fact:

Dear [Customer's Name]:

I think I understand your confusion regarding the total due on the invoice. We have carried over $XXX from the previous billing cycle and have added that to this month's invoice total, which comes to a combined total of $XXXX. That is the cumulative total now due.

Sincerely,

Unsatisfactory Service

Customer satisfaction is never open to dispute. Either the customer is satisfied or she is not. The underlying reasons for the dissatisfaction may be debatable, as when a customer claims that a product is defective but objective testing shows that it is operating up to spec. While you can argue the fact that the product is not defective, you cannot argue that the customer is "wrong" to be dissatisfied. After dealing with the factual basis for the customer's complaint, accept the dissatisfaction and address it as effectively as you can.

> "I'm sorry that you are dissatisfied with the repair work we performed on your unit. I have just completed a thorough retest of it, and I can find no problems. It is operating up to spec. However, that does not change the fact that you are dissatisfied. There is a very slight possibility that your unit has an intermittent or transient defect, which would not necessarily show up in test results. There are two ways we can address this possibility: I can return the unit to you with every expectation that it will perform properly. Or you can leave the unit with me for [state the time period] so that I can run a continuous "burn in" test. This should reveal any intermittent flaw. I realize that this is inconvenient for you, but it is a way to get at a definitive answer."

EDUCATING YOUR CUSTOMER

Persuading customers that they should be satisfied with your merchandise or service is not a matter of eloquence or mastery of debate. It is a project of education. Ensure that your customers understand the benefits of your product or service and that they understand how to derive these benefits. Ideally, the more a customer knows about what your product or service can and cannot do, the more satisfaction he should derive from it.

By educating your customers you'll enable them to appreciate, understand, and enjoy the full value of your product or service. It takes no understanding to know what your product costs. But it may require a degree of education to understand its value—the ratio of cost versus benefit. If you provide your customers with this understanding, you will enhance their satisfaction and greatly reduce the areas of potential dispute.

Deal with Your Vendors

*Using effective communication to create profitable
partnerships with your suppliers and vendors.*

You don't just sell goods and services to others, you also buy them. However, a good "buy" negotiation is, in essence, a good "sales" negotiation. In making a purchase for your business, you should do your best to *sell* your suppliers on the proposition that they should give you great value and service of the highest quality.

Money, runs the cliché, talks, and it is undeniable that your prospects for getting the best possible deal are often proportional to the amount of business you do with a given vendor. Money doesn't just talk. It talks persuasively. However, making a big deal is no guarantee of value—nor should you *have* to make a huge purchase in order to get first-class treatment. The secret is to make an argument that persuades the vendor to treat you right.

WORDS TO USE

Find words that define you and the vendor as partners—collaborators in a mutually profitable relationship. Here are some suggestions.

alternatives	discuss	options	schedule
best	estimate	partner	select
careful	expect	quality	service
comparison	expectation	relationship	specifications
deadline	long-term	reliable	unacceptable
deal	lowest	reliability	value
dependable	negotiate	responsive	

WORDS TO AVOID

Avoid using words that limit options or devalue the vendor's goods or services—words such as the following.

| absolute | cheap | immediate | nonnegotiable |
| bargain | excited | no | |

AT STAKE

The poet John Donne wrote, "No man is an island." The same is true, of course, of any business enterprise. To survive and prosper, each business requires customers, and each requires suppliers. Just as it is critically important to develop productive long-term relationships with customers, so it is mandatory to develop the same with vendors. Your objective, of course, is to get the best deal—the greatest value. Just don't mistake price for value; it is only part of the equation. Value also includes reliability of service and long-term availability of whatever your business needs. At stake, then, is a business relationship over time. Persuade your vendors to become your faithful partners in business.

YOUR GOAL

The goal of communication with vendors is, first of all, clarity. Communicate what you need, how much you need, and when you need it; secure complete agreement on costs and prices as well as all other terms. This achieved, your next goal is to create an empathetic bond with the vendor. The more thoroughly he understands the nature of your business, the more efficiently he can serve as your partner in business. Persuade him that you represent more than a sale. Persuade him that he has a stake in your continued success. This is the basis of an ongoing relationship that will contribute to the long-term prosperity of your enterprise.

YOUR APPEAL

The foundation of all communication with vendors is the appeal to reason. Ensure that everyone understands the facts involved in each communication. Ninety-nine percent of any communication with a vendor involves the exchange of facts: merchandise, model numbers, quantities, prices, financial and delivery terms, and so on. These issues must be nailed down with absolute certainty. As important as the remaining one percent is—and we will get to that in just a moment—you want to be in a position from which you can address, first and foremost and without ambiguity, the facts of the matter. This will minimize the chance of error and miscommunication and will greatly reduce the amount of time and energy squandered on "argument" in the all-too-common sense of the word: a fruitless shouting match.

In dealing with vendors, the appeal to reason is paramount, but you should not neglect the ethical appeal. Between vendor and customer there should be an assumption of goodwill and good faith. You should be able to appeal, if necessary, to your vendor's pride in his reputation, and the vendor, in turn, should be confident of yours. You should feel that you have a right to receive good value, and the vendor should feel that he will receive good value in return—including timely payment for goods and services.

To a large extent, the ethical appeal is implicit; however, do not hesitate to remind the vendor that you value his good reputation as a supplier:

> "I'm confident you'll deliver what you promise. Your reputation in the industry was a big reason for our choosing you over your competition."

In communicating with vendors, the appeal to emotion comes in third, behind the appeal to reason and the ethical appeal. Where the transfer of money and goods is concerned, emotions tend to cloud the issues. Quality, quantities, schedule, and cash should be managed and manipulated as efficiently and directly as possible. Appealing to personalities and emotions tends to get between you and the facts you need to manage. This said, it is always helpful to make a vendor feel good. Compliment your vendors on a job well done. Tell them that you are pleased with their product or service:

> "I am very impressed with the features of your new model widget. Your design is very innovative, and I look forward to getting the installation completed so that I can start using the unit."

STRATEGIES TO ENSURE CLARITY

Begin your persuasive argument from the very first contact with the vendor. When you first call to solicit information from a vendor, describe your business, emphasizing your reputation, special needs, and so on. Be very specific about what information you require from the vendor. If appropriate, you may want to submit (perhaps by e-mail or fax) a written list of your requirements. If the product or service in question must meet formal specifications, these should always be submitted in writing.

When you are ready to take the next step with a vendor and solicit a bid, it is prudent to back up all verbal requests with an e-mail or other form of memo itemizing the specifications and requirements. A written record of specifications is absolutely necessary when you are soliciting competitive bids from more than one vendor. Even when you send a full spec sheet, consider making a phone call as reinforcement. On the phone you can highlight any points you may wish to emphasize in your spec sheet, or you can ask for information that may have been omitted from it (e.g., "What is your customer-support policy?"). Close by inviting the vendor to ask you questions or to make follow-up calls as necessary. End the call by establishing a firm deadline for submission of the bid.

STRATEGIES TO CREATE EMPATHY

When you describe your business to a prospective vendor, detail the specific challenges and problems you face. Help the vendor understand your business. Then, in a polite but straightforward manner, challenge the supplier to measure up to the requirements of your business. You may add here a compliment concerning the vendor's reputation or any positive reports or word-of-mouth you may have encountered.

After the vendor makes his presentation, offer compliments on the presentation as well as the product. Let him know that *he* has persuaded you to expect great things from him; however, also let him know that you have solicited bids from other top firms—if this is indeed the case.

Here is an example of an argument intended to create an empathetic relationship with a vendor:

> "We are a specialist marketing service with a very select client list. We serve just fifty-two clients, for whom we drop about 400,000 national mailing pieces per month. Right now, we are looking to significantly upgrade our list-maintenance software, which we run on an XYZ platform. We want to replace our off-the-shelf software with something tailored to our specific requirements. Now, I have heard very good things about your product, your pricing, and your customer-support and training programs. I want to send you our spec sheet and get a bid from you. I can e-mail the spec sheet to you by the end of the week. I will need a detailed bid by [date]. Are you interested in working with us?"

MOVING VENDORS TO GIVE YOU THEIR BEST

No one wants to be treated like a number. Indeed, everyone wants "extra special" treatment. So how do you persuade a vendor to treat *you* as a special customer?

As always, the most persuasive rhetorical strategy is to appeal to the *other* person's self-interest. You want something special for yourself. Your task, therefore, is to persuade the vendor that giving *you* what you want will benefit *him*.

Begin by approaching the vendor in a pleasant and professional manner. Some customers believe that it is necessary to come across as hard-nosed, hard-to-please taskmasters. Although it is important to make clear your concern for top quality and high value, presenting yourself as nearly impossible to satisfy will alienate rather than ingratiate. The approach is not likely to produce exceptional quality or value, but rather a feeling of resentment and an attitude suited to dealing with impossible people: *If this guy cannot be satisfied, I'm not even going to try to satisfy him.*

Without making any promises, be clear that it is your desire to establish a regular, ongoing working relationship with this vendor. Give him a stake in the relationship by suggesting that your satisfaction now will result in more business for him later. Let him know that you want to be a satisfied customer, a good customer, a regular customer. You are interested in finding a business partner, not just someone to supply a single piece of merchandise or do a single job. Do not "guarantee" endless amounts of business. You need do no more than establish a stable, dependable, mutually productive working relationship. Here is a sample argument:

> "We buy about three gross of widgets each quarter. That represents a very nice piece of business for our supplier. Price is very important, of course, and you have very good prices. But that is only part of the value picture. We also need a supplier who will *be there* for us, who will go the extra mile when we need him to do so. That means expediting delivery and being available for quick-turnaround odd-lot orders from time to time. That also means accuracy in filling our orders. Any time I have to go back to fix an order, I am making my own customer wait. I can't afford that.
>
> "As long as we maintain a great working relationship—as long as I can depend on you as a partner—you'll have my business."

APPROACHES FOR MANY SITUATIONS

The achievement of clarity and empathy are the twin objectives of every communication with a vendor. The following are some examples of how to achieve both in typical situations.

Negotiating Price

Many books have been written on the art of negotiation, including the specialized art of haggling or negotiating price. For the purposes of persuasive argument with a vendor, it is necessary to know only three "secrets" to negotiating the best price:

1. *Become thoroughly familiar with the competitive field.* Make it your business to know what others charge for the products or services you seek. These days, in many fields, researching a wide array of vendors has been made relatively simple thanks to the Internet. The more prices you get, the better. It will allow you to negotiate from authority. Being able to state that "the average price for that item is $XXX" is a much stronger argument than saying, "Your price sounds a little high to me."

2. *Stay focused on value.* The object of negotiating is to buy the product or service you want at the best price you can get. It is *not* to defeat vendor. Keep your focus on the product or service, not on the personality of the individual from whom you are buying it.

3. *Vote with your feet.* The most persuasive argument you can make in any negotiation doesn't use your voice, but your feet. If you go into a negotiation prepared to walk away from it, you will find your position considerably strengthened.

The more thoroughly you know prevailing prices before you walk into a negotiation, the less you will need to rely on your ability to gauge the honesty, integrity, and negotiating skills of the stranger with whom you have to deal. Know the competitive field, and you can focus on value, not the personality of the salesperson or vendor. Only after you have gathered sufficient data, open negotiations with the vendor or vendors who seem to offer the best value.

And do remember that the objective of the negotiation should not be price, but value. Value is an expression of price in proportion to benefits derived from the product or service. A cheap product (that is, a product with a low price) may or may not be a good value. If the cheap product offers few benefits, it is a poor value and will probably create more costs in the long run. Targeting value will help you negotiate far more effectively by focusing your argument on a well-defined goal.

Finally, use the best price you were quoted during your research phase as a starting point for getting an even better price.

If you find that you and the vendor are far apart in price or value, you may have to apply your most persuasive argument: your feet (or, if you are communicating by telephone or e-mail, announcing the end of the discussion). Unless the gap is indeed hopelessly wide, chances are that your gesture of withdrawal will push the vendor to make his best offer. Even if it does not, there is no shame in calling back later if you cannot find a better deal elsewhere. This is why you should keep personalities out of the negotiation. Do not alienate a vendor with anything that even smacks remotely of a personal attack.

When you return to a negotiation, make certain that you recap your last conversation. For example:

> "We were talking about a price on twenty-four widgets. You were at $XXX, and I offered $XX. Have you given any further thought to price?"

You need not *begin* by agreeing to the vendor's last offer. Provoke him to move downward. Perhaps you will be able to meet somewhere in the middle. If not, accepting his last offer is not an admission of defeat. It is, rather, the best price you could get.

Negotiating Terms

Another alternative to walking away from the deal is to accept the vendor's bottom-line offer, but go on to negotiate the most favorable payment terms you can. Indeed, it is often the case that price is less of an obstacle than impact on your cash flow is. Even if the price of goods or services is higher than you would like, you may be able to negotiate sufficiently satisfactory terms to make the deal work. Generally, the best negotiation strategy is to settle on a price, then proceed to terms. If the vendor has been able to secure a price favorable to him, he will be that more strongly motivated to arrive at finance terms that will make it possible for you to conclude the deal.

Although negotiating credit with a vendor is similar to talking to a bank or other financial institution about a loan—in both cases, your objective is to persuade someone to have confidence in you and your ability to meet your financial obligations—you enjoy two advantages when you deal with a vendor rather than a bank. First, the decision to loan you money is a decision to go into partnership with you. This is a fact, but one that a bank may choose not to recognize. A vendor, however, has no choice but to think this way. To make it possible for you to do business with him, the vendor knows that he must find a way to extend credit, to make you, in effect, his partner. Second, vendors are usually not subject to the formal and restrictive regulations that govern banks. Most vendors are willing to take greater risks in order to make the sale.

When you negotiate credit terms, always identify the positive—what you've been offered—and negotiate to improve the terms however much you can.

> "I'm reviewing your proposal for the widgets. I think we're just about there, but I need you either to give me a break on the finance charge—down to X percent—or more room on the payment schedule. If you stay at XX percent, we will need at least XX payments over XX months, not X payments over X months. I can't tie up that kind of cash. Work with us on either of these options, and we're ready to close the deal."

If the vendor has doubts, always work with whatever positive elements you can find:

You: Thanks for sending your proposal. You've made the first cut, but we are going to need better terms. We can do XX payments over XX months, not the short-term schedule you propose.

Vendor: I don't know if we can stretch the payments out that far. [This is an expression of doubt, but not a definitive no.]

You: Give it some hard thought. If you can stretch just a bit, I'm ready to close the sale. How about calling me back later on today? We're ready to get moving.

Rejecting a Proposal—Constructively

Diplomacy, it has been said, is the art of disagreeing without being disagreeable. When it is necessary to reject a vendor's proposal, it is in your best interest to do so in the spirit of this definition. Reject the proposal without rejecting the vendor.

One of the great lessons the ancients taught about argumentation is to separate issues from personalities. Although the classical rhetoricians prized the ethical appeal highly, they generally disdained the *ad hominem* argument, which addresses issues of personality and character rather than fact. This is a good example to follow, because almost every difficult, unpleasant, or sensitive business communication is made easier—or more effective—by such a separation. Do not be tempted to assume that just because someone is in business, he will not be personally disappointed by rejection. Remember, no one does business with a business. People do business with people—and people have feelings.

It is to your advantage to give the vendor the right feelings—positive feelings—

even if you have to reject his proposal. After all, you may want, or need, to call on the rejected vendor again, at another time. Moreover, done correctly, rejection can actually serve a very positive purpose. It can deliver a strong message to a vendor, alerting him to what he *must* do to get your business in the future. Offend the vendor and he will not hear this message. If the rejection ends the relationship, its positive value is lost.

Do you owe the vendor the courtesy of an explanation for turning his proposal down? Not necessarily, and certainly you do *not* owe him a justification. However, you will probably benefit from taking the time to explain your reasons for rejecting the proposal or for choosing one proposal over another. This information will educate the vendor by suggesting to him how he might serve you better in months or years to come.

Here is an example of saying no to the proposal, but not to the vendor:

> "You delivered an impressive proposal, but the approach outlined is just too costly, and we are going to go with a scaled-back version. Thanks for a terrific effort, and I will certainly be calling on you in the future for other projects."

If it is possible and appropriate, offer hope for future business, but only if the encouragement has a basis in realistic expectation, not as a pro forma matter. Your objective is to get the vendor to perform for you—next time:

> "We have completed reviewing your proposal for project XYZ. Unfortunately, what you proposed is not up to spec. Obviously, we are looking at other suppliers, but we won't be making any final decision for at least two weeks. Would you like to revisit your proposal and submit a revision by [date]?"

Complaining—Constructively

Just as it is a mistake—nonproductive and even downright destructive—to confuse the common understanding of the word *argument* (a shouting match) with the rhetorical sense of the word (an exercise in persuasion), so it is a bad idea to think of complaining as simply giving a vendor hell by venting your irritation over mistakes in billing or shipping or whatever. Before you begin to speak, the classical rhetoricians counseled, determine what you hope to achieve. In the case of complaining to a vendor, if all you want to do is let off steam, fine. Go vent. But you can't run a business on that kind of steam. It is far more productive to make a complaint if your objective is the correction of an error or the solution to a problem. If that is what you wish to achieve, consider approaching the complaint with the following steps:

1. Unfold the *narratio*—the orderly exposition of the facts of the error and the problem the error has created. Don't speculate as to fault, motives, or motivations. Instead, simply narrate such details as the duration or frequency of the problem or error, as well as the *material* (not the emotional) effect the problem or error

caused: that is, the impact it has had on your business. Always strive to *quantify* the scope and the consequences of the problem: "Late shipments this month have cost us upwards of $XXX."

2. Propose a solution to the vendor or solicit one from him.

3. Do your best to transform the complaint into a dialogue about a genuine business partnership. Avoid the "I" and "you" of the typical complaint and instead speak in terms of "we." Persuade the vendor to work with you—not in opposition to you—to correct the error or fix the problem.

Probably the complaints most commonly leveled against vendors concern time—specifically unforeseen delays and slipped deadlines. In complaining about scheduling problems, it is best to begin as gently as you can. This is a situation in which you want to persuade the vendor to cooperate, to work with you toward a solution. For example, a shipment has arrived late, which has had an impact on your manufacturing division. You call the vendor, who offers some explanations and excuses. How do you reject the excuses without cutting loose a vendor who offers you favorable prices?

You: We ordered a dozen widgets on [date 1] and forwarded with the order a deposit of $XX. It is now [date 2] and we don't have the widgets. We were promised a two-week turnaround. What's going on?

Vendor: I'll investigate and get back to you.

You: When will I hear from you? Here is the problem: If we don't get delivery by [date 3], we will be forced to cancel the order and recall our deposit.

Vendor: I *will* get back to you as soon as I can.

You: I really do not want to cancel this order. I also assume you don't want to lose the order. I want the widgets. Let's work together on this—starting with your giving me a definite time when you will get back to me.

Vendor: You'll have the information before the end of the day.

You: I'll be here. Just call. Thanks.

Repeated errors are symptoms of something wrong with a vendor's systems. By complaining about these problems constructively, you can make it clear that the situation is unacceptable and must not continue; you can also offer help, advice, or suggestions to improve the vendor's systemic problems. Be careful to keep the focus on the issues and away from personalities or character. For example:

You: We have been doing business with you for a good while, so I feel that I can talk to you about a problem we've been experiencing lately. The performance of your shipping department over the past sixty days has been just plain unacceptable. Of fifteen shipments we received since [date], six have been late by at least three days, and nine have been incomplete, and of those, two included items we did not order. These mistakes have cost us time and effort. They have even inconvenienced some of our own customers.

I am more than slightly interested in hearing your take on this situation. Can we set up a time to discuss shipping? Maybe I can even offer some suggestions you might find helpful. In any case, we need to find a definitive fix for these chronic problems. We cannot keep doing business this way.

Bumps in the Road

The relationship between vendor and customer goes two ways, and if you make a mistake or create a problem for a vendor, it is important to address the situation constructively in order to preserve—and even to build—the relationship.

In business, most problems have to do with money: late payments, missed payments, neglected bills, errors of calculation, even bounced checks. These situations can be embarrassing and certainly threaten to undermine a business relationship. However, they do have the advantage of being generally straightforward in nature—a matter of dollars and cents, after all—and an honest admission of financial error or difficulty puts you in a stronger position than may be immediately apparent to you:

> A frank admission and apology are often greeted with respect and gratitude. Such an admission is an ethical appeal, a testament to the character it requires to accept responsibility for a situation resulting from your error or failure.
>
> Admitting a problem and asking for assistance or even patient indulgence empowers the creditor-vendor. It gives him the opportunity to be gracious, understanding, and human. It may actually strengthen his partnership with you.

The one strategy guaranteed to fail where money is concerned is the "let sleeping dogs lie" approach. No creditor wants to be ignored. Fail to communicate, avoid answering the phone or replying to e-mails, and you will create a crisis where none exists, or else you'll magnify a looming crisis into an outright catastrophe. If you are having financial problems that affect your ability to pay a vendor, go out of your way to communicate and to keep the lines of communication open.

The time to begin communicating is when you first anticipate a payment problem. In this situation, take the following steps:

1. Advise your lender, vendor, or supplier of the problem.
2. Explain the nature of the problem.
3. Explain how your problem will affect payment to the vendor.
4. Explain how you propose to deal with the problem.
5. Ask the vendor for help and cooperation, which will benefit both of you.

Of course, it is not always possible to foresee or anticipate cash-flow problems. When you are blindsided, your only available option is an after-the-fact apology. This is, in effect, an argument for understanding, cooperation, and aid:

1. Begin by explaining the nature of the problem.
2. Explain how you propose to deal with the problem.
3. Outline how you would like the vendor to help.
4. Propose a solution to accompany the apology.

As important as persuasive communication is, actions do speak louder than words. If the problem is a late payment, send a check for whatever portion of the money due you can pay, then make that phone call to tell the vendor a check is on the way.

Informing a vendor of an impending payment problem can be emotionally stressful, but it is also an opportunity to demonstrate that you are on top of the situation and that it will not spin out of control.

Put together an argument that incorporates an element of apology, but maintain a tone of calm control rather than anguished contrition. You are not a criminal or a sinner, so don't invite the vendor to heap blame on you by crying *mea culpa* too loudly and too long. If you do this, the vendor will conclude that you really are terribly at fault, and he may accordingly decline to give you the cooperation you seek.

Avoid emotionally charged language. Instead, present the facts straightforwardly. If you have a specific request to make, make it directly after explaining the situation. An apology is in order. Just be certain not to apologize for the request that you make. Take care to avoid emotional words that tell the other person how to feel. Also avoid telling the person how to judge your request. A statement such as "I realize this is a lot to ask" invites the vendor to agree with you and conclude that you are asking too much of him. Instead of self-sabotage, present the facts, make the request, and let the vendor decide whether what you ask is reasonable.

It is natural to want to tell the vendor how bad you feel, but avoid doing so. Sure, you feel bad, but why should your creditor be made to feel bad, too? Isn't it enough that he is not getting his money on time? Don't burden anyone with negative feelings. Focus instead on making things right.

The best way to think about working with a vendor to solve your payment problems is to approach the conversation not as crisis resolution, but as a routine renegotiation of terms. This approach is best to take when you anticipate problems *before* they actually occur. For example:

"We want to extend payments on our account an additional three months, reducing our monthly payment from $XXX to $XX, but retaining our present rate of interest. Our operating costs have increased faster than our client list. I need to improve cash flow in the short term. That's what I need. You will collect another three months of interest—and I'm happy to pay it to you for the convenience of those extra three months."

Here is a how you might make a phone call advising of an impending problem:

"Hello, John. This is [your name] at XYZ Company. I'm calling in reference to our account with you, account number 12345. I am hoping you can help us. We have experienced a series of equipment breakdowns, which has put us behind in order fulfillment and given us some heavy and unanticipated expenses. It would be a big help in managing our cash flow if we could reschedule our payment due dates for the next six months. At present, we pay on the first of each month. I would like to push that back to the twenty-fifth of the month."

If you are going to make a partial payment—a payment less than the agreed amount—advise the vendor with a phone call as well:

"I just put into the mail a check for $XXX toward your invoice of [date]. I am in a cash-flow crunch here, and I wanted to send you a partial payment immediately rather than making you wait another twenty days or so for the whole thing. I will be sending you the balance by the twenty-seventh of the month. Will this work for you?"

If you cannot advise your creditor in advance of a payment problem, you should apologize for any problems that have already occurred. An apology for a late payment, missed payment, or some other misstep always helps to defuse a potentially destructive situation. Make it clear that you *are* apologizing by using such phrases as "I hope you will accept my apology" or "I'm sorry." However, always include with the apology some positive steps toward remedying the error. If possible, advise the creditor that you are sending partial payment immediately. Propose a definite—and doable—plan for settling your account or rectifying the error.

The apology should include a brief and direct explanation of whatever has caused the problem. It is a very good idea to include the vendor in the solution. Ask what *she* would like you to do. Use phrases like "How do you want to proceed?" and "What would be best for you?" A simple approach is typically the most effective:

"This is [your name] at XYZ Company. I've just put into the mail a check for $XX, which, I'm sorry to say, is overdue by more than a week. I wanted to let you know that the money is on the way, and to apologize for being late with it. It won't happen again."

For more serious lapses, at least some explanation is helpful:

You: I've been swamped with work and am just now hustling to get my payables out the door. I just sent you a check for $XX, which, I know, is late.

Vendor: Yes. I was about to call you.

You: I'm sure you were, and I'm glad I got to you first. My apologies, and I will not let it happen again. Thanks for your patience.

Responding to Referral Requests

One of the most powerful arguments you can make to develop and build a great working relationship with a vendor is to offer positive word-of-mouth advertising.

This not only helps out your vendor (and it is always to your advantage when a trusted vendor does well), it also gives you an opportunity to extend your influence and judgment among your colleagues and throughout the business community. Moreover, when you send a good vendor to a colleague, you build a stronger relationship not only with the vendor, but with the colleague as well.

Take the initiative and *offer* a referral. Don't wait for the vendor to ask:

> "You always go the extra mile for us. I want you to know that I am referring my good friend, [name], who runs [name or type of business], to you. I think he'll give you some very nice business, and I know he'll be just as satisfied with your work as I am."

When you make referrals, be specific. Avoid vague adjectives. Instead, mention specific events, projects, and accomplishments relating to the vendor you are recommending. Above all, never make a referral unless you can do so without reservation. If you have any doubts about the vendor, don't offer to make a referral, and don't say okay to any request to make one.

If a vendor asks you to call a colleague with a recommendation, make the call easier by asking the vendor to tell you what he would like you to mention or emphasize. Here's an example of what you can say when making a vendor referral:

> "[Name of contact] at WXY Widgets asked me to give you a call to tell you a little something about her and her company. I have been doing business with XYZ for [time period], and I use them exclusively. They offer great prices, and their service is top-notch and highly responsive. Just last month, I needed a rush shipment of an odd lot. I put in a call to [name of contact] and she had real-time inventory information up on her computer screen instantly, and the goods were out the door later that same day. That is not exceptional. It is typical. I know you will enjoy working with her and with XYZ."

Close with Your Investors and Lenders

Promoting your enterprise clearly,
persuasively, and ethically.

Winning investment is really what the classical rhetoricians and orators had in mind when they formulated the rules of persuasion. To be sure, the details of how businesses and other enterprises got funded were different in ancient Greece and Rome than they are today, but the principle was the same: *A* had to persuade *B* to finance the future of *A*. The objective of arguments for investment is not merely to compel intellectual, emotional, or theoretical agreement with a position. It is to compel someone to stake money on that agreement. And this, of course, sets the bar of persuasion quite high.

WORDS TO USE

Build positive relationships with investors and lenders by using words that emphasize the value they will receive by investing in you and your enterprise. Here are some suggestions.

advice	evaluate	opportunity	problem
advise	expertise	options	proceed
aggressive	explain	outline	quantity
alternatives	future	plan	safe
caution	growth	possibility	safety
checklist	imagine	potential	satisfaction
consult	invest	precise	strategy
develop	issues	precisely	study
enterprise	negotiate	present	vision
entrepreneurial			

WORDS TO AVOID

Never let your own doubts and anxieties find their way into the words you use when communicating with lenders or investors. The following are common deal killers.

certain	generally	risky	urgent
desperate	guaranteed	sure thing	

AT STAKE

At stake in arguments intended to move lenders and investors is your future. That much is obvious. But just because it is obvious doesn't mean that it is compelling. After all, although you are intensely interested in your future, why should an investor be?

To answer this question, raise the stakes by persuading the lender or investor that, yes, your future is on the line, but so is *his*. The lending/investing argument must lay out what the funding will do for you *and*, even more important, what it will do for the lender or investor. Persuade him that *his* future is at stake just as much as yours.

YOUR GOAL

Another question: *Why doesn't everyone get rich investing in stocks?* The answers are doubtless many, but perhaps the most meaningful is the simplest: Very few people understand what it means to invest in the future.

To most people with a little cash to invest, putting money in a mature company with a proven track record seems safe and prudent—very nearly a sure thing. Although an investment in an established enterprise is to some extent an investment in the future—at the very least, an investment in the continued success of the firm—it is mostly an investment in history, in the company's past. As such, prospects for a high return on the investment are limited. That is, while investing in an established firm is relatively safe, it is also only *relatively* profitable, if at all. The future of a mature company will probably be little different from its present; therefore, investments will probably enjoy only modest growth, if any. Mature markets may be proven, but they are also limited, their future pretty well foreclosed.

Your goal in communicating with investors and lenders is to educate them about your future, and once they are sufficiently educated, to *sell* them a share of that future so that they perceive your future as theirs as well. Persuade investors and lenders that, while the past may be comforting, it is also limiting. The future presents risks, but it also offers far greater opportunity.

YOUR APPEAL

All three modes of appeal are required for arguments presented to lenders and investors. In isolation, none is sufficiently persuasive.

The appeal to reason presents the contours and details of the proposed deal. Clarity and thoroughness are essential, but it is vital to keep the presentation from becoming an exhaustive laundry list. Maintain control of the investment presentation so that the principal benefits to the investor are always uppermost and are not suffocated in a blanket of qualifiers and other minutiae.

The appeal to emotion should convey your vision of, confidence in, and passion for the enterprise in which you are asking others to invest. All investors need to understand the prospective investment intellectually, but they also need to sense what some call the "fire in the belly," the passion that drives success. Your argument should convey enthusiasm.

Finally: the ethical appeal. You will not attract investment solely by demonstrating your high ethics, but you cannot attract it without instilling confidence in your good character. The ethical appeal also goes beyond character and extends to expertise and experience. Perhaps the best phrase to describe what an investor looks for in the principals of an enterprise is "the right stuff," the phrase used by test pilots to describe the constituents of the character of a good pilot. For the leader of a young enterprise, the right stuff includes ethics, expertise, passion, confidence, and courage. A strong ethical appeal conveys these qualities.

SELLING IT

All persuasive argumentation is selling, and every communication with an investor or lender is an attempt to sell. As any sales professional knows, there are two broad approaches to making a sale:

1. *The soft sell.* This approach emphasizes the appeal to reason. It is especially effective with more sophisticated investors who are accustomed to making up their own minds.
2. *The hard sell.* This approach makes its case more directly and stresses the emotional as well as the ethical appeal.

Both approaches can be effective, and really, most investment arguments combine elements of the two. Tailor your choice of one or the other (or the proportions in which you combine the two) to the nature of your business and the kind of investor you approach.

The soft sell is largely an attempt to open the door to further discussion, whereas the hard sell tries to open the door, enter the room, make the sale, and leave with the cash. While that may sound very appealing to the entrepreneur in search of fast money, be aware that the hard sell will typically elicit a more definite response from the prospect, which may be a more definitely *positive* response or a more definitely *negative* one. In contrast, the soft sell is less definite and immediate, but also less risky. Knock politely on a door and you may initially be refused admittance, but at least you won't get *kicked* out.

Whether you employ the soft sell, the hard sell, or a blend of the two, you must attain seven objectives to be successful:

1. Provide prospective investors or lenders with a good reason for your having approached them. It is often effective to employ a certain amount of flattery by identifying the prospect as a member of an elite group—one of a group of discerning and historically successful investors, for example.

2. Make a compelling case for the investment opportunity by (for example) identifying a hitherto unmet need for which there is a lucrative market.

3. Explain how your project or company will meet this need.

4. Make the ethical appeal, persuading the prospect of your personal ability to meet the need and your qualifications for leading the company or project.

5. Enumerate the benefits—to the investor or lender—of the proposed investment or loan.

6. Lay out a clear course of action. In a hard sell, it may mean asking provocative questions of the prospects (which you always answer for them) and announcing that you will follow up personally to solicit a response. The soft sell does nothing more than lay the groundwork for a follow-up.

7. Invite questions. An effective presentation need not answer all of the prospect's questions, but it must elicit any questions it fails to answer. The more a prospect asks, the greater his interest in what you have to offer. Be grateful for questions, and answer them enthusiastically.

Define

The classical rhetoricians regarded definition as a basic (and highly effective) mode of persuasion. Definition is especially important in presenting novel projects or ideas to investors. After all, what is new is, by definition, unknown. It is up to you to define it and to do so in a manner that compels intense interest.

Compare

Comparison is another classic topic for argument, and it is highly useful in presenting new projects. Comparing your new way of doing something with the old way of doing the same thing can be a persuasive case for getting behind the new approach. New enterprises are not born in a vacuum. Make your case by comparing your company or project to others and demonstrating the superior potential of what you propose.

Show the Past, Offer the Future

Studies of what makes some product advertisements work and others fail invariably cite the word *new* as powerfully appealing to prospective consumers. Similarly, there is a natural tendency on the part of entrepreneurs to sell novelty and innovation to the exclusion of the traditional and the proven. Novelty and innovation are important; they are at the core of most investment opportunities. However, it is a mistake to neglect the past.

Ideally, every investor wants something entirely new that has worked well in the past. This is, of course, an impossibility, a contradiction in terms, but it presents an important lesson for the entrepreneur. For it is possible—and desirable—to present the new idea, project, or company in the context of the past. As the ancient orators realized, precedent makes for a compelling argument. So, be ready to present your track record and compare your proposal to past or current success stories. Analogy is powerful in this context:

> "When the XYZ widget was introduced ten years ago, it captured 70 percent of the market within three years. The new design we propose builds on the phenomenal success and acceptance of the XYZ widget but provides [list new benefits], which will make it a must-have replacement. Our projections suggest that, within the first year of introduction, the new design will capture 25 percent of the current XYZ widget market."

THE TWO APPROACHES

Here is an example of a soft-sell approach to a potential investor:

> "Whenever I need help, I go straight to the top. That's why I'm calling you, a leader of this city's business and cultural community.
>
> "Last year, some 520 small presses in the United States and Canada published approximately 4,800 books they hoped would appeal to a wide audience. Few of these presses, however, had access to a distribution service capable of getting their products to this audience.
>
> "My plan is to change this situation with a company I call Bookoffer, a distribution and warehouse service for independent and small presses. The publishers are crying out for such a service.
>
> "Of course, they won't be the only ones who will profit from the enterprise. Bookstores will gain access to vast, enticing new stocks, readers will benefit, and so will you—as an investor in Bookoffer. Our business plan suggests that investors will realize profits within three to four years after start-up. How do I know? I've been in book distribution for twenty-three years and am currently general manager of XYZ Company, one of the nation's most successful distributors.
>
> "I would like to set up an appointment to speak with you in person and present to you a detailed business plan."

Alternatively, there's a hard-sell approach:

You: I know of 520 companies that need your help, and that are willing to give you a fair share of their profits for helping them. Last year, some 520 small presses in the United States and Canada published over 4,800 books they intended for the general reader. Because few of these presses had access to a decent distribution service, the "general reader" never saw the majority of these books, let alone had the opportunity to buy them.

My plan is to change all this with a company called Bookoffer, a distribution and warehouse service for small presses. After working more than twenty years in book distribution—I'm currently general manager of XYZ Company, one of the nation's most successful distributors—I know I can make Bookoffer work for small presses, for book dealers, for the reading public, and for you: the investor. Do you want to hear more?

Prospect: I'm listening.

You: I want to introduce myself in person to bring you a detailed business plan that explains how you can expect to realize a profit on your investment in just three to four years. I want to explain how, with your help, we will revolutionize an industry, perform a cultural service, and make money in the bargain. I will be in town . . . .

PRESENT A WINNING PROSPECTUS

Getting Your Way Every Day is not a book about writing an effective investment prospectus or business plan. Peruse any online or brick-and-mortar bookstore and you will find plenty of books on the subject. Two time-tested standards are:

> James B. Arkebauer, *The McGraw-Hill Guide to Writing a High-Impact Business Plan* (New York: McGraw-Hill, 1994)
>
> Joseph Covello and Brian Hazelgren, *Your First Business Plan* (Naperville, IL: Sourcebooks, Inc., 1993)

There is also a variety of business-planning software, including Palo Alto Business Plan Pro 2006 Edition (Palo Alto Software, Inc.) and Business Plan Writer Deluxe 2006 (Nova Development). The books and software will save you time by helping to keep you from reinventing the wheel, but do remember that there is no silver bullet or one-size-fits-all prescription for writing a business plan. However you go about creating your prospectus or plan, be certain to tailor it to *your* business, venture, or project, as well as to the kind of investor you are seeking. Do *not* try to adapt your business or your target investor to whatever ready-made business plan you may have on hand. As with all other offers of a persuasive argument, begin by knowing what your goals are and what your audience wants.

One other rule: Don't start fishing before you have a boat. Be certain that your prospectus and plan are ready before you approach prospects. Once the investor's interest is piqued, you must present your prospectus or business plan without delay. Momentum is one of the keys to unlocking capital.

However you finally decide to compose and structure your business plan, don't skimp on details, but do strive to be concise. The plan should be readable in a single sitting, which means that it should be about twenty to thirty pages for most projects or ventures. Steer clear of vagueness and pie-in-the-sky predictions, but don't smother the prospective investor in details. Detailed breakdowns, test-market results, focus-group numbers, and other information should be available in a backup document for the investor who asks to see these things. At most, include highlights of these items in your prospectus.

In addition to a business plan, be prepared to furnish a more specifically detailed marketing plan, a document that covers, at minimum, ten key issues:

1. The customer
2. The product or project
3. The market (its size and growth potential)
4. A strategy for distribution of the product or service
5. A strategy for pricing
6. A strategy for promotion
7. How your company and product relate to the established industry
8. How you propose to compete—and win
9. The environment (political and regulatory, legal, cultural, economic)
10. The technological context

If you don't present your prospectus or business plan in person, at least make a phone call to alert the prospect to the arrival of the document:

> "I've overnighted the business plan for Bookoffer. It speaks eloquently for itself, but the highlights I don't want you to miss include: probable return on your investment within six months, profit on start-up capital within three to four years, a client base of 300 to 500 firms, and diversity within a focused, targeted market.
>
> "It has been a pleasure speaking with you about this project, and I look forward to your response to the business plan. I will call you early next week to discuss it."

You can also use your phone call to once again emphasize how your plan addresses specific issues the investor may have expressed concern about:

> "After our great conversation yesterday, I must tell you that I'm not surprised you asked to see the business plan. You'll have it before the end of the day. Read through it, and you'll understand why I'm so excited about the company. Now, it's true, as you pointed out, that small presses can't afford to put much money behind promotion. But that is the beauty of our business model: The key to selling books is not advertising but distribution—which is precisely what we are all about.
>
> "You might also bear in mind a few other highlights as you read through

the prospectus: probable return on investment within six months, profit on start-up capital in three to four years, client base of 300 to 500 firms, and diversity within a focused, targeted market. It's a winner—but you'll see that for yourself. I'll call you early next week to discuss."

Not all the investment you are likely to seek is for a start-up venture. When you are looking for investors to fund an ongoing business, make your annual report a primary exhibit in support of your case. An effective annual report speaks for itself, but that doesn't mean you can't help it along with a preparatory phone call. Calling key investors or new investment prospects in advance of sending the annual report should achieve three goals:

1. It should personalize the report, providing the vivid impression that you regard this investor as a key player and partner in your enterprise.
2. It should highlight the achievements of the year.
3. It should explain and put into perspective any disappointments during the year.

Here is a phone call intended to get your annual report the attention you want it to command:

"I've just sent out to you the first annual report of Bookoffer. As a charter investor, you'll find it not only interesting but—I'm delighted to say—extremely *enjoyable* reading. Before you go to the bottom line, please take time to look at the growth of our client list, which exceeds the prospectus numbers by 18 percent.

"[Investor's name], I am grateful for your support during this past year, and I hope that you are looking forward to the next year as much as I am. Give me a call if you have questions about the report."

Sometimes it's not all good news. A timely call can help put problems into perspective; just make certain that you don't come across as making excuses or trying to cover up the hard facts:

"[Name of investor], I just sent our first annual report out to you. You don't need that report to tell you that we have come through a rough start-up year. But I ask that you take a good, hard look at the numbers. What you'll see is that the growth of our client list is right on target, and while our retail penetration has fallen 5 percent behind what we expected, it has picked up with each quarter. These numbers are all about the future, and they suggest increasingly rapid growth. Call me if you have any questions."

FOLLOW-UP STRATEGIES

Sales professionals do not need the classical rhetoricians to convince them that follow-up is an important part of the persuasion process. Nevertheless, the Greek and Roman orators put great emphasis on ensuring that each argument concluded with a call to action. It is not sufficient to present your case, they pointed out; you must also enable others to act according to your wishes. The follow-up is an extension of the call to action. It tells your prospect what to do next.

Follow-up calls are valuable in the following situations:

- During the interval between initial contact with a prospect and the next contact, a personal interview, or the transmission of a business plan
- When a prospect fails to return your calls
- When a prospect who has agreed to take the next step fails to do so
- When a prospect declines to invest

Moving the prospect to action may require keeping the level of involvement and excitement high. A follow-up call often makes an appeal to emotion:

> "I enjoyed our telephone conversation yesterday, and I look forward to our meeting a week from Tuesday.
>
> "The questions you asked were challenging, shrewd, and right on the mark. I am confident that the business plan I will present Tuesday will answer them all.
>
> "You know, what really excites me is that our conversation convinced me that you are just the kind of investor Bookoffer needs. You evaluate and think several moves ahead. I understand that you are not about to throw money at a project."

Resistance must be refuted by a strong appeal to reason; however, the most difficult form of resistance to counter is indifference. Don't give up easily. Here is a follow-up left on the evasive prospect's voice mail:

> "Hello, [name of prospect]. Looks like you've been too swamped to get back to me on the Bookoffer proposal. It's an exciting venture, and I don't want to see us both miss an opportunity because we couldn't make contact. I hope you will find some time to examine the business plan I left with you. I'll check back early next week. In the meantime, if you have any questions, please call."

The strongest form of resistance is a *no*. There is no magic formula for converting this response into a yes, and, indeed, it may be time to move on—politely—to the next prospect. The word *politely* is important. The prospect who says no to a proposal today may say yes to another proposal on another occasion—unless you alienate him by a rude remark or a scolding. ("You will live to regret your decision. . . .") Do not badger a prospect who says no, but do follow up if you are not certain that you gave the initial pitch your very best shot. Such a follow-up is your opportunity to amend the pitch by adding new information or an emphasis you may have neglected earlier:

"I am grateful for the time you gave me to present my proposal for Bookoffer. Naturally, I'm disappointed by your decision, and I can't help thinking that, in my eagerness to present a detailed plan, I may have caused you to lose sight of a few essential points that might otherwise have influenced your decision positively. Please, let me just double-check. Did I make the following clear?

"First—that you can distribute your investment capital over a dozen quarters. Second—that your voting privileges on the board of directors are proportional to your investment. And third—that you retain the right to review the list of publishers and titles we will carry.

"Are there any questions I left unanswered?

"As I say, I appreciate the time you've given me. Of course, I'd appreciate any more time you might devote to reconsidering the proposal."

Following up with lenders, in contrast to prospective investors, mainly serves to get the loan officer off the dime. Banks often seem to crawl when you need them to sprint. Make an argument to get the prompt attention you need—without annoying or alienating someone you want on your side. If you push too hard for a quick answer, you might just get the quickest answer of all, which is no. When following up with a lender:

1. Begin the call by letting the loan officer know that you realize how busy he is.
2. Explain why you need a prompt answer. Appeal to reason, not emotion. No whining, please. The loan officer should feel that you are asking for help not from a faceless bureaucrat, but from an individual who is about to become your de facto business partner. The remarkable truth is that most business people welcome opportunities to be helpful. It is human nature. Keep this in mind when you make the call. You are persuading a person, not a business.
3. Gently nudge the loan officer into action by giving him an opportunity to be helpful.

Here is an example of a call you might make. Begin with the facts. Avoid personalities:

"It has been X days since I submitted my application for this loan. I faxed you on the [date], but I received no reply. I understand that processing a business loan is a painstaking process, but I am confident that you appreciate the impossibility of maintaining responsible financial management in the absence of complete financial information. That is why I need your help—in the form of an accurate update on the status of my loan application."

REFUTING RESISTANCE

We have already touched on refuting resistance. Let's return to the subject. Most resistance must be refuted with the facts—an appeal to reason. However, no matter how persuasive an argument you may present, it is not likely that you will convince any conventional lending institution to give you funds unless you have a decent balance sheet, prospects for a bright future, and a reasonably clean credit history. You cannot change the facts, but you can often put them into perspective so that the positives outweigh the negatives and the lender feels ready to give you the answer you *both* (after all) want.

Most banks and conventional lending institutions request a formal letter explaining any questionable episodes in a loan applicant's credit history. Even before this process, however, you should be prepared with a calm and well-reasoned verbal explanation of any credit glitches. Don't make excuses, and don't appeal to emotion. Use facts to create the appropriate perspective.

Do not rush to explain. This is one situation where it does not pay to be overly proactive. Unless the blemish on your credit history is very substantial and very obvious, let the lender decide whether it is worth discussing. Do not volunteer your opinion that an incident might "cause trouble" or "require explanation." That doesn't mean you should be unprepared to address any issues that you yourself identify. Just keep them to yourself until you are asked about them.

If you go into a credit application with what you know to be substantial and obvious credit-history problems—bankruptcy, legal judgments against you, obviously heavy debt load, substantial losses—you should be more proactive. Meet with the lender when you discuss terms or at the time that you file your application. When you are asked about specific episodes of your credit history, respond calmly. Adopt an even, businesslike tone. Avoid defensiveness and, above all, avoid a confessional tone. Asking for funding should not be a religious experience or a purgation of the soul. In face-to-face meetings, be aware of your body language. Make and maintain eye contact; avoid biting of the lips, bringing the hands to the face or mouth, and head shaking. Nervous laughter is fatal.

Do not make any ham-handed attempts to deny, dismiss, or otherwise minimize any incident in question. You will need to explain it. You will need to demonstrate that it is not a critical failing. But you cannot deny that the lender *believes* it may be important. Make a convincing argument that proves the episode is not especially significant. If you merely assert that it is not, the lender will assume the opposite, and you will likely be denied the loan.

When you explain a credit problem, keep your remarks concise and factual. Be certain to include all mitigating circumstances. Do not lie. Do not distort. Be very careful that what you say verbally does not conflict with anything you have put (or plan to put) in writing. Be aware that even if you give a persuasive verbal explanation of credit-history glitches, you will almost certainly be asked to provide a written explanation as well. You are speaking for the record.

The goal of your argument is not to deny the existence of the glitch, but to put it into perspective. Paint a picture of the problem as a small blot on an otherwise exemplary history of a prosperous company. End the explanation by soliciting further questions—now or later.

Are these arguments worth making? The effectiveness of a good verbal explanation of credit-history difficulties depends on the nature and seriousness of the problem in question. The biggest hurdle is the perception of a pattern. If you clearly make it a habit not to pay your bills, no amount of explaining is likely to get you a loan. But, if you have an isolated problem or two, the perspective argument is more likely to succeed.

Here are typical verbal responses to questions about irregularities in credit history. Note that the response must not be vague or evasive, but neither should it smother the loan officer in details. Give the minimum amount of information needed to answer the question. If the loan officer requires more information, she will ask you.

> **Lender:** I noted that you had a late payment on your corporate credit card last quarter.
>
> **You:** That's correct. From [date 1] through [date 2], both principals of our firm were out of the country. The explanation for this isolated late payment is that neither my partner nor I was present when the bill arrived, and this bill was shuffled to the bottom of the heap. That was careless, but it was an accident— and it cannot happen again because we have put all recurring payments on automated electronic payment schedules. I should point out that the payment was made only ten days beyond the thirty-day limit. We've held the credit card for X years, and this is the single instance of a late payment.

Another example:

> **Lender:** I am concerned about three late payments your credit report turned up. Are you aware of these?
>
> **You:** Yes, I am. You may have noted that all of the late payments occurred during the March–May period. During that time, we lost two of our major clients: ABC Company failed to secure anticipated funding for a project contracted with us, and DEF Company petitioned for Chapter 11 bankruptcy at the end of March. These unforeseen events, as you might expect, impacted our available cash for a short time. Of course, we contacted the credit officers at the three creditors in question and arranged deferred payments. I can furnish, in writing, the details of these arrangements. The bottom line is that all of those accounts are currently up-to-date and in good standing.

Epilogue: When Rhetoric Hits the Speed of Light

The ancient Greeks knew a lot about a lot of things, and many of their most profound ideas on philosophy, government, and communication are as relevant today as they have always been. But not even Plato or Aristotle could have imagined digital communications. To be sure, the word *revolutionary* is chronically overused, but surely we must apply it to the advent of e-mail and instant messaging in the workplace.

Despite the revolutionary technology, the principles of classical rhetoric still apply—perhaps more than ever. The availability of electronic communication has been a boon to all of us, but it also presents a formidable challenge. Think of it this way: You are thankful for the vacuum cleaner, the automatic dishwasher, the clothes washer and dryer—all the modern labor-saving devices. Would you swap any of these for a broom, a washboard, and a sink? Not likely.

At least, not until you gave the proposition a little thought.

Take the vacuum cleaner. It is doubtless faster and more thorough than a broom, but together with those other "labor-saving devices," it has also raised the standards by which we judge a clean house. And therein lies the problem.

In the old days, cleanliness was defined by what a broom could do. Now, a "clean house" is a thoroughly vacuumed house. While it is true that a vacuum cleaner can get a house "broom clean" faster than a broom can, a broom will get that same space broom clean faster than a vacuum cleaner will get it "vacuum cleaner clean." The truth is actually pretty ugly: By raising expectations, some of our so-called labor-saving devices have actually created more, not less, labor.

Now, consider another labor-saving technology: digital communications—e-mail, instant messaging, and the like. These technologies make it easy for many people to reach you, and you them. Easy, yes. But each of these easy communications invites—or even demands—virtually instant replies. E-mail generates many more messages to you, together with the expectation of a reply.

If digital communications technology has created at least as much labor as it has saved, it also applies a considerable degree of pressure on us. The very speed and accessibility of e-communication that saves us so much time also places demands on our time. The arrival of an e-mail demands, or at least tempts, immediate response. E-mail speeds everything up—not just the mechanics of communication (which is good), but also the thought processes that should go along with it (which is not so good).

The principles, rules, and guidelines of classical rhetoric can be used to salvage some of that lost thinking time by making it easier for us to structure "instant" messages. The best place to start is with an update to the word of caution that is the foundation on which classical rhetoric was built: Before you put fingers to keyboard, know what you want to say, know who your audience is, and be certain that you really have something of value to communicate.

These slightly modernized admonitions from two-and-a-half millennia ago may save you from sending what might be called knee-jerk e-mails. Think before you type and click. Too many e-mails take too much time to sort through and read. Useless e-mails bury important e-mails. As we begin to drown in a sea of digitally generated communications, we simply stop paying attention. In 1998, Computer Associates International, a major software company, discovered that its managers received between 200 and 300 e-mails each and every day. This information (or noninformation) overload was not only time-consuming, it also created a climate in which people stopped talking to each other. They substituted e-mails and instant messages for face-to-face talk.

Before you write, ask yourself: *Is this message necessary?* Before you send, ask yourself: *Does the recipient really need to have this message?* Think especially hard before you "cc" recipients: *Do all these people really need to receive the message?* (Use "cc" to respond to anyone who must receive a copy, according to company procedures or policies. Also include those who will be affected by the content of the message. No one else needs to be included.)

E-mail is a potentially great messaging medium, but it is not well suited to genuine discussion and even less suited to argument or debate. An issue that requires deliberation demands a phone call, a conference call, or, better yet, a face-to-face meeting. Don't use e-mail as a way of avoiding real talk, real debate, and real argument—that is, argument in the rhetorically productive sense of making a persuasive case.

Familiarity, runs the cliché, breeds contempt. We have become so familiar with e-mail and instant messaging that we often thoughtlessly abandon standards of good business communication when we dash off an e-message. Grammar, syntax, and even spelling evaporate. Worse, we say things on the spur of the moment that cannot be retracted once the send button is clicked. The illusion of intimacy created as we face not a man or woman but a computer screen tempts many of us to be careless, even indiscreet online.

Be on guard. Take the time to reread your message before you send it. Fix the grammar, check the spelling, and sharpen the words. Then think one more time before you click *send*: Do you really want to let this missive go?

And, when you do let it go, think about who is there to catch it.

The message you sent to your pal in the next cubicle, the message with the snide remark about your boss, will materialize on the screen of your intended recipient all right. But it will also remain tucked away on your hard drive and, most likely, in an electronic file within the bowels of some network server. In a corporate setting, there is no such thing as privacy in digital communications. Any message you send is automatically the property of the company who owns the computers and owns the network that connects them. Court case after court case has upheld this legal concept, and the people who have been fired for their electronic indiscretions have stayed fired.

E-mail brings out two opposite tendencies in people. Some emphasize the *electronic* part of the communication and write in a staccato, telegraphic style:

> Joe: Meeting 2 pm 5/22 my office

Others are drawn out by the casual intimacy of e-mail and become quite conversational:

> Hey, Joe, we're having a meeting at 2 in the afternoon on Wednesday. Love for you to be there. Can you make it? Oh—my office this time. Okay? See ya!

What's the better approach? As with any persuasive communication, suit the style and tone to the purpose and the recipient. If you are transmitting a single piece of simple information, be brief—but clear. Complete sentences are preferred. If your message is more complex, take the space and the words you need. The tone you adopt with your boss will probably be different from the tone you use with a colleague who is also a friend.

As for small talk, while it is important during the business day, e-mail and instant messages are not the proper venues for it. Save small talk for actual conversation in the break room or while waiting for the copy machine.

Increasingly, e-mail has become more closely identified with spoken conversation than with paper memos or letters. In digital communications, informality is both expected and tolerated to a greater degree than in business letters or even telephone calls. Since the conversational model figures so importantly in e-messaging, you may find it helpful to picture your correspondent when you write an e-mail or instant message. You may even find yourself speaking out loud as you type. Of course, at that point, you should consider getting up from your desk, walking across the hall, knocking on the door (or the cubicle partition), and having the kind of conversation the Greeks, the Romans, and the Renaissance rhetoricians had centuries ago. We can be sure that such talks were smart, productive, and very lively. Even in the digital age—quite possibly now more than ever—there's no substitute for flesh-and-blood face time with the people you need to persuade every day.

Index